SHAME

SHAME

The Exposed Self

Michael Lewis

THE FREE PRESS
New York   London   Toronto   Sydney   Tokyo   Singapore

The Free Press
A Division of Simon & Schuster Inc.
1230 Avenue of the Americas
New York, N.Y. 10020

First Free Press Paperback Edition 1995

Printed in the United States of America

printing number

1 2 3 4 5 6 7 8 9 10

Library of Congress Cataloging-in-Publication Data

Lewis, Michael
       Shame: the exposed self/Michael Lewis.
          p.   cm.
       Includes bibliographical references and index.
       ISBN 0–684–82311–X
       1. Shame.   2. Shame—Case studies.   I. Title.
       BF575.S45L48   1995
       152.4—dc20   95–30552
                                                    CIP

It all means nothing at all, and howling for his milky mum,
for her cawl and buttermilk and cowbreath and welshcakes
and the fat birth-smelling bed and moonlit kitchen of her
arms, he'll never forget as he paddles blind home through the
weeping end of the world.

—Dylan Thomas, *Under Milkwood*

For Leah, Anna, Barbara, Rhoda, and Felicia,
the women of my life

Contents

Acknowledgments

This book is more than an intellectual exercise, a continuation of my study of self and emotion development. It is a journey into my own life, a journey that started with a mother dead and a child shamed, who became orphaned, searching for himself and for the meaning of life. For the past thirty years, my wife, Rhoda Lewis, has been my companion on this journey. I have consistently drawn for sustenance on her intelligence and sensitivity, her deep understanding of human behavior and life. Indeed, some of the ideas that follow originated with her, and all were improved by her comments. This book would not exist without the collaboration of Rhoda Lewis.

I wish to thank all my students and colleagues who have helped me formulate my theory, and who have served as a sounding board for these thoughts. I owe particular gratitude to Margaret Sullivan and Linda Michalson Brinker. In the last two years I have lectured about shame to many audiences on three continents. The comments and criticisms of the nameless crowd are here remembered and thanked. Most recently, I spent a week in Australia giving the Westmead Lectures at the University of Sydney, where I received encouragement and suggestions that helped me to finish this work. I also wish to extend my thanks to the lonely pioneers whose work on shame enlightened me, the late psychoanalysts Helen Block Lewis and Silvan Tomkins, both of whom saw clearly the central role of shame in human life. Newton once said that the fate of a good theory was to become the limited case of another theory. If a more articulated theory emerges in these pages, it is because I had broad shoulders to stand on.

I have learned much as a teacher, a psychotherapist, and a researcher. Each of these roles has given me a different perspective on shame. As a teacher I come in contact with a large number of students, varying in age from adolescence to early adulthood. This experience allows me to observe how young people interact with authority and react to standards. As a research scientist interested in developmental questions, I observe children's development, sometimes through a one-way mirror, but often by interacting with them in talk and play. This experience enables me to explore the origins of shame. Studying the parents of these children allows me to observe the socialization of the shame process and, at the same time, to consider intergenerational shame by means of questioning and interview techniques. Finally, as a therapist, I have been able to explore my patients' experiences and to see how maladaptive some ways of coping with shame can be.

I could not have written this book without the untiring help of my secretary, Ruth Gitlen, who received assistance from Stacey Fanslow. She not only typed and retyped the drafts, but in her way, gave meaning to sentences in need of her keen eye. To Barbara Louis, who proofread the manuscript, many thanks. Andrew P. Morrison, Carolyn Saarni, June Tangney, and Lawrence Pervin read an earlier draft of the manuscript. To them, I owe my appreciation for helping me make clearer what I wanted to say and for pointing out what I had forgotten to include. My editor, Susan Milmoe, provided support for my effort and demonstrated intellectual vigor and command of our language while editing my text. My work has been supported by many grants but two foundations have been particularly helpful: the Robert Wood Johnson Foundation and the W. T. Grant Foundation. The latter, headed by Robert Haggerty, has provided my colleagues and me with the resources to conduct our longitudinal studies, from which much of the material of this book was gathered. Finally, I am grateful to David Carver and Norman Edelman for their continued support of my work.

1

Shame in Everyday Life

She took of its fruit, and did eat, and gave also unto her husband with her and he did eat. And the eyes of both of them were opened, and they felt that they were naked.

E motions, our own and those of others, affect us during every waking moment. It is difficult to construct a sentence or to look at a person without feeling some emotion. While there are many glib references in popular books to the importance of getting in touch with our feelings, we really know little about feelings. Recently, following up the pioneering work of Darwin, systematic research on emotional development, individual differences in the expression of emotions, and the impact of emotions on social behavior has begun. However, progress has been slow and difficult. The primary concern of academic psychologists in the last three decades has been cognition. No doubt, the computer as model is partly to blame. The primary concern of psychiatrists has been clinical problems and, increasingly, their biological substrates. But the study of emotions for their own sake is vital if we are to understand human motivation and behavior.

We all recognize the opening quotation as part of the biblical story of creation, and specifically as the Genesis version of the origins of shame. Shame is one of the quintessential human emotions. It affects all our feelings about ourselves, and all our dealings with others. But what is shame, when and how does it occur, how does it develop, and do men and women differ in their shame feelings? A few psychoanalysts have specu-lated about these questions over the years, but psychologists and psychia-trists have begun to explore them more systematically only in the last decade.[1]

The general lack of attention to shame does not reflect its esoteric nature. Shame touches on many themes in contemporary psychological thought. Shame is related to guilt, pride, and hubris, all of which also require self-awareness. Shame bears on narcissism; indeed, the narcissistic personality is the personality of the shamed. Shame underlies many of our relationships with others: marriages, for example, are often environments of shame.

I believe that the species-specific feeling of shame is central in our lives. Shame, more than sex or aggression, is responsible for controlling our psychic course. Shame guides us into depression or antisocial behavior. Our internal struggles are not battles between instincts and reality, but conflicts that typically involve the understanding and negotiating of shame, its elicitors, and its frequency.

Consider a married couple. The husband asks the wife, "So when are you going to go on that diet you keep talking about?" Or consider a professor who comments to a student, "I found much that was good in your paper, but I thought your argument went seriously astray." In both of these everyday exchanges, the speaker causes the listener to feel shame. Shame can be defined simply as the feeling we have when we evaluate our actions, feelings, or behavior, and conclude that we have done wrong. It encompasses the *whole of ourselves;* it generates a wish to hide, to disappear, or even to die.

Responses to shame can be varied: anger, depression, or withdrawal. The wife, criticized, becomes angry; the student, criticized, becomes embarrassed, loses confidence, and vows to avoid taking courses given by that professor. Cultural differences, past and present, can be viewed as differences in the ways in which shame and self-consciousness are experienced and addressed. Recent "theorists of narcissism," those who have informed us of the possibilities of self-actualization and personal freedom, have focused us on ourselves; this focus is associated with an increase in shame. Narcissism is the ultimate attempt to avoid shame.

Shame has an impact on diverse human phenomena, from the level of the individual to that of culture and society. The conflict between self-actualization versus commitment to community involves shame, as well as anxiety. To understand shame is, in some sense, to understand human nature.

Shame Is Everywhere

Let us consider a few examples that demonstrate shame's ubiquity and its chameleon nature.

Angry Donald

I am in an observation room in my laboratory, watching a mother playing with her 3-year-old son. I have asked her to teach the child a game called the Hanoi puzzle, which involves moving doughnut-shaped circles from one stick to another. It cannot be solved by a three year old, but the mother does not know this.

She begins by showing her child how to perform the task. "Look," she says, "take this doughnut and move it from here to there." The child complies. "Very good, Donald, you're a good boy." "Now," she says, "take the second doughnut and put it on this one." The child does as she requests. She slowly goes through each step of the task as the child watches intently. Although she occasionally smiles, her face is usually serious. She often praises the child, using such comments as "Good boy, you're really smart." Now she rearranges the puzzle and presents it to the child to solve by himself.* She starts the timer, which I have given her, "to clock her child's speed in solving the puzzle." The child puts the first piece on the wrong shaft, smiles, and looks up at his mother, who now yells, "No, no, no! What is wrong with you?" Our cameras focus on her face, with its nose raised and nostrils flared. I know that I will later score her expression as a look of contempt and disgust. The child looks confused by his mother's reaction and then turns back to the task. But now his body is hunched, his smile is gone, and he no longer appears interested in the puzzle. His mother insists that he go on. He reaches for a ring and throws it across the room.

The mother's expression of disgust has shamed the child, who has responded with what Helen Block Lewis called "humiliated fury."

Paul's Public Performance

I am sitting in a high school auditorium next to the father of a friend of my daughter. Both of our children perform with the school orchestra; my daughter plays the violin, her friend Paul, the oboe. We are parents, admiring our children's performance and skill. Paul has a solo piece, and he stands up to play. But something is wrong: perhaps suffering from stage fright, he seems to have forgotten the opening passage of his solo. After what seems to be an interminable delay, but in truth just long seconds, Paul finally begins to play. When Paul finishes I look at his father and say, "Once he got it, he played really well." I notice that Paul's father is

---

*I use male or female pronouns in random order throughout this book. Using "she" sometimes and "he" at other times allows me to employ the first-person singular.

blushing, and that the blush extends from his face to below his collar. He does not look back at me, but does manage a faint smile. At the end of the concert, he quickly gets up and leaves. He does not stick around to mingle with the other parents.

Paul's father had been shamed. Like many of us, he had experienced shame, not because of some action of his own, but because he was associated with someone else who had failed.

Sol's and Rita's Self-Concern

I always have a private conversation with each student in my seminar to review their papers. Sol, a first-year graduate student, had come to the university with good recommendations. His undergraduate professors judged him to be bright and conscientious, although one noted that Sol had trouble accepting criticism. His paper was ambitious, and demonstrated considerable effort, but it was marred by some problems I wanted to discuss with Sol so that he could make it better. Knowing Sol's sensitivity to criticism, I started by saying I had really enjoyed his paper and thought he had done a fine job. He smiled brightly and thanked me. I went on to say that I thought he had covered the literature well and, in fact, had demonstrated real understanding of the problem. Again he beamed at me. He seemed happy with himself and very pleased by my comments. I then brought up what I thought was a logical error in his paper. "Sol," I said, "while I enjoyed the paper, and thought you did a good job, your analysis of sex differences in the socialization of emotion was not well developed." Sol's face dropped. He tightened his hands around the arms of the chair, almost forcing himself to sit upright. "Professor," he started to say, "I don't think you're correct. . . ." He never finished the phrase. He seemed unable to go on with our conversation. I tried again. "Sol, I really liked the paper, and I think that overall you have done a fine job." Again, he seemed to brighten. Seeing him relax, I thought I would try again. "Sol, I think your analysis needs more work. You have not developed the role of sex differences in socialization." Once again, Sol tensed. This time he turned toward me. He appeared angry and his voice was loud and intense as he said "I just did what you told us to do in class." I thought of arguing with him, but I could see that it would do no good. I handed him the paper and told him that I would like him to make the corrections indicated and then return it to me. Sol never corrected the paper and, in fact, he let his B grade stand. Sol was shamed by my disapproval, and did not want to risk more disapproval and further shame by resubmitting his paper to my judgment.

I had a similar experience with Rita. Her paper appeared hastily done: she had not reviewed the literature, and had not even bothered to proofread her work, which was poorly typed and full of spelling errors. Rita was a good student, so I was surprised by her poor job. When she entered the room and sat down, she appeared tense and worried. "Rita," I said, "this paper is missing references and is poorly typed." I paused, because I recognized that Rita was going to cry. She turned to me, wiping her eyes, and said, "Dr. Lewis, why don't you like me?" I responded, "Rita, I *do* like you. I am not talking about *you*, I am talking about one paper that you have done." She burst into tears, and many minutes passed before she could compose herself enough to leave.

Sol and Rita had both interpreted my negative comments as criticism of them as people, not as criticism of their work. The two were ashamed in my presence because they confused their roles as my students with their identities as individuals.

Minority Status and Billy's Anger

Some time ago, I was working with a young Hispanic man who had been arrested after a confrontation with a policeman. He had been innocently sitting on the steps of his apartment house with several other boys when a police car stopped in front of them. One policeman asked, "What are you doing here?" He responded, "I'm waiting for a friend." The policeman did not reply, but got out of the car and walked toward him, accompanied by another officer. Billy heard one policeman say, "These Spics are all the same." Angered by this ethnic slur, Billy stood up to the policeman who had uttered the statement, and said, rather tamely, "You shouldn't say that. It's not a very nice thing to say." The policeman repeated his ethnic slur. Billy kept quiet, and the policemen returned to their patrol car and drove away. Billy next remembered kicking over a large number of garbage cans and scattering them across the street. The police soon returned and arrested him.

Billy was shamed by the policeman's ethnic slur and his inability to do anything about it. As he told me later, "Doctor, I felt so helpless, I felt so bad. The only way I felt I could feel better was to go and kick those garbage cans over." In this case, Billy's shame at not being able to defend his ethnic origin resulted in antisocial behavior.

The Teasing of David

David, a 16 year old, was so unhappy that his parents feared he was suffering from depression. They sent him to me for treatment. After a visit or two, during which he told me about his life, David described his home situation. David's family lives in a small apartment. He had started to masturbate, and to guarantee privacy, he used his time in the shower to do so. Four days earlier, David had been showering and masturbating when his father banged loudly on the door and said, "You have been in there over half an hour. Will you stop playing with yourself and get out of the shower!" David said to me, "I was so angry at what he said, but worse, I was so ashamed. I didn't feel like ever coming out of the bathroom."

I listened quietly and asked him if he could recall any other situations in which he felt this way. He answered, "I always feel this way." I asked why. He responded, "My father is one of the world's worst teasers." I asked him, "What do you mean, a teaser?" David replied, "He's always doing that kind of thing. Whenever there is anyone around, he is always saying things like that to me. I can remember when I was talking to a girl who lives next door, who's about my age. When I came back into the house, my dad said, 'David's got a girlfriend' in a sing-songy voice. My mother and older sister smiled, and I felt absolutely terrible."

On the receiving end of his father's jokes, David is continually humiliated by him in public. He is ashamed. David is the victim of a shaming environment.

Dyadic Shame Games

A couple, who had been married for some years but who appeared to be having a rough time getting along in their marriage, came to me for help. The wife said, "Doctor, I don't think I can stand it any longer. He is always criticizing me. Everything I do is wrong. I don't feel there is anything I can do to please him." She continued in a similar vein for a few moments. I turned toward the husband to give him his turn to complain. "Doctor," he said, "I don't know what is wrong with her. Half of the time she is depressed, the other half of the time she is furious with me. I don't know what it is that I am doing. Just last night, for example, I said to her, 'Why did you use this old tablecloth, it's threadbare. Why don't we use the new one?'" He was just barely able to finish this report when she turned on him and said, "There, you see, Doctor, he's always critical, he's always hostile, he's always dissatisfied with me." The husband turned quickly and said, "No, I simply suggested that you use another tablecloth."

Unbeknownst to the husband, his "suggestions" are shaming for his wife. He thinks he is only making suggestions. She reads his "suggestions" as criticism, and feels shame. She responds to her sense of shame with withdrawal, depression, and anger. He reads her withdrawal as the withdrawal of love, and he, in turn, is shamed by it. They, like many couples, have created a shame environment in which each shames the other.

Poverty and Shame

Recently, I was reading a newspaper story about poverty in Russia that made the point that beggars existed even in this country.[2] Mrs. V. was described as an elderly woman living on a skimpy monthly pension. To survive, nearly every day she eats in a cafeteria for poor people. When asked if she would mind being photographed, Mrs. V. said it would be all right as long as the picture would be printed abroad and would not appear in the local papers. She did not want her picture to appear in the local papers because her neighbors would then know that she used the poor people's cafeteria. She said, "I would be so ashamed if they knew."

We rarely think of the poor and unfortunate as being shamed by their condition. When we pass beggars in the street, we do not think of their shame, but, in fact, do we not turn away our eyes because we are ashamed of their shame?

Arnie and His Aging Body

Not too long ago, a fifty-year-old man came to my office. Arnie was a tall, robust-looking fellow who told me in the first session that he felt depressed and anxious. After 3 or 4 sessions, I learned that Arnie was very proud of his physical appearance. He had played football in high school and college and was still quite an active athlete, playing tennis every weekend. His physical ability was very important to him. He described how much he liked to play tennis and how he hated to lose. He said, "When I lose, I feel terrible, even though I know that I've beaten my partner before." Arnie's facial expression during our discussion of his lost match led me to suspect that he might have strong feelings of shame arising from a sense of physical inadequacy.

The next time I saw him, I questioned him concerning how he felt about getting old. He laughed when I broached this topic and said that he did not feel that he was getting old in his body, just in years. I smiled and asked him if he thought that he was immune to aging? He argued that he was feeling just as good as when he was 27. I let the matter go, since he appeared to be irritated and distressed by this topic. At our next session, he appeared anxious. He said, "Doc, our last conversation got me thinking about something that I haven't mentioned to you." He averted his gaze, which indicated to me that he wanted to tell me something that was shameful. He went on, "You know, you were talking about aging, and I guess that may be what's at work." He paused for a long time. "Yes, Arnie?" I said, smiling and trying to reassure him. Arnie then told me that in the last six months he had been, on occasion, having potency problems. "I just can't get it up," he said. I asked him what was happening. After describing the situation, he looked at me and said, "I felt so ashamed. I haven't wanted to have sex with Sue [his wife]. Is this what you meant by getting older?"

The Good Provider

Larry, a patient suffering from depression, worked two jobs in order to make enough money to support his wife and two kids. He was quite proud that, through his effort, he was able to earn enough money to provide for his family's needs, that he was what he called "a good provider." Larry's symptoms of depression appeared after he overheard a conversation between his wife and oldest son, who had come home for the summer and was working to earn money for next year's college expenses. "I heard him ask her for some money to buy new boots. She said that he could use the money he was earning. He said that he needed it to pay for his expenses next year at school. He then asked for the money for the boots again, and my wife said, 'I just don't have it. Dad hasn't been getting the kind of tips he used to [Larry drove a cab at night], and we're short of money.' " Larry went on, "I looked at my son's face, and the disappointment and frustration made me feel terrible." Larry began having trouble sleeping. The good provider could not provide. Shame and depression were the consequences.

———— • ————

As we can see, shame exists in our everyday lives. It influences our interpersonal relationships and affects how we think and behave. Given its power in our lives, it deserves study. Below I outline the course of our exploration.

The Plan of This Book

In chapter 2, I discuss emotional life, with particular emphasis on the difference between primary and secondary, or self-conscious, emotions.

Primary emotions, including joy, sadness, anger, disgust, interest, and fear, appear early in human development and, while requiring cognitive activity, do not rely on self-consciousness. The secondary emotions, such as shame, guilt, and pride, all involve self-consciousness. It is not possible to feel shame without comparing one's action against one's standards or beliefs. I will also consider the behavioral manifestations of shame, and the history of their study, starting with Darwin's description of blushing as a species-specific behavior. While I touch upon the psychiatric view of shame, full discussion of this topic will be deferred to chapter 4, when I present my own model of shame.

In chapter 3, I focus on such issues as self-awareness, consciousness, and, from an attentional perspective, objective self-awareness. All systems, from the simplest to the most complicated, regulate themselves. Regulation requires that a system be aware of itself, at least at some level. Thus, awareness is a property inherent in life, one that cannot be claimed as something unique to adult humans. However, not all living beings possess what we adults refer to as "consciousness of ourselves." I propose that there are three different levels of self-awareness. Subjective self-awareness exists on two levels, the reflexive and the representational, which allow for self-regulation and control—even of highly complex actions. Objective self-awareness exists on a third level that allows for the consciousness of ourselves. These levels correspond to emotional states (the subjective self) and experiences (the objective self). Moreover, each level involves different areas of the brain to support different functions.

Awareness develops during the first two years of life. While one level follows another, the final structure of the self system includes all three. All three are involved in our daily functioning. In part, we may understand intrapsychic conflict as the interactions of these different levels.

In chapter 4, I present a cognitive attribution model of shame, guilt, hubris, and pride. The model is based on the general proposition that shame and guilt are the consequences of the self's failure in regard to a standard, goal, or rule. Hubris and pride, in contrast, are the consequences of the self's success in regard to a standard. Shame can be distinguished from guilt: a *total* self failure vis-à-vis a standard produces shame, while a *specific* self failure results in guilt. A similar analysis allows us to distinguish between hubris and pride. In this chapter, I contrast my specific hypothesis about the cause of shame, cognitive attribution, with psychoanalytic theories relating shame to the failure to control impulses in accordance with the dictates of the ego ideal.

The processes that allow for the emergence of shame can be traced over time. The developmental analysis presented in chapter 5 involves both the primary emotions and the cognitive capacities that account for the emergence of the self-conscious emotions. I discuss two classes of self-conscious emotions: those that involve self-exposure and those that require both self-exposure and evaluation. Self-exposure, the development of objective self-awareness, gives rise to embarrassment. Although embarrassment appears to have an evaluative feature, people can and do show embarrassment when no self-evaluation takes place. For example, we are embarrassed when we are complimented or when we perceive that we are being looked at by others. Developmentally, after further cognitive elaboration, children are able to form goals and construct standards that can be compared to what they are actually doing. Failure or success vis-à-vis these standards gives rise to the self-conscious evaluative emotions. The development of these emotions takes place over the first three years of life, although they are elaborated over the life course. Using the biblical creation story, I argue for the proposition that emotions give rise to thoughts about emotions, which, in turn, give rise to new emotions.

Although the development of shame requires maturation, socialization is the eliciting force. In chapter 6, I suggest that shame results from comparison of the self's action with the self's standards, and that socialization provides the wherewithal for the process of comparison as well as the standards themselves. The goals and rules that govern our lives are learned from those around us, and our evaluation of success or failure also involves learning. Our parents teach us how to set standards and how to evaluate performance. Parents also play a teaching role that is more indirect but just as important. Parents who practice love withdrawal or who express contempt and disgust affect their children's sense of pride and shame. The available data indicates that girls and women are more likely than boys and men to make global self-attributions—"I am bad," not "My performance was bad"—when they fail. Thus, girls and women may experience more shame than boys and men.

Having analyzed the fundamental processes and developmental changes in the production of shame, I turn in chapters 7, 8, and 9 to how people deal with their shame. Chapter 7 reviews two kinds of shame experiences, felt and bypassed shame. In the former, people experience their shame and develop strategies to cope with this intense and unpleasant feeling—forgetting, laughing, and confessing are just a few of these strategies. We "own" the shame, but learn ways of dealing with it. In bypassed shame, people repress the initial experience of shame and focus their attention elsewhere. They feel sadness or anger instead of shame. The problems that are associated with bypassed shame include the inability to prevent shame from reoccurring since, not recognizing it, we do not see its causes nor are we able to read others' shame.

Of more serious consequence are the effects of prolonged shame. As we

see in chapter 8, depression and rage are the most likely ⟨
prolonged shame. Prolonged shame is best understood in it
Those who suffer prolonged shame experiences are li
shame-producing environments. Men and women, ofte
what they are doing, shame each other. Shamed women aɪͨ ···ᴜɪ·ͨ ······ʸ
respond with depression, shamed men with rage. Depression following the
loss of a love object appears to involve shame as an intermediate step. I
contrast this view with those held by object relations theorists.

I pay considerable attention to the shame-rage axis, since violence is
becoming more and more prevalent in this society: witness the rise in
murder, suicide, and child abuse. I distinguish between anger, a response
to the blockage of a goal, and rage, a response to an attack on the self. The
data support the belief that shame may underlie much of the violence we
witness.

The extreme pathology of prolonged shame produces narcissistic disorders and the disintegration of the self system. These topics are considered
in chapter 9. Narcissistic disorders generate a wide range of symptoms
including grandiosity, rage, inferiority, overidealization, entitlement, and a
lack of empathy. For me, the inability to cope with shame and humiliation
underlies these pathological disturbances. Narcissists seek to avoid shame,
and, when avoidance fails, engage in emotional behavior that masks their
underlying feeling.

Multiple personality disorders (MPD) are directly related to early
intense shame experiences. In almost all cases, MPD patients have
experienced prolonged sexual abuse. As a defense against their shame,
they develop a coping strategy that allows them to believe that "it is not me
that this (sexual abuse) is happening to, it is someone else." MPD, the
ultimate disassociative disorder, enables us to probe how shame affects all
disassociative processes.

The sex differences I have noted suggest the "two world" hypothesis I
advance in chapter 10: the emotional lives of men and women may differ
because they have different strategies for coping with shame. Regardless of
their individual degrees of empathic ability, men and women are unable to
understand the opposite sex's emotional response. Intergenerational
difficulties, the Oedipal myth, and the intimacy and anger of the
mother-daughter relationship, for example, can also be interpreted as
problems arising in the negotiation of shame.

I devote most of my attention to shame as it is manifested in the lives of
those in contemporary Western societies. But a complete understanding of
shame and its impact on individuals and societies requires that we step
back from where we stand. In chapter 11, I examine shame in other
cultures and at other times. My conclusion is both reassuring and

alarming. Shame is universal. To feel shame is normal. There is comfort here. But too little or too much shame may produce unique difficulties. Some cultures and some times seem to produce more shame than others—and concomitantly more narcissistic disorders and violent behavior.

Both narcissism and violence characterize our culture and time. In a philosophical epilogue, I consider the evolution of the existentialist conception of self-alone. As Erich Fromm pointed out in his book, *Escape From Freedom,*

> The whole social history of man started with his emerging from the state of oneness with the natural world to an awareness of himself as an entity separate from surrounding nature and man. Yet this awareness remained very dim over long periods of history. The individual continued to be closely tied to the natural and social world from which he emerged. While being partly aware of himself as a separate entity, he also felt a part of the world around him. The growing process of the emergence of the individual from his original ties, a process which we may call individuation, seems to have reached its peak in modern history.[3]

How can we more effectively meet the challenges of coping with shame? There is no clear answer; but it does not seem unwise to suggest that beside love and work, we need to look toward commitment and community, to move away from our exposed selves.

2

Our Emotional Lives

E motions are not thoughts, yet we think about them. They are similar
to physical sensations such as hunger and pain in some ways, but
different in others. Hunger goes away when we eat, and pain disappears
when we remove its immediate cause. The study of emotions is complicated
by definitional problems. Our emotional life is familiar to us and we have
developed a great deal of folk knowledge about it. But this folk knowledge,
while adequate for our everyday needs, fails us when we try to analyze
emotions.

Are Emotions Feelings?

I start with the terms *emotion, affect,* and *feeling*. These terms need to be
distinguished, since they are often used interchangeably. The first two are
rather easy to define. Like others, I assume the major distinction between
emotion and affect to be the difference between the specific and the
general. By affect, I mean all states that are not cognitive in nature. Thus,
such bodily sensations as hunger, fatigue, and pain are affects. However, I
restrict certain affects and call them emotions. Here I include the simple
everyday emotions that I will call primary emotions, such as joy, sadness,
fear, disgust, interest, and anger, and the more complex emotions, such as
empathy, sympathy, envy, guilt, shame, pride, and regret. As we will see,
primary emotions can be distinguished from the more complex emotions
because the latter require self-reflection. There are many more emotions;
indeed, I could compile lists of terms referring to emotions that would fill
many pages. It is not my intention here to define dozens or hundreds of
terms referring to emotions or to argue whether particular ones are
properly affects or emotions. I will focus on the self-related emotions.

The term *feeling* has at least two meanings. For example, when we say "I am feeling happy," we mean, first, "I am in a state of happiness" and, second, "I am aware of this state".[1] Some researchers have argued for a restricted meaning of feeling and have therefore suggested that feeling refers only to the condition described in the first statement, "I am in a state of happiness." This restricted meaning implies that feeling is something real, an internal state that, given the proper observational techniques, could be measured and described. This view of feeling as an internal emotional state has preoccupied theorists since the earliest writings on emotions.[2] Several different physical locations for this internal state have been proposed.[3]

Defining feeling as an internal emotional state that is physically real and measurable allows us to conceive of internal emotional states as independent of cognition. The eliciting stimulus event simply acts in some manner so as to produce an emotional state.[4] Although some type of cognition may be necessary to link these eliciting stimulus events to feeling, neither feeling nor the emotional state itself depends on cognition. One needs cognition for perceptual discrimination or for the interpretation of emotional elicitors, but one does not need cognition to experience or be aware of the state itself. For example, cognition enables us to discriminate a doctor's white coat from a coat of another color, and to associate the white coat and past pain, but is not involved in the resulting emotional response of fear.

By *emotional state* I mean a specific internal bodily response that has a unique correspondence in some one-to-one fashion with discrete emotions such as fear, empathy, anger, disgust, shame, etc. I postulate such a hypothetical state in order to make clear that emotional states are not epiphenomenal: they have a unique and specific location within the biological system.

Unfortunately, measurement of these unique emotional states remains extremely difficult. Most early research in psychophysiology was concerned with locating foci in the central or autonomic nervous system bearing some one-to-one correspondence with these unique emotions. For example, the work of Cannon and Bard seemed to indicate that stimulation of the hypothalamus in cats produced an anger or rage response. This finding was used to argue the existence of unique brain sites for emotions that can be mapped. In this sense, then, feelings are "real."

The second statement concerning the meaning of the term feeling—"I am aware of feeling happy"—has more to do with thinking and with the self. While emotional states may exist independent of cognition, awareness of such states of being in and of themselves is very important: such awareness is itself cognitive. Analogous to knowing about knowing is knowing about feeling. Thus, we may be in a physiological state of happiness but we do not feel happy, that is to say, we are unaware of our happiness. There are many emotional states at many different times of which we are not aware.

Two examples illustrate potentially different processes via which the thinking or awareness aspect of feeling and the emotional state aspect of feeling are disassociated.

While she is driving her car at 60 miles per hour, Gloria's front left tire blows out. For the next 15 seconds she struggles with the steering wheel to try to bring the car safely to a halt on the side of the road. Once having succeeded, she observes that she is fearful. She further observes that her fearfulness started at the point when she noticed that her hands were shaking and that she was reflecting on the last 15 seconds' events.

The first question to be answered is: Was Gloria, from the point of the blowout until she noticed that she was fearful, feeling fear? It seems reasonable to assume that, had we the proper measurement instrument, we could have determined that she was in a state of fear during that time period. The second question to be answered is: Was she feeling fearful? If we mean by "feeling," "was she *in* a state," then we must answer yes, she was feeling fearful. If, however, we mean "was she *aware of or did she think* about her fearfulness," then we must answer no. Since she was attending to outside stimuli, how could she have been *aware* of her internal state? During those 15 seconds when she was bringing her car to a stop, she was focusing on the proprioceptive feedback from the steering wheel or the tires on the road. She was listening to the sounds her brakes were making, and watching objects in front of her on the road. Given that she was attending to all of these external stimuli, could she also have been attending to her internal state? Admittedly, it is possible to attend to one's internal state during the course of attending to the external complex array of stimuli; however, attending to one's internal state is costly since it detracts from the ability to attend to those external stimuli that are necessary for survival. Thus, while it is possible, and while individuals do sometimes attend to their internal states during times of action, for the most part they do not. In this particular case, given Gloria's situation and her need to attend to and process external stimuli, it is reasonable for us to assume that while she was *in* a state of fear, she was not *aware* of feeling fearful.

I had a patient named John who received the news that a very dear aunt had died. At first, he reported experiencing great sadness at the loss. But then his sadness seemed to dissipate. Several weeks later, he felt agitated and experienced some trouble eating and sleeping. When I asked John how he felt, he replied that he felt tired. When I asked him whether he was depressed, he said that he did not feel depressed.

John reports that he feels, that is, he is aware of, a particular emotion. In this case, the emotional state that he is aware of and reports is fatigue. Here, rather than distraction (that is, attending to other stimulus events), we see a different mechanism that can disassociate the feeling as self-awareness from the feeling as state. John is engaged in an active attempt to pay attention to and focus on one feature or aspect of his emotional state rather than another. By focusing on his fatigue, John diverts attention from the more serious feeling state, depression. What might be the mechanisms that cause someone to focus on one aspect of his emotional state as opposed to another or, in some cases, cause him to state that he is feeling fine, rather than sad or depressed?

I can imagine two. The first is an active and, perhaps, unconscious mechanism that seeks to prevent one's conscious self-awareness from engaging in the "true" emotional state of sadness. The process takes the form "I am unaware that I am aware of a feeling or an internal state." For some intrapsychic reason, one aspect of the self prevents another aspect of the self from being aware of a particular emotional state. Such a mechanism requires both cognitive self-awareness and a cognitive unconscious endowed with the same abilities that the conscious self has.[5] In this mechanism, these unconscious cognitive structures, called unconscious self-awareness, act on one's self-conscious self-awareness as it pertains to emotional states. Such a model has been articulated by others. I am not sure how one would go about putting such a conception to empirical test. Nevertheless, the notion of unconscious mental processes has had great appeal and has been used widely as an explanatory device because it accounts for a wide range of phenomena. Consider the following: I inform John that his awareness of being tired is an incomplete self-awareness. In fact, I tell him that he is really sad or even depressed because of his aunt's death. My understanding in some fashion acts to alter John's self-awareness and he suddenly discovers that my observation is correct. John realizes that he is more than just tired: he is depressed.

Whether this change in awareness represents bringing into consciousness that which is unconscious or simply John's willingness to succumb to the suggestion of another remains an important distinction—one that is of some concern in the psychotherapy literature. If it were the former, we would have evidence of an unconscious awareness that is different from conscious awareness; if it were the latter, it would simply mark a change in his conscious awareness.

The second mechanism that can be evoked to explain why John focused on fatigue rather than sadness has to do less with a topology of components of the self in conflict or the mechanism of repression and more with simple learning processes. I have suggested elsewhere that during socialization children are given specific verbal labels and are responded to in a unique fashion when they exhibit certain emotional behaviors in certain contexts.[6] Parental response to emotional states and their associated behaviors should result in children learning to think about their emotional states. Parents may in effect teach children to have an awareness not in agreement with their internal states. For example, as a child John may have exhibited certain behaviors in a situation of loss. When he did, his parents informed him that these behaviors meant that he was tired, not sad. In other words, past experience may be capable of shaping people's self-awareness about an emotion, even to the extent of producing an awareness that is idiosyncratic in relation to the actual emotional state. This type of learning is likely to account for differences termed pathological. Perhaps it also accounts for familial, group, and cultural differences in emotional experience.

To summarize, "feeling" means having an emotional state, *and also* means being aware of that emotional state. These meanings are too often assumed to be the same. All emotions can be experienced. What we need to consider now, however, is how emotions differ from one another.

Primary Versus Secondary Emotions

The notion of primary, or basic, emotions has a long history dating back to Descartes's six primary passions and to Spinoza's three primary affects. The idea that there is a basic set of emotions grows out of the idea of human instincts or propensities. If they are basic, prewired, or genetically given, they have to be limited in number. While we recognize an enormous variety of emotions we describe in giving accounts of our lives, the existence of each one as a unique and discreet "wiring" is too burdensome a characterization of the nervous system. Instead of positing this complex set of emotions, most theorists have argued that there are only a select number of basic, primary, or pure emotions, and that all the others to which we refer are mixes of these original few.

Robert Plutchik offers perhaps the best discussion of this problem.[7] He offers six postulates that set the stage for all other discussions: (1) there is a small number of pure or primary emotions; (2) all other emotions are mixed, that is, they can be synthesized by means of various combinations of the primary emotions; (3) primary emotions differ from each other with regard to both physiology and behavior; (4) primary emotions, in their pure form, are hypothetical constructs of idealized states whose properties can only be inferred from various kinds of evidence; (5) primary emotions may be conceptualized in terms of pairs of polar opposites; and (6) each emotion can exist in varying degrees of intensity or levels of arousal. Plutchik, in his analysis of emotions, uses a color wheel analogy to explain how the eight basic emotions become elaborated into all others: just as all complex and varied colors are derivatives of three primary colors, all complex and varied emotions derive from eight primary emotions.

The idea of primary emotions as the basic building blocks from which all other emotions are constructed seems to be an idea with both heuristic value and conceptual simplicity. The problem here, however, is that Plutchik postulates eight primary emotions, and his candidates do not agree with those postulated by others. Carroll Izard, for example, offers six primary emotions, while Silvan Tomkins offers eight, but a different eight than Plutchik.[8]

The problem of deciding which emotions are the basic, primary ones and which are the derived ones is not easily solved given the diversity of opinion. Plutchik offers three decision rules. He suggests that for an emotion to be considered primary, first, it must have relevance to basic, biological, adaptive processes. I could argue, post hoc, that almost any emotion has such relevance, and therefore Plutchik's first rule does not help us much. Second, Plutchik suggests, a primary emotion must be found, in some form, at all evolutionary levels. Exactly why this should be a requirement for a basic emotion is unclear to me. For example, Darwin pointed out the uniqueness of blushing for humans; although blushing is evolutionarily unique, nonetheless it is basic and specific to humans. Plutchik's third suggestion, however, is useful: he argues that basic emotions, by definition, are not dependent on introspection. Presumably, he means that some emotions are dependent on introspection. Self-conscious emotions, shame in particular, would not be basic or primary emotions according to this definition. Plutchik stands in opposition to Darwin and Tomkins, both of whom argue that shame *is* a primary emotion.

One possibility for solving the problem of primary emotions is to look at emotions that emerge early. We can make a logical claim that these emotions are the primary or the basic ones and argue that those that emerge later are the secondary, derived, or mixed ones. Such a view would be satisfying except for two counterarguments. First, based on simple biological principles, there is no reason to assume that because something emerges later it is less biologically central than something that emerges early. We know that over the life course different biological functions appear—functions that are prewired and genetically coded, and influenced little or not at all by socialization—and that these functions occur, not only at the beginning of life, but all through the life course. A good example is sexual maturity in adolescence. Clearly, puberty is programmed and genetically triggered, yet it does not occur in the beginning of life. Thus, the argument of temporal position as a significant factor for determining primary versus secondary emotions will not suffice.

Second, given that we accept early emergence as a defining sign of the primary emotions, how do we determine at what point in the developmental sequence emotions belong to the primary set versus a latter set? In other words, do all the primary emotions emerge in the first 3 months of life, or the first 6 months, or 18 months, or at some other point? How do we determine a terminus? I think that the timing postulate will not do as a method for defining emotions, since we do not know what *early* means.

In fact, there is no clear way to differentiate primary from secondary emotions. Thus, even though this idea has appeal, its practical utility remains doubtful. But Plutchik's distinction between emotions that require or do not require introspection gives us a clue to a system that might prove workable for separating and defining categories of emotions. I suggest that emotions can be classified in relation to the role of the self. The elicitation of fear, joy, disgust, surprise, anger, sadness, and interest does not require introspection or self-reference. Therefore, let us consider these emotions as one set. The elicitation of jealousy, envy, empathy, embarrassment, shame, pride, and guilt does require introspection or self-reference. These emotions constitute another set. By simply differentiating emotions on the basis of the use of the self we are able to produce two groups. Note also, in reference to the timing postulate, we find that the second set of self-referential emotions emerges later than the first set of non-self-referential emotions.

The ontogenetic difference is supported by a phylogenetic difference. Although some theorists might disagree, I believe that all animals possess the emotions that do not require introspection, but only the human animal (and perhaps the chimpanzee) marked by self-introspection, is capable of having the second group of emotions. This method allows us to divide emotions both ontogenetically and phylogenetically along a single dimension, that being introspection. I will take this approach, though I recognize that, while it has heuristic value, it is only one of a number of possible approaches. Thus, I propose that the difference between primary and secondary emotions is that secondary emotions involve self-reference. Secondary emotions will be referred to as *self-conscious emotions;* shame is a self-conscious emotion.

Emotional life has three major aspects: emotional states, emotional expressions, and emotional experiences. I will discuss each with special reference to shame. I have already discussed emotional states. Emotional expression relates to our public action; emotional experience relates to introspection and self.

Emotional Expression

Emotional expression is the external manifestation of internal states. Although I define emotional expression in this fashion, others believe that emotional expressions themselves constitute the unique bodily activity associated with the unique emotions that we have. So, for example, Tomkins, Izard, and Ekman, following Darwin's initial observation, have argued that the unique expressive behaviors of the individual constitutes, in some one-to-one fashion, these unique emotional states. I certainly am sympathetic to such a view; nevertheless, emotional expressions rarely bear a one-to-one correspondence to internal states. There are three modalities for emotional expression: the face, the voice, and the body. The complex interaction of these three modalities has not been adequately analyzed.[9] I will focus illustratively on facial expression.

Facial expressions center on the eyes and the mouth. They include the movement of eyebrows and the degree of eye openness. In the mouth they involve tension: lips pulled up, down, and back or into an oval-like or square shape. It is not my intention here to elaborate on facial configuration possibilities. Paul Ekman has argued that there are over 33,000 possible facial expressions that can be articulated given the various muscle groups. Clearly, however, human beings cannot discriminate such a vast number of facial expressions.[10]

Of some concern to this discussion is the ability to produce facial expressions at will. If we wish to hold that facial expressions have some one-to-one correspondence with internal states, then we must be prepared to argue and demonstrate that facial expressions always mean what they seem to mean. Such a proposition is unreasonable. At very early ages, children are capable of altering facial expression to serve their needs.[11] In our adult lives, we encounter many situations in which our facial expression bears no resemblance to our internal state. Look at a common, and very simple, example:

My wife returns from a sale where she has bought a dress that cannot be returned. It is obvious to me that she really likes her new dress and thinks she looks good in it. She asks me my opinion. I think the dress is hideous and not the least bit becoming, but it is important for me to pretend that I like it. My task, then, is to produce the appropriate facial and postural behaviors which should convey my intended, rather than my real, feeling. This I can manage without any trouble!

We are, of course, moderately successful in carrying out these forms of pretense or deception. The question is how good are we and are such deceptions detectable? Remember, if we believe that there is a one-to-one correspondence between facial expressions and internal states, then we should be able to detect false facial expressions. In general, detection of pretend faces has met with relatively little success.[12]

While facial expressions *may* bear a one-to-one correspondence with unique internal states, there is no reason to assume they do. In fact, socialization rules are designed to disassemble the relationship of facial expression to the internal states they may initially represent. Ekman and Friesen, as well as others, have articulated some of the rules of masking the face.[13] These rules are quite complex and include producing no facial expression, producing a facial expression that is unrelated to the internal state, and even producing an exaggeration of the internal state so that the receiver is likely to think that this exaggerated face cannot represent the true internal state. I will not elaborate on the rules that adults use to mask their faces nor upon the process by which children learn them. It is obvious from any number of studies that these rules are acquired early, and that after the first few years of life children are quite knowledgeable about the societal scripts necessitating the use of particular faces in particular situations.

The Behavioral Measures of Shame

What behaviors may indicate shame? Because emotional expressions are only partially correlated with emotional states, any description of shame based on behavior is bound to be limited. As we search for manifestations of shame, we can look at various external manifestations, that is, the behaviors that are visible to others. Or we can look at the internal states, the physiological, including autonomic, biochemical, and central nervous system, responses that occur during the shame experience. Finally, we can study language, starting first with sounds and then looking at words themselves.

We can dispense with internal states and language relatively quickly. Little is yet known about either. While recent data suggest that some emotions are associated more with activity of the left than the right hemisphere of the brain, this work is restricted mostly to the emotions of fear and enjoyment.[14] There may well be specific central nervous system activity associated with particular emotions; however, this unproven possibility does not really help our study of shame. Some researchers have looked at different responses that index select emotions. It seems reasonable to believe that if a person is shamed, we should be able to measure some sort of physiological change associated with the shame emotion. It also seems reasonable to believe that the physiological changes associated with shame should differ from those associated with another emotion, anger, for example. Unfortunately, after a hundred years of psychophysiology, neither a simple physiological response nor a set of such responses correlated with specific emotions has been found.[15]

Vocal expression and language also do not appear to index specific emotions. In exploring the question of whether sets or patterns of vocal cues are associated with the discrete emotions that we experience, Klaus Scherer seems to suggest that judges can differentiate emotional expressions.[16] But the evidence for such an association exists only for two emotions that have readily discernible vocal indicators, anger versus grief or sadness. No vocal patterns specific to shame have been suggested. Thus, we are left to explore surface manifestations of shame in the face and in the body.

I turn first to Darwin's *Expression of Emotion in Man and Animals,* in which shame is described as being expressed facially, like most emotions, and also through head movement and body posture. The primary emotions, such as happiness, fear, or anger, can be detected by observation of selected muscles around the eyes and mouth; however, the expression of shame is indexed more by other parts of the body. Darwin said that when one is ashamed the head is averted or bent down with the eyes wavering or turned away (what is now referred to as gaze avert). Darwin noted that facial blushing is a manifestation of shame, and he also pointed out that the reddening of the skin, the bringing of blood vessels to the surface, takes place not only in the facial region but all over the body.

In Victorian times, even scientists were subject to the age's prudish standards. Darwin had no opportunity to observe naked humans, so he had to rely on reports from physicians. From them, he concluded that the blushing response is not restricted to the face, although the extent and degree of blushing elsewhere on the body is difficult to determine. Possibly, because the face is the seat of one's identity, and one wishes to conceal oneself during shame, the face becomes the focus of the shame. By logical extension, the degree to which other parts of the body become the focus might influence the degree to which they also would blush. Darwin relates the case of a physician examining a woman. During the preliminary, fully clothed part of the exam, the woman's face blushed. As the examination progressed, the physician removed the top part of the woman's gown. At this, her blush traveled down to her now-exposed breasts. Darwin claimed that any area of the body will blush if it becomes the focal point of attention.

Darwin suggests that the shame response is associated with a strong desire for concealment. He quotes from the Old Testament and Ezra, who cries out, "Oh my God, I am ashamed and I blush to lift up my head to thee, oh God!," and Isaiah, who says, "I hide not my face from shame." Darwin also notes the responses of turning away, lowering the eyes, or the restless moving of the eyes from side to side—all of this to escape the painful gaze of others.

Although his description of shame appears to be consistent with more modern descriptions, it is broad enough to fit most self-conscious emotions. He does not distinguish between shame and guilt or, for that matter, between shame and shyness, or modesty, or embarrassment. For him, all were self-conscious emotions characterized by what he called self-attention. Consider shyness. When Darwin talks about measures of shyness, which he considers false shame, he mentions blushing, eyes averted or cast down, and nervous movements of the body. Both shyness and shame appear to involve the same bodily movements. Although Darwin does not make much of the distinction between shyness, embarrassment, and shame, he does distinguish these three emotions from guilt. He considers guilt more like regret over some "fault committed."

Because Darwin believed the blushing response was species-specific and related to shame, he was particularly interested in it. He inquired into situations and conditions that were likely to lead to blushing. He did not think that blushing would occur if you gave money to a beggar but might occur if you became aware of someone watching you while you gave the money. Darwin believed that such a blush is caused by attention directed toward ourselves by another. But his beggar example more reasonably illustrates a case of embarrassment—exposure plus a positive action—

than shame—exposure plus a negative action. This important difference will be considered in more detail later.

Darwin also observed that children do not blush before age two or three. Others have made the claim that shame can be detected earlier, that the turning away of the child at the approach of a stranger by 8–10 months is indicative of shame, but I do not think it is.[17]

McDougall, an early investigator of the role of emotions in human life, was particularly interested in the relationship between emotions and cognition.[18] Although he was more interested in curiosity, he also considered shame a complex self emotion. The behaviors that he used to index shame were similar to those that Darwin had used before him. McDougall talks about the shame response as bashful behavior. He also saw blushing and the lowering of the eyes both as a literal, behavioral representation, and as a figurative representation of the feeling.

The relationship between body posture and emotion has attracted some attention because so few facial expressions appear to be unique markers of the secondary or self-conscious emotions. For example, pride is often referred to as being "puffed up," and the bodily behaviors in the service of pride include holding the head high, making strong eye contact, and external thrusting and puffing of the body. Shame, in contrast, is more characterized by gaze aversion and a shrinking or a compressing of the body, consistent with wanting to disappear or to hide. The coding systems for bodily activity suggest that facial expression alone is insufficient to index all emotional states.

In the second volume of Silvan Tomkin's *Affect, Imagery, and Consciousness,* he devotes a considerable amount of space to the self-conscious emotions. Tomkins, like Darwin, did not distinguish between shyness, shame, and guilt. For him, these emotions are of the same class. Though evoked by different experiences, the three states are fundamentally the same, even if the conscious awareness of each is different. Thus, for Tomkins, all the self-conscious emotions, which also include contempt, guilt, and humiliation, are subsumed by a particular state that serves the function of "inhibiting the continuing interest and enjoyment of the person." He goes on to say that shame is designed to inhibit interest and enjoyment: "the innate activator of shame is the incomplete reduction of interest and joy."[19] Unfortunately, though there is little empirical support for this assertion, the idea that shame is the result of the incomplete reduction of interest and joy has been widely accepted.[20]

The behaviors that Tomkins sees as indicative of shame are those pinpointed by Darwin and, as we will see, almost all others. Tomkins makes little attempt to locate specific muscle movement in the face; rather he sees the dropping of the head and upper part of the body, including the eyes and eyelids, turning away, and, of course, blushing as an emotional set designed to reduce facial communication.

Next to blushing, hiding is mentioned most often as a behavior indexing shame. Recently this response—collapse of the body, including the hunching of the head and the squeezing of the shoulders together—has been used to systematically measure shame.[21]

Carroll Izard has long been interested in observing facial expression and developing a coding system in order to understand emotional development.[22] He has made considerable progress in the nearly twenty years that he has been working on this problem. In his earlier work, he saw shyness, embarrassment, shame, and guilt as the same; however, by 1977, while he still identified shame with shyness, he recognized guilt as a separate entity. By 1986 he had ceased even to regard shame and shyness as the same, though embarrassment and shame remain similar. For Izard the measures indexing shame are the same as those reported by others: a lowering of the eyes, or gaze avert, a lowering of the head, and a collapse of the upper torso as it moves in toward itself. He also notes that shame is accompanied, on occasion, by blushing. While Izard differentiates shame, shyness, and guilt conceptually, his measurement system, focusing on the facial musculature, does not as yet provide a way to differentiate them in practice.

Recently, others have begun to develop coding systems for such self-evaluative emotions as shame, pride, submission-shame, which is similar to self-deprecation or guilt (regret), and dominance (or self-enhancement).[23] Zahn-Waxler has been looking at children's responses to mistakes and has focused on behavior that may provide useful indicators of guilt (regret) and shame. In her work and in our studies following her, young children are given a toy. Unbeknownst to the child, the toy is designed to fall apart after a few minutes of normal play. Children's responses are quite varied.[24] Some children simply do nothing and go to another toy, while others become upset and cry. Neither of these two responses are of particular interest to us. But two other responses, which may differentiate guilt from shame, are. Some children show the typical shame response: they avert their gaze and their bodies appear to collapse. They stop moving and remain quite impassive. Their behavior seems disrupted; their thought processes appear confused, or at least inhibited. Other children, at the moment the toy falls apart, avert their gaze and show tense facial expression, but their bodies do not collapse. Rather than "disappearing," these children try to fix the toy. Their attempts at reparation suggest guilt rather than shame. For these children, the object of concern is not themselves but the toy. For me, the attempt at reparation, the focus upon the toy rather than the self, constitutes the most important behavioral distinction between shame and guilt.

I have been trying to see if it is possible to distinguish embarrassment from shame. Margaret Sullivan, Cathy Stanger, and I have been looking at children's behavior during embarrassing rather than shameful situations.[25] In this particular set of studies, which I will discuss in more detail later, we had children aged from 8 months to 3 years and their mothers come to the laboratory. When they arrived, we greeted them, and, in the course of discussing what we were going to do, repeatedly praised the children for a variety of actions: what they were wearing, what they looked like, and what they were doing with the toys we gave them to play with. The experiment was designed to follow a fixed procedure in which the experimenter said "I like the way you combed your hair," "What a pretty skirt [or slacks] you're wearing," "That's a lovely——" (——being the toy or object the child brought), and finally "You put the pieces of the puzzle together very well, you must be very smart."

Observation of the children's behavior indicates a pattern that we have labeled as embarrassment. This pattern is consistent with others. The children averted their gaze but, unlike children who were experiencing shame, their turning away was for a brief period of time only. Moreover, this gaze aversion often was repeated in a turn-away-and-then-back pattern. At the same time they averted their gaze, the children smiled broadly. This smile seems to differentiate embarrassment from shame. Finally, some children nervously touched their bodies with their hands, although they did not cover their faces with their hands.[26] These three behaviors occurred in rapid succession, with gaze aversion and smiling usually occurring before the nervous touching of the body. When the children were complimented we observed no collapsing of the body or other shame behavior that was seen when we asked the children to perform some task they could not manage or when the toy they were playing with broke. It does appear that embarrassment can be differentiated from shame, at least in some situations.

Nevertheless, over one hundred years of research make it quite clear that there is no single measure, or set of measures, that is likely to bear a strong one-to-one correspondence with the experience of shame. This result (or lack of a result) should come as no surprise. We know that the correspondence between external manifestations of emotion and internal states of emotion is at best minimal. But we will continue to try to find them.

Emotional Experience

Emotional experience can be defined as a person's evaluation and interpretation of her own perceived emotional state, through observation of physiological changes, such as increased heart and breathing rate, facial flushing or blushing, sweating, etc., or through evaluation of facial neuromuscular activity like smiling. We have ample evidence that people have control over, and therefore feedback from, the muscles of their faces.

We can also observe the situations in which we find ourselves in order to aid in our perception of our emotional states. Thus, for example, if Larry is quiet and not moving and he is at a funeral, he is likely to interpret his emotional state as sadness, whereas if he is quiet and not moving and is in an auditorium listening to a lecture, he is likely to interpret his emotional state as interest. Emotional experience, therefore, requires that we attend to both sets of stimuli previously discussed as emotional states and expressions, at two levels. At the first level, which I will call the subjective level, the body attends to itself. Like all complex machines, various parts have to monitor and track other parts for the whole to work. Our bodies track the CO_2 level in our blood and, if it is too high or too low, cause a series of complex responses that address and correct the difficulty. All complex organisms attend to their functioning and regulate themselves. This first level of experience I will call *subjective experience.*

But it is the second level of experience, which I will call *objective experience,* that will be focused on here. In objective experience we consciously reflect on ourselves. For many reasons, we are not always experiencing at the objective level. Competing stimuli often draw our attention away from ourselves. When, as described earlier, Gloria was trying to bring her car to a stop, she was not attending to her internal state. I do not mean to suggest that she was not in a state of fear: she was in a state of fear as soon as the tire blew and her car began to go out of control. But she could not really experience her fear until she safely brought her car to a stop and could attend to stimuli emanating from her own body.

Emotional experiences require organisms to attend to a select set of stimuli. Without attention, objective emotional experiences may not occur even though we are in a particular emotional state. I have no trouble reconciling the fact that there are emotional states and expressions that organisms do not objectively experience, with the fact that these states and experiences nonetheless may affect our perceptions, thoughts, and interactions with others and motivate us to particular action. For example, patients may undergo painful treatment at the dentist's but may not experience pain if they are distracted through the use of earphones and loud music. A painful state does exist within the patient, but it is simply not objectively experienced.

Let us return to the issue of being in a state and not experiencing it. I suggest that this is what is often meant by unconscious motivation.

> *A patient of mine took his car to a repair shop and was told that he could have his car back at 2:00 P.M. When he arrived at 2:00, he was informed that the car was not ready. He reported that he was unaware that he was angry or that he looked angry. However, the mechanic interpreted his expression as anger and responded with a sharp, angry statement that amazed the patient. Now my patient became angry at what he perceived as the anger of the mechanic. He said to the mechanic, "What are you angry about? I'm the one whose car is not ready!"*

I was able to show the patient how his unexperienced anger had consequences for his interpersonal interactions, even when he was unaware of his emotional state.

Emotional experience occurs as a result of the interpretation and evaluation of states and expressions, and is therefore dependent upon cognitive processes. It is impossible to talk about interpretation and evaluation without discussing both the cognitive ability to interpret and evaluate and the rules governing the interpretation and evaluation that are the products of particular socialization. The cognitive processes in question are complex and involve perception, memory, and elaboration.[27] Events like changes in autonomic activities need to be perceived, compared with previous experience, and then labeled. Socialization strongly influences labeling. Thus, parents, for example, can aid or harm their children in their emotional experiences by their interpretation of them.

> *We recently saw a 2-year-old girl in our laboratory first with her mother and then with her father. During the course of playing with her mother, the child sat down, became very quiet, and stopped playing with the toys. Her mother asked, "What's the matter? Are you sad?," instructed the child to come and sit in her lap, and then stroked and hugged the child. The mother's response was obviously related to her interpretation of the emotional state of the child. Later, while the father was playing with the child, she exhibited the same behavior. He asked her "Are you tired?," and urged the child to get up and to play more vigorously with a particular toy.*

It seems reasonable to assume that different families and different cultures make different affective interpretations. In some, explanations of internal states either are not given or are given around particular themes. I have a close friend who rarely uses emotional terms to characterize his young children's behavior. For him, his children are hungry, tired, overstimulated, and the like; they are hardly ever sad, happy, excited, or angry.

The Role of the Self in Shame

It is clear that all emotional experiences require objective self-awareness. As we have seen, it is possible to be in an emotional state but not to experience that state, whether the emotional state is a primary or a self-conscious one.

Self-conscious emotional states differ from primary emotional states. By definition, they come about through self-reflection. While primary emotions require a self to experience the state, self-conscious emotions require a self both to produce the state and then to experience it. For example, a loud noise may put me in a state of fright. But to experience this state, I need objective self-awareness. Moreover, to be in a state of shame I must compare my action against some standard, either my own or someone else's. My failure, relative to the standard, results in a state of shame and requires my objective self-awareness. Once in the state, I may or may not experience it. To experience it depends on whether I focus my attention on my state. Again, this requires objective self-awareness. Others have suggested that the state of shame can be produced in a more automatic fashion, one that does not require objective self-awareness.

Consider the case of a 30-month-old child who has a bowel movement in his pants. We could assume that this event automatically causes a state of shame, that is, that there is some connection between the bowel movement and shame. Alternatively, we could think of shame as the consequence of what the child was thinking, either about the accident or about his parent's response to it. Obviously, I prefer the latter explanation, because I believe that most examples of shame-eliciting events cannot readily be explained by an automatic process. Consider another example, this time involving adults. A man asks an acquaintance who claims to be well read if he has read John Updike's latest novel. The well-read friend has not read the Updike book, but answers that he has read it in order to maintain his reputation for being cultured. In other words, he lies so as not to be shamed by his lack of knowledge. Clearly, here the event leading to a state of shame has to do with how the second man thinks rather than with some automatic process.

The confusion resides not in the nature of the process but in the likelihood that some events lead to the state of shame more readily than others, perhaps because they are more likely to elicit specific thoughts than are others. Toilet accidents are more likely than knowledge gaps to lead to disapproval from others. The suggestion of prototypicality in regard to shame-eliciting events must rest on the assumption that certain events lead to a shame state because they are more likely than others to lead to shame-producing thoughts. But in most discussions these factors have remained somewhat confused.

Darwin's own discussion illustrates the confusion. He believed that blushing could be produced in some automatic fashion by drawing attention to a particular part of the person: attention to the face would cause the face to blush. But Darwin also believed that blushing was caused by how we appear to others—as he put it, "the thinking about others thinking of us . . . excites a blush."[28]

His observation in regard to blushing and shame indicates his concern with two issues: the issue of appearance and the issue of consciousness. In his model of blushing, the personal appearance of the individual and the consciousness that others were attending to it were the critical elements. He repeatedly made the point that shame depends on sensitivity to the opinion of others, whether good or bad. Thus, self-conscious emotions require the organism's own sensitivity. Even so, Darwin repeatedly returned to the point that shame is specifically related to external appearance. Darwin did not distinguish between embarrassment and shame, but he did point out that praise, admiration, and even disapproval can cause blushing! He was quite specific in this regard. Somehow, personal appearance, and not moral conduct, was what produced blushing.

Darwin's description of shame and guilt indicates that he saw them as distinguished by their eliciting events, although he could not find the specific behaviors that would mark the difference. He saw guilt as regret over some fault committed; a person's relationship to others could then turn that guilt into shame. So, for example, he pointed out that one can feel guilty in solitude but would not blush because "it is not the guilt over an action, but what others think or know about our own guilt which leads to the blushing [shame]."[29] It was the social significance of the act, the eye of the other, that produced shame. He did note that a blush might occur in solitude, but only because we might be thinking about what others might be thinking of us. Again, the opinions of others about our appearance, especially the appearance of our faces, or our conduct, are Darwin's elicitors of shame.[30]

Although Darwin could not distinguish behaviorally between shyness, shame, guilt, and embarrassment, he did offer a variety of possible stimuli likely to elicit these emotions. He was clear in specifying that action per se is not the cause of the shame state: shame arises from how others see us. Understand here that the metaphorical "see" means "evaluate." Once again, Darwin's discussion presages others a century or more later.

Tomkins both elaborates on and develops the Darwinian view. For Tomkins, the self-conscious emotions are not readily distinguished from each other at the level of affect; however, they are distinguished at the level of conscious awareness and by the stimuli that elicit them. Having said this, Tomkins spends most of his discussion considering shame, and directs relatively little attention toward shyness, disgust, contempt, embarrassment, or guilt.[31] All of these emotions are incorporated into an overview of interconnected constructs. It is therefore difficult to separate one from another and claim that one pattern represents shame as opposed to embarrassment or guilt.

The definitions of shame that Tomkins gives vary from the prototypical, which is automatic in its ability to produce a shame state, to more specific situations and events. Tomkins's model utilizes the idea of an automatic elicitor, one that does not require thought. Thus, he has no difficulty assuming that infants experience a shame state. His automatic eliciting event is any event that inhibits interest and enjoyment: "Shame is an innate auxiliary affect and a specific inhibitor of continuing interest and enjoyment. The innate activator of shame is the incomplete reduction of interest or joy."[32] Interestingly, we could transpose the elements in this statement and argue that it is shame that interrupts and terminates excitement and enjoyment. The automatic causal connection that Tomkins makes is predicated on an attempt to understand the utilitarian nature of shame in its evolutionary niche. Such a definition of shame makes its elicitation much more mechanistic and controlled by particular inhibitory mechanisms, rather than by any conscious or self-conscious attribution or process.

Tomkins's prototypical and automatic elicitors of shame are barriers to enjoyment and excitement. I think the term "blocking of desire" would approximate Tomkins's meaning of shame. Just as there are many different desires, there are many different shames, each one caused by a particular desire's blockage. Tomkins suggests a variety of specific situations likely to elicit some of these many shames: failure at work, loss of friendship, loss of close relationships through death, and feelings about the body. In particular, "unattractiveness is seen as producing shame because it produces a loss of interest in pride in our own bodies."[33] Tomkins does not consider shame from the point of view of violation of social norms. Because of the breadth of his idea of interruption, and because of its causal nature,

Tomkins's theory of the elicitation of shame is unique. For him, the prototypic shame event is any event that leads to the reduction of interest. Here, then, is prototypicality at the level of function, not in terms of specific events.[34]

In considering what causes the shame state, Izard vacillates between the notion of an automatic elicitor in the manner of Tomkins and a phenomenological position developed more fully by H. B. Lewis.[35] Shame can occur from an unrequited smile: excitement is interrupted, positive emotions and enjoyment are reduced, just as Tomkins believes. But shame, for Izard, also has another dimension. Shame becomes a heightened consciousness of the self, an unusual and distinct form of self-perception. The self is seen as small, helpless, frozen, emotionally hurt. Although Izard does not explore the question himself, we should ask by whom is the self seen as small, helpless, frozen, emotionally hurt? It appears that Izard is prepared to see shame as elicited by some belief or thought of the person. It is more than an interruption, it is an idealization. Izard defines shame phenomenologically "as a heightened degree of self-conscious self-awareness, or self-attention: our consciousness is filled with self and we are aware of some aspect of self *we consider innocuous or inadequate.*"[36] Here, then, is the precipitating event, not only an interruption or reduction of positive emotions, but also a heightened awareness of some aspect of self. Thus, the elicitation of the shame state requires objective self-awareness; the precipitating stimulus is that which we consider in ourselves to be innocuous or inadequate. It is what we could think of as contempt for the self.

Central to H. B. Lewis's notion of shame-eliciting events is the belief that shame is a state of self-devaluation that can, but does not have to, emanate from "out there." Shame for her involves self-consciousness and self-imagery, that is, the idea of the other's feelings. She distinguishes shame, which is about the self, from guilt, which is about action related to another. For her, shame and guilt are confused because of their common origins as modes of correcting lost affective bonds. They are fused under the heading of guilt but do not represent the same phenomena. One of H. B. Lewis's major contributions is her stress on the belief that shame is produced by events located in the head of the person experiencing it. While it is true that she suggests that shame arises out of, and in large part is caused by, the loss of approval of a significant other, the source of the shame is our thoughts about our selves. The stimulus eliciting the state is self-thought about the self. For example, the disapproval of a significant other leads to thoughts about self-degradation, and these thoughts, in turn, lead the person to feel shame. This model is very different from one in which the shame state is the natural consequence of the specific action directly eliciting the state.

One of my students came in crying and said that she could not finish her term paper in time to meet my deadline. When I asked her what the difficulty was, she said that she had had a fight with her boyfriend and that it "made me feel as if I'm no good, inadequate. All I want to do is sleep."

The analysis of such statements leads me to believe that they really are expressions of disguised shame, the shame here being produced, first, by the fight with her boyfriend and, second, by her feeling that she is not any good because they had this fight. Her self-contempt and self-evaluation of unworthiness was triggered by the loss of affection from a significant other. We can conclude from this that the elicitors of shame appear to reside in one's evaluation of the negative evaluation of others. The particular reasons are varied. They can include failure to adhere to standards, like failure to meet the requirement needs of neatness and cleanliness as described by Erikson; physical appearance issues as described by Darwin; or the loss of a significant other, as pointed to by Klein and the object relation theorists.[37] In all cases, however, it is the focus of the self on the self's failure, and an evaluation of that failure, that leads to shame, not some automatic elicitor.

A Phenomenological Sense of Shame

Clearly, the stimuli that elicit the state of shame can best be understood if we consider shame from a phenomenological point of view. It would ease our task if we could define the state of shame by compiling a list either of a set of unique behaviors, or of a unique set of stimuli likely to elicit the particular feeling, or of some combination of the two. But I hope I have made the point that this is impossible.

A combination of behaviors and situations offers us a very powerful matrix in which to define, observe, and study individual differences in shame. If we could come to understand a coherence between events and behaviors, we could perhaps articulate them into a useful theory of shame.

Consider the case in which two students each received the same grade on a paper. Elizabeth is overjoyed at an 85, but John is disturbed. Clearly, one

*could not define students' reactions to their performance on an exam without
knowing what their expectations were and how they would evaluate the
grade they received.*

People's responses to events and situations are, obviously, specific to their
unique histories of experiences, expectations, desires, and needs.

Theorists from such diverse backgrounds as evolutionary biology,
clinical psychology, and psychiatry all seem to arrive at a similar
phenomenological view.[38] Shame is like a subatomic particle. One's
knowledge of shame is often limited to the trace it leaves. Nevertheless,
from Darwin forward, theorists have proposed the desire to hide or to
disappear as one very important feature of the phenomenology of shame.
That is, that desire is an overpowering component of the experience. A
second feature in descriptions of shame is intense pain, discomfort, and
anger. In fact, these distinguish shame from embarrassment and shyness.
A third feature is the feeling that one is no good, inadequate, unworthy. It
is a global statement by the self in relation to the self. And a fourth feature
is the fusion of subject and object. In shame, we become the object as well
as the subject of shame. The self system is caught in a bind in which the
ability to act or to continue acting becomes extremely difficult. Shame
disrupts ongoing activity as the self focuses completely on itself, and the
result is confusion: inability to think clearly, inability to talk, and inability
to act.

This fourth phenomenological feature enables us to differentiate shame
from guilt. As described above, shame is the complete closure of the
self-object circle. However, in guilt, although the self is the subject, the
object is external to the self. The focus of the self is upon the behavior that
caused the interruption, namely the inadequacy to meet certain standards,
and upon the object who suffers from that failure. Many have used terms
like *concern* or *regret* as synonyms for guilt, suggesting a focus on something
external to the self rather than on the self itself.

This four-feature phenomenological definition will be used throughout
the remainder of this book. Nonetheless, I shall not forget nor neglect the
behaviors and situations likely to be associated with shame and its
companion emotions of guilt, embarrassment, and pride.

Before I leave the phenomenology of shame, I must ask an important
question: What is the function of these particular negative feeling states?
While functional analysis is always difficult, it is reasonable to ask, with
Darwin and Plutchik, what adaptive significance these emotions have. The
function of guilt and shame is to interrupt any action that violates either
internally or externally derived standards or rules. The internal command,

which I call bringing into consciousness, says "Stop. What you are doing violates a rule or a standard." This command, then, serves to inhibit that action. The difference between shame and guilt resides in the nature of the interruption. In guilt, the command is essentially "Stop. What you are doing violates the standard or rule. Pay attention to what you did and alter your behavior." Guilt is designed to alert the organism that the behavior violates some rule or standard and to alter that behavior. Its function is to alert or to provoke anxiety. In addition, it directs behavior toward alternative action patterns that repair the inappropriate behavior that has been called into question.

In shame the command is much more severe: "Stop. You are no good." More important, it is about self, not about action; thus, rather than resetting the machine toward action, it stops the machine. Any action becomes impossible since the machine itself is wrong. The shame interruption is more intense given the identity of the subject-object. That the violation involves the machine itself means, functionally, that all behavior ceases. Its function, then, is to signal the avoidance of behaviors likely to cause it. Its aversiveness functions to ensure conformity to the standards and rules. While shame, more than guilt, should be likely to change behavior, thought, or feeling, its aversiveness may be so extreme that shame is bypassed. If bypassing occurs, a shame state may be ineffective in producing a change in behavior. There is some evidence from the work of Janis that too intense a message will be disregarded.[39]

In reviewing ideas about shame, we have come to see that shame involves specific behaviors associated with certain phenomenological experiences. These behaviors are elicited by two classes of events: those related to specific physical events, like exposure of the genitals, and those related to thoughts about the self. While both classes have been recognized, they have not been separated, in part because no careful analysis of the cognitive aspects of shame have been undertaken. Without introducing objective self-awareness and thoughts about standards, our understanding of shame remains inadequate. In the next chapter I will articulate more clearly what I mean by objective self-awareness and how this cognitive capacity develops. Without a concept of self, we can make little progress in understanding the self-conscious emotions.

3

The Self and
Its Development

The subtitle of this book is *The Exposed Self*. What is an exposed self and to whom is it exposed? The self is exposed to itself, that is, we are capable of viewing ourselves. A self capable of self-reflection is unique to humans.[1] As I pointed out earlier, human beings are complex, multilevel, self-regulating organisms capable of perceiving, emoting, thinking, remembering, and learning. We possess elaborate feedback loops, but these loops do not require our objective awareness of them in order to operate. We regulate our bodily functions as well as our cognitive functions without focusing on the fact that we are doing so (indeed, most of the time we are unaware of this aspect of our being). All living creatures have similar capacities. However, at some point phylogenetically and ontogenetically, human beings gain a new capacity: awareness of their own operations. The capacity for objective awareness allows humans to process information and to decide on the best action (whether motor behavior, thought, or emotion). The objective self can reflect on and reject any solution generated by the subjective process. The objective self uses metaphors; the subjective self operates with a simple sign system. The objective self allows us to stand back from our own processing and thereby increases the possibility of generating new solutions.

Although human adults possess this capacity for objective awareness, or reflection, most of the time, for most of our organizing and regulating functions, we do not avail ourselves of this capacity. Moreover, there are times when its use can actually lead to difficulty. For example, when we try to listen to what we are saying while we are talking, we block our ability to continue to talk.

36

Much has been written about this complex capacity, only some of which will be referred to here. I have already indicated the importance of self for emotions in general, and for shame in particular, and I will return to this topic when I focus more narrowly on shame. Here I am concerned simply with the capacity for self-reflection. As we will see, this aspect of the self goes by many names: consciousness, the me, the objective self as opposed to unconsciousness, the I, the subjective self.

This chapter constitutes an effort to define the reflecting self. I will consider the different levels of self, different ways of knowing, and the issue of consciousness. Freud's conceptualization of the conscious and the unconscious mind and his later tripartite theory of a self constituted of id, ego, and superego represent his continuing attempt to understand the different levels of self and to define the psychological self.[2] Others have made similar attempts within the frameworks of cognitive theories and theories about interpersonal connectedness.[3]

I will also refer to empirical data, some of which I presented in my book *Social Cognition and the Acquisition of Self*.[4] I hope to show that the ability to view the self does not exist at birth, but develops over time. The developmental process requires maturational changes that are both genetically and socially influenced. We are born helpless and survive only through the efforts of others. The human child's self necessarily exists within the nexus of other selves, particularly adult selves with the capacity for self-reflection. Within this nexus of selves the child's maturational process gives rise to the ability to reflect on the self.

Modes of Self-Consciousness and Ways of Knowing

The notion of a self and its development is vitally important for under-standing shame. A mechanistic model of human behavior can ignore the self, but human beings are not simple mechanisms that operate like switchboards: information coming in, information going out. All of us consider ourselves. We not only know ourselves, we know ourselves in many different ways. We know our names, we know what we look like, we know what it feels like to be us, and so on.

A doubter might say, "Well, animals have emotions. They experience fear and happiness. Moreover, animals seem to know about themselves and their place in time and space. They do not crash into walls but are able to move around objects in search of food. They seem to have plans and goals. What is this special thing that you are calling self, and why is it so important for understanding human emotional life?"

I think the answer is relatively simple. Clearly, we have emotions and engage in actions of which we are not consciously aware. When we walk across the hall to get a glass of water, we are not aware that we are moving our muscles in a particular way. Yet, we carry out this action. If, by self, we mean a capacity for unreflective yet complex actions, then certainly it can be said that animals have selves. However, there are many different kinds or modes of selves. Aspects of the self emerge ontogenetically, so that infants lack many features of selves that adults have: the infant self is not as complex as the child self, which in turn is less complex than the adult self. Likewise, animals have some features of the selves that human beings possess, but are unlikely to have certain other features.

Attempts to delineate features of the self are not new. Freud's contributions, especially his conception of the unconscious mind, extended and broadened our idea of self, enabling us to understand diverse behaviors as a product of the self's action.[5] He forced us to recognize that the self acts, plans, knows, and believes without apparent awareness. There are, of course, problems with the psychoanalytic notion of an unconscious. The tripartite division of the self into id, ego, and superego, each with a life of its own, competing and warring with one another, is both appealing and puzzling. Such a division requires these features of the self to stand as separate entities with separate goals and desires, and also necessitates some overall and overriding mechanism by which they are controlled. Freud assigned the ego the task of keeping peace; and he gave the ego both a conscious function, that of monitoring the world in which we live, and an unconscious function, namely controlling and organizing libidinal impulses.[6]

The idea of a multifaceted self, of one that has many components, is at the heart of psychoanalytic theory. Traditionally, however, Western society has viewed the single self, characterized by a unity of purpose, goals, and functions, as the apex of human maturation and mental health. I believe that the concept of the unified self, despite the esteem it has enjoyed, is a cultural artifact; a variety of evidence supports this view that the self can best be understood by means of the concept of multiple selves.[7]

My earlier discussion of the distinction between emotional experiences and emotional states is helpful in framing the problems of a complex self. Emotional states operate at the level of subjective self-awareness. These states have goals; they learn and profit from experience; they control functions and react to events, including people. The processes are unknown to us, but they require learning and can be made to change. The experience of our states is the equivalent of objective self-awareness. The distinction between states and experiences or between subjective versus objective self-awareness can be explored at a biological level. Recently, certain states (rather than experiences) have been tied to the stimulation of different locations in the brain.

Karl Pribram describes a patient in whom the medial part of the temporal lobe, including the amygdala, had been removed bilaterally.

> Because of the removal of this area, humans and animals are known to gain large amounts of weight, sometimes as much as 100 pounds. He asked the patient how it felt to be so hungry, and one patient who had gained more than 100 pounds in the several years since surgery, he spoke to at lunchtime and asked her "Was she hungry?" She answered, "No." "Would she like a piece of rare, juicy steak?" "No." "Would she like a piece of chocolate candy?" She answered, "um-hum," but when no candy was offered she did not pursue the matter. A few minutes later when the examination was completed, the doors to the common room were opened, and she saw the other patients already seated at a long table eating lunch. She rushed to the table, pushed the others aside, and began to stuff food into her mouth with both hands. She was immediately recalled to the examining room, and questions about food were repeated. The same negative answers were obtained again, even after they were pointedly contrasted with her recent behavior at the table. Somehow the lesion had impaired the patient's feelings of hunger and satiety, and this impairment was accompanied by excessive eating![8]

Here we can see a distinction between the patient's objective self experiences and her behavior and state of hunger.

More recent work by Joseph LeDoux and his colleagues also points to specific brain regions as responsible for what I have called specific emotional states (mediated by subjective self-awareness) and also emotional experiences (mediated by objective self-awareness).[9] Working with rats, LeDoux and his colleagues found that even after the removal of the auditory cortex, the animals were still able to learn an association between an auditory signal and shock. After just a few trials, the rats showed a negative emotional response to the sound. Removal of the visual cortex followed by a visual signal and shock also resulted in learning. These findings indicate that fear conditioning—the production of a fear state—is mediated by subcortical, probably thalamic-amygdala, sensory pathways. Similar findings have been reported in humans and point to different brain areas for experiences and states. Weiskrantz, among others, has reported on a phenomena called blindsight.[10] Patients found to lack a visual cortex, at least in one hemisphere, are asked if they can see an object placed in their blind spot. All such patients report that they cannot. When, however, they are asked to reach for the object they cannot see, they show that they have the ability to reach, at least some of the time, for the object. These findings suggest that separate brain regions are responsible for the production and maintenance of emotional states and the experiences of these states. LeDoux believes that emotional states and emotional experiences may be mediated by separate but interacting areas of the brain. "The computation of stimulus significance takes place prior to and independent of conscious awareness. . . . the amygdala may be a focal structure in the affective network. . . . Emotional experiences, it is proposed, result when stimulus representations affect representatives, and self representations coincide in working memory."[11]

Consciousness and the Self

Like many of the common terms we use, *consciousness* has a variety of meanings. Consider the following situation:

> *A woman gets into her car and drives a familiar route to her office. As she pulls into her parking space, she suddenly realizes that she was not paying attention to her driving, and she is quite amazed that she has arrived at her destination. She cannot remember crossing the familiar bridge and stopping at the various stop signs along the route. Nevertheless, she has done so.*

How are we to interpret this woman's surprise at arriving at her destination without being aware that she was making the trip? We could, of course, talk about it in terms of some kind of psychopathology, disassociation or the like. The subject does not remember actions because she has a problem with recall. However, this situation and others like it are such common experiences that we would be in error to call her experience psychopathology. We know that the woman intended to go to her office. She set her alarm clock for 8:00 A.M.; she got out of bed, dressed, and collected her briefcase; she got into her car. Obviously, the woman was enacting a planned strategy to achieve a definite goal, namely, to get to her office. But the question remains, how is it that she was able to achieve this complex task without being aware that she was doing it?

If driving were a simple reflex task, such as walking, we might say that particular movements led to other movements in an automated process. But driving is not a simple reflex action. If the woman was truly unaware of the complex mechanical task of driving her car, how did she manage to get to her office without breaking driving laws or doing harm to herself or others? We have to think about various ways of knowing or of intending.[12] I think it is reasonable to assume that the driver has knowledge of how to drive, how to stop at the particular points along the route, how to turn her car, and perform all the actions necessary to get her to the parking lot. In some sense, this knowledge of actions is possible without awareness. Still, what do I mean by "awareness?"

She must be aware of the lights and aware of her foot on the brake or the accelerator. That awareness does not solve the problem, which may be more semantic than anything else, that there appear to be different ways or modes of knowing, as well as different modes of intention. These different modes have to do with aspects of our selves.

Consider the possibilities. We might say that an organism knows something even at the level of a reflex: certain kinds of stimuli result in certain kinds of responses. This stimulus-response pairing, almost like a prewired program, might be considered as the simplest mode of knowing. The most complicated mode of knowing occurs at the level at which we know we know something, that is, when we have turned our attention toward contemplating our awareness of what we know. There are, of course, a variety of intermediate modes. So, for example, I might know something but pay no attention to the fact that I know it. Regarding the driver example, she knows how to drive and she knows how to follow the route to her workplace, but she has not paid attention to her knowledge. This distinction of levels must be maintained when we seek to analyze consciousness, because it is quite clear that different modes of consciousness are evoked by differing situations. For example, there are some situations and some occasions when I know that I know—that is, I have objective self-awareness—and other times when I know but I do not know that I know. Unfortunately, we use the term *consciousness* to describe both states of being.

The term *conscious* is usually restricted to the sense of knowing that one knows, a turning inward to observe what it is that we know. The term *unconscious* is usually restricted to the sense of knowing but being unaware that one knows. Differential use of these two terms gives rise to some confusion. From an epistemological point of view, I question such a restricted use of the term conscious. I would argue that the degree to which organisms act, plan, and show lawful behavior is the degree to which they are conscious, that is, aware of the events in their world, even if those events themselves are only registered in the unconscious. This gets us back to the problem of who in the unconscious world is conscious of what is happening in the real world?

We can avoid this problem by talking about different modes of consciousness or by avoiding the term consciousness entirely and considering, as we have, the different types of awareness. I follow Duval and Wicklund in using the term *objective self-awareness* to mean the organism's act of turning attention toward the self, to what the self knows, to what plans or desires the organism has; I use the term *subjective self-awareness* to mean processes and systems that know about the world but to which we do not or cannot pay attention.[13]

Objective awareness can be contrasted with subjective awareness in order to capture the directional nature of consciousness. When attention is directed inward, we focus on ourselves: we are the objects of our own consciousness. This is objective self-awareness. When attention is directed away from us, we are the subject of the consciousness that is directed toward external objects. Then we have subjective self-awareness. In both cases we are aware. In the latter case, we are aware of the events occurring *out there*, that is, we have consciousness of external events. We can plan, alter plans, and correct action. We, in fact, can learn and create and retain new memories and structures. One reaction to events out there can produce internal structures, states, and stimuli that, if attended to, would constitute objective self-awareness or consciousness directed toward the self. Thus, I allow for consciousness to be a property of all organisms, and, although others have used that term in a different sense, I will continue to use the term objective self-awareness to refer to a unique feature of consciousness.[14]

From an epistemological point of view, we have knowledge of many things, but it is our human capacity to have knowledge of knowledge that constitutes a unique mode of consciousness—from an ontogenetic and a phylogenetic sense, the highest mode. The same applies to the self system that has knowledge and therefore can function in the world, but also has the capacity to reflect upon itself. The uniqueness of shame (and hubris, guilt, and pride) is its relationship to a self that can reflect on itself.

This notion of modes is important. By modes, I mean to indicate that individuals can accomplish the same task through different but related processes. To analyze modes of ability, we could consider such problems as how a rat and an adult can both make their way through space/time, or how children and adults appear to be equally capable of obtaining an object by reaching for it, or how individual adults can accomplish the same task in different ways. Approached in another way, these different modes bring us to the issue of equivalence of behavior. Though especially pertinent to studies of development, this issue is relevant to all work on behavior. Examining mature creatures, we often assume that a particular behavior has a particular meaning. Moreover, we also assume, for the most part, that the meaning of the behavior, the mechanisms that produce it, and the behavioral system in which it is embedded are the same. But such an assumption misses the importance of modes. Although anthropologists recognize that the same behavior can have different meanings in different cultures, they often mistakenly believe that the same behavior exhibited by different people will have the same meaning within a culture. Clinicians, unlike anthropologists, do appreciate that particular behaviors may be caused by different, and often competing, mechanisms. In the study of development this problem of equivalence has received much attention, since similar behaviors often, indeed usually, are caused by and are embedded in different processes.

In the discussion to follow, we will pursue the issue of modes. I will argue that adults utilize different modes of "self-ability," that is, sometimes we experience subjective and sometimes objective self-awareness, depending on the needs of the moment. Moreover, the various modes observable in adult functioning have a developmental sequence: objective awareness emerges after subjective awareness.

The Duality of the Self

The development of the self is a topic that has received much thought and has a long history. I cannot do justice to this history, but I will attempt to touch on some significant theories. One hundred years ago, William James, in *The Principles of Psychology*, considered the problem of self, and mentioned its duality:

> Whatever I may be thinking of, I am always, at the same time more or less aware of myself, of my personal existence. At the same time, it is I who am aware, so that the total self of me, being as it were duplex, partly known and partly knower, partly object and partly subject, must have two aspects discriminated in it, of which, for shortness, we may call one the "me" and the other the "I."[15]

James went on to distinguish a hierarchy of selves, with a "bodily me" at the bottom and a "spiritual me" at the top, and various social selves in between. He envisioned a developmental trajectory, from the earliest physical experiences of the self as an entity to the later spiritual or nonmaterial experiences.

James's duality of self can be noted in the philosophical literature stretching from Descartes to Wittgenstein. As Wittgenstein himself points out, Descartes considered two classes of experience, with pain as an example of one, grief of the other.[16] The first, pain, comes to us through our senses, or what we might refer to as James's "bodily me." Grief, in contrast, does not arise from immediate sense impressions.

James's thinking about the self and self-development branched in two directions, one cognitive, the other social. Within a cognitive framework, Baldwin, writing at the same time as James, and Piaget, writing much later, describe the development of the self, although they do so in somewhat different terms.[17] Baldwin preferred to see the development of the self in terms of its relationship to others, while Piaget viewed this development in terms of the evolving mathematical/logical constructions, as the child moved from egocentrism to decentering. Though Piaget's discussion focuses on ages beyond the period of most interest for study of the emergence of the objective self, his views are still intriguing. If we ignore the fact that he is talking about children between the ages of 2 and 6, his formalization fits with those of others who are talking about 2 year olds. Piaget writes,

> That the child being ignorant of his own ego, takes his own point of view as absolute, and fails to establish between himself and the external world of things, that reciprocity, which alone would ensure objectivity. . . . Whenever relationships dependent upon the ego are concerned—they are at the crux of the matter—the child fails to grasp the logic of relations for lack of having established reciprocity, first between himself and other people, and between himself and things.[18]

According to Piaget, it is not until age 2, and sometimes as late as age 6, that the child is able to decenter, that is, to take the perspective of another, and thereby come to view himself as others might view him, thereby indicating movement from a subjective to an objective self point of view. Other epistemological-cognitive theorists have also articulated the issue of duality.[19]

At about the same time as James, Charles Cooley, a sociologist, struggled with similar problems concerning the self and its origins. Cooley, writing about the social nature of human beings and social organization, posited a reflector or "looking glass" self.[20] The self is reflected through others; thus, other people are the "looking glass" for oneself. In addition, Cooley stressed the idea that self and society form a common whole, with neither existing in the absence of the other. Cooley believed that infants are not conscious of the self, or the "I," nor are they aware of society or other people. Infants experience a simple stream of impressions, impressions that gradually become discriminated as the young child differentiates itself, or "I," from the society, or "we."

Following Cooley, George Herbert Mead also drew a distinction between the objective and the subjective self, using James's "I" and "me." The "I" is the subjective self and the "me" the objective self reflecting upon the "I." Mead assumed that the movement from the subjective "I" to the objective "me" takes place within a social nexus and is made possible only by social learning. Mead saw taking the perspective of another as the way the child was able to develop an objective self, and, like Cooley, believed that knowledge of the self and others developed simultaneously, with both forms of knowledge dependent on social interaction. Heavily influenced by Darwin, he felt that the human infant is active rather than passive, selectively responding to stimuli rather than indiscriminately responding to all events. Hence, Mead believed that the infant actively constructs the self (here he is referring to the objective self). He stated,

> Self has a character which is different from that of the physiological organism proper, the self is something which has a development; it is not initially there at birth, but arises in the process of social experience and activity. That is, it develops in the given individual as a result of his relations to that process as a whole and to other individuals within that process.[21]

The similarity between Mead's and Cooley's ideas is great: they share belief in the duality of self, subjective and objective, and the role of the child's social interaction in promoting his development from subjective to objective.

Although I cannot present psychoanalytical views of the self in detail, we need to keep in mind two of Freud's central ideas concerning the self's conscious and unconscious processes and tripartite structure. The id and ego can be characterized as representing a subjective and an objective self, although Freud's ideas about this tripartite division of personality have recently been questioned.[22]

In general, classical psychoanalytic theory has not paid much attention to the self, although self psychology has redressed the balance.[23] I will restrict my discussion of self psychology, only briefly mentioning the work of Erikson, Mahler, and Stern. Each takes a developmental perspective like my own. Erikson does not deal directly with self development except from the point of view of the self's struggle at each stage. Nevertheless, the challenge of the stages bears directly on issues of self development. Mahler and her colleagues articulate a self system that clearly develops in a sequence.[24] There is some similarity between Mahler's point of view and

Erikson's in that she describes the development of the self as a struggle between separateness and relatedness and calls this the separation/ individuation process. This process and struggle continues across the life course. Of special interest for us is Mahler's description of the child in the last half of the second year. She posits an increased awareness of self, and a concomitant heightened concern with the mother. In addition, she feels that both empathy and understanding of what it means to be separate and autonomous emerge between ages 18 and 24 months. The child's "love affair" with the world is modified as he learns about frustrations and limitations. In the third year, individuality is consolidated, separations from the mother become easier to bear, and the ability to take another's role becomes more pronounced. The child has developed a self that is separate from, but also related to, others.

Daniel Stern speaks of four kinds of self, which, while developing over time, are all available to both child and adult: the emergent self, the core self, the subjective self, and the verbal self.[25] While such a scheme is useful, it also presents difficulties. Stern's view of the infant's development of a differentiated sense of subjective and objective self follows that of other investigators. He also sees different developmental periods although the developmental sequence he describes can be called into question.[26]

The Development of Objective Self-Awareness

For the last 15 years, first with Jeanne Brooks-Gunn, and more recently with Linda Michalson and Margaret Sullivan, I have been studying the problem of self development and emotional life.[27] Our interest in empirically exploring the origins of self started with our interest in self-recognition. Given that infants and very young children do not have the capacity for language, it is very difficult to study the acquisition of these concepts of the self that I have been discussing. While it is true that we can observe mother-child interaction, or children's interactions with objects, our observations, while informative, do not give us a clear idea of the developmental sequence. Accordingly, I decided to look at children's behavior in the presence of reflective surfaces. It seemed to me that if children could be shown to recognize themselves in a mirror without any prompting, then it might be said that they were able to view themselves, to refer to themselves; I saw this self-referential behavior as the best possible marker of objective self-awareness. My colleagues and I undertook a large number of studies starting more than a decade ago. Our results indicate that true objective self-awareness as defined by self-referential behavior does not emerge until the second half of the second year of life. Thus, our experiments support what has been suggested by others.

In our procedures, we watched children's responses to mirrors, as well as their responses to television images and still photographs. The rather simple mirror technique we used was developed by Gordon Gallup in his work with nonhuman primates.[28] It involves placing some dye on the animal's nose without its awareness of this marking, and then observing its behavior in front of a mirror and classifying this behavior as either mirror-directed or self-directed.

Many animals react to their mirror images as though the images were other animals. For example, chickens eat more when in the presence of other chickens and also when in the presence of a mirror image of themselves than they do when alone.[29] Furthermore, animals behave as though the mirror images are not only social objects but animals like themselves. For example, fish, birds, and monkeys will display aggression to their mirror image just as they do to others like them. Some species, specifically primates, respond as though the images were unfamiliar, rather than familiar, members of their species. Self-directed behavior in the mirror indicates that the organism recognizes that the image in the mirror belongs to the self in another space. Thus, when the dye is applied to the animal's nose, we can observe whether the animal uses the mirror to touch its own nose. This is called self-recognition or self-directed behavior. Gallup's findings are interesting from a phylogenetic point of view. He found that only higher primates, in particular chimpanzees and perhaps orangutans, are able to recognize and direct their action to the mark on their face. Lower primates, including monkeys, gibbons, and baboons, are unable to do so.

My colleagues and I decided to apply these techniques to the study of infants. Although they might seem farfetched, analogous situations do occur in everyday life. Consider, for example, the following two young children:

David is a 2 year old who loves helping his mother bake brownies. Being a little overenthusiastic, he gets more flour on his hands than in the bowl and is asked to go and wash up. Upon looking in the mirror over the sink, he discovers, to his glee, that there is flour on his cheek, and he tries to wipe it off with his hand.

Another toddler, this one 18 months old, has fallen while chasing her older sister and has bruised her forehead. Later that night, when the tears and pain are forgotten, she passes a full-length mirror in the hall, sees herself and the bruise, says "oh" and starts to cry, apparently remembering the fall and pain.

Children do have mirror experiences. In fact, in a survey we conducted 10 years ago, we found that almost all children had some sort of mirror experience at least several times a week. More recently, a whole variety of infant toys have emerged in which children are given the opportunity to observe themselves in reflective surfaces.

Using the same technique as Gallup, we found that infants from 15 to 24 months of age touched their bodies or faces when placed in front of a mirror after their faces were marked, with more infants touching their faces following the marking process than before. Their reaction was similar to chimpanzees' use of the mirror to visually locate and touch marked parts of their bodies. Infants begin to imitate their marked image by making faces, sticking out their tongues, or watching themselves disappear and reappear at the side of the mirror around 15 to 18 months of age. These behaviors seem to indicate a growing awareness of the properties of reflections. At the same time that they begin to imitate, children also start to touch the mark on the face. The results from several of our studies were surprisingly consistent: mark-directed behavior was never exhibited in infants younger than 15 months. Between 18 and 24 months, a dramatic increase occurred, with approximately 75% of the 18 month olds and all of the 24 month olds exhibiting mark recognition.

We also studied visual self-recognition using pictures of the self. Studies of pictorial recognition almost always concentrate on the face because even adults have considerable difficulty recognizing body parts other than their face. The ability of preverbal children to recognize their faces in pictures is best inferred by comparing their responses to pictures of themselves to their responses to pictures of others. The "others" used for comparison purposes were as similar to the subjects as possible, to guard against differential responding based on aspects other than self-perception. Infants respond quite differently to adults than to children, for example, and therefore may differentiate between themselves and adults on the basis of age features, not features specific to themselves.

The earliest developmental research we found that used pictures was performed by Zazzo, who showed his son pictures of himself throughout the first years of life to see when he would recognize them.[30] Zazzo reported such recognition around 3 years of age. Using a more sophisticated procedure, my colleagues and I presented 9- to 24-month-old infants with slides of themselves, same sex peers, and opposite sex peers. The pictures we used showed only the face and shoulder area. Children under 2 years responded differentially to pictures of themselves and other babies: they smiled more to their own pictures. Early pictorial self-other differentiation may require perceptual-cognitive support structures other than feature recognition. Some of the infants differentiated between pictures of themselves and pictures of infants of the opposite sex, but not between pictures of themselves and pictures of infants of the same sex. Pictorial self-other differentiation in the first year of life seems to be dependent on perceptual structures, such as age and gender. In the middle of the second year of life, children seem to be capable of recognizing their own pictures on the basis of feature differences alone.

We also studied children's verbal responses by asking infants to point out and label their own picture in a set that included their own and others' pictures. As many language researchers have found, comprehension preceded verbal production. Almost all infants could point to their own picture, as opposed to another's picture, by 18 months of age. But most infants did not label their own pictures until 21 to 24 months of age, though a few exceptions labeled as early as about 15 months. Personal pronouns, although appearing at the end of the second year, were not used by a majority of the children until 30 to 36 months of age, a finding also reported by Gesell.[31] Personal pronoun usage is an interesting milestone, not only in the acquisition of subjective self-knowledge but also in terms of a linguistic representation of self. Although children are referred to by others as "you," "he," or "she," and never as "I" or "me," and although they hear others refer to themselves as "I," but not as "you," "he," or "she," most children do not refer to themselves as "you," or to others as "I." Interestingly, autistic children and blind children have been observed to use personal pronouns incorrectly, employing "I" for others and "you" for self.[32]

Examination of the use of personal pronouns seems to indicate that the first person pronoun, "I," appears around age 20 to 24 months, and second and third person pronouns, "you," "he," and "she," appear about two months later. When asked questions like, "Where is my hair?," "Where is your hair?," and "Where is her hair?," toddlers responded to the second-person-pronoun question earlier than to the first-person-pronoun question, even though in spontaneous conversations they used "I" correctly earlier than they used "you." It seems that toddlers focus on the consistencies in speech, using "I" and "you" appropriately, rather than just imitating others' speech. Additionally, when the self is being referred to ("I," when the child is speaking, "you" when the adult is speaking), personal pronoun usage is more likely to be correct and to occur earlier than when another is being referred to ("you" when the child is speaking, "I" when the adult is speaking).

We also observed children's self-recognition responses in movies and videotapes. In Zazzo's study of his own son, home movies as well as pictures were shown to the child. He was found to recognize himself in these home movies in his third year of life. Today, videotapes have replaced home movies as the preferred medium for studying self-recognition and moving representations. In one of our videotape studies, infants of ages between 9 and 24 months were seated in front of a television screen and saw, among other tapes, a videotape of themselves in the same setting made a week earlier or a videotape of a same-sex, same-aged infant in the same setting. In another videotape, the same procedure was utilized, with one interesting addition: an unfamiliar person silently approaches either the self or the other infant from behind, with the approach being visible on the television screen although, of course, the person was not actually present in the room. Infants were more likely to pay attention to and turn toward the stranger when they saw the videotape of the other than the tape of themselves, while they were more likely to make sounds in response to and to imitate play with the tape of themselves than with that of the other. Differential responses to the tape of themselves and those of others occurred at around ages 15 to 18 months and reflect objective self-awareness.

These studies suggest an ontogenetic sequence of self-recognition, which I use as an index of the acquisition of self-referential behavior, or objective self-awareness. Our observations, along with other information collected on children's development, allow me to trace the construction of the different modes of self. While I present these modes as an ontogenetic sequence, it is important to remember that the end result is the existence of all modes in the adult. The achievement of a higher mode does not necessarily mean the destruction of a lower one. Thus, as the child develops new and different modes of self, earlier modes continue to exist. Earlier modes are not replaced by later ones; in fact, the various modes of development are likely to be elaborated over the life course.

Modes of Self: From Reflexes to Objective Self-Awareness

Borrowing from Kurt Fischer's theory of levels,[33] I will define the three modes of self that each adult possesses as (1) sensorimotor affective ways of knowing, (2) representational knowledge, and (3) abstract knowledge.

While forms of knowing develop over the first two years of life, once they emerge, each continues to exist and is elaborated in its own fashion. Thus, while they have a maturational basis they are also linked to the organism's transaction with its environment.

Sensorimotor Affective Knowledge

The period from birth to eight months is the period dominated by sensorimotor affective knowledge of the self. The first half of this period is characterized by sets of reflexes that govern the child's transactions with the environment. These reflexes, or action patterns, are designed to be evolutionarily adaptive, that is, they allow the child to survive in her world from the moment of birth. Children need some abilities immediately after birth. They do not have time to acquire these abilities gradually because sometimes they must be able to act without prior experience. Adaptive reflexes include blinking to bright lights or objects moving toward the infant, smiling from internal pressure, and crying when distressed. Feeding reflexes, such as swallowing and sucking, are vital to allow the child to take in nourishment.

The second half of this period involves reflexes, behavior patterns, or ways of knowing that involve the child's commerce with both her social and object environment. One example is the reaching action pattern. The child seems to know, in some sense, its place in space, since she is able to reach for and obtain objects located in particular space/time, and to sense distance, since the reaching response seems to be affected by whether objects are near or far.[34]

Toward the end of the first eight months of life, representational knowledge begins to emerge and thereafter functions alongside reflexive knowledge. Representational self-knowledge also emerges and coexists with reflexive self-knowledge, in particular the knowledge implicit in recognizing one's position in space/time in terms of objects and the ability to recognize other as opposed to self.

Representational Knowledge

The second mode of knowledge emerges at about eight or nine months. The development of active memory is a major cognitive milestone. Memory allows the child to develop significantly different aspects of self-knowledge. It releases her from complete dependence on the here and now, the only form of knowledge obtained by means of sensorimotor affective knowledge. Memory at this stage is limited to actual representations of people and objects; it does not encompass abstract representations, which will come later.

Representational ability, even of this limited type, has other significant implications. Children's knowledge about objects no longer is dependent upon their sensorimotor affective level. The child will now reach for objects that she can no longer see but that she remembers were hidden. The child *represents* objects, even those not in sight. Even more important, however, is the effect of memory, and therefore representation, upon more sophisticated cognitive activity such as the creation of means-end and the learning of causality.[35]

The child's knowledge of herself, given memory, is enhanced since she can remember actions that led to certain consequences in the object world. The same, of course, is true for her actions in the social world. Now that behaviors and people can be remembered, the child has the capacity to repeat successful actions. During this period the representations in memory, because they are abstract, often conflict. Thus, for example, sometimes the child has interactions with her mother that lead to positive affective states and desired goals, and other times the child has interactions that lead to negative affective states, failure to achieve goals, and frustration. These representations must coexist since the child is not yet capable of organizing and combining these representations. From the point of view of her social relations, this means that the child has knowledge of a good and a bad father (or mother) as well as of good and bad action. Failure to integrate these aspects of parents and actions initiates psychic problems for the child.[36]

Memory allows the child to build up permanent representations of self, of significant others, and of interactions. The social exchanges we witness in children aged 8 to 15 months demonstrate sophisticated and complex social patterning, based in part upon the reflexive sensorimotor affective knowledge of the first level and in part on the memory-based representation of the second level. The knowledge that the child exhibits about self, other, and interactions between self and other is sophisticated and appears from the point of view of a third person to be complex and adultlike in structure. Indeed, for many behaviors, children of this age do show adultlike patterns, even though children of this age have far less representational knowledge, memory duration, and ability to abstract.

What does a child of this age know? She knows that certain actions lead to certain consequences, knows what it is like when she engages other people, and knows when she fails. That is, she has an elaborated representational knowledge of her own actions, those of others, and the ability to differentiate, and knowledge about interaction. The child shows in her social exchange that (1) she knows of events that have *it* as center (called self in time/space), (2) she is differentiated from others (called self-other), (3) she has enduring patterns (called permanence), and (4) in certain interactive exchanges she knows which actions coincide with actions of the other. This knowledge of the self, however, is representational. As such, it is subjective. The infant has an *I* but not yet a *me*. The objective self emerges only with abstract knowledge.

Abstract Knowledge

From approximately the second half of the second year on, children develop the ability to abstract. Their representations are no longer limited to the realistic: now the child can create representations of representations. Abstraction allows the child to categorize both objects and people, and to consider both future and past events. It also allows the child to merge and reconcile discrepant events.

Now the child can remember over relatively long periods of time. Even more important, the memory system itself has become abstract. Abstract knowledge allows for the creation of language and, with it, the continued development of abstractions. In the representational period the child had representations or memories of events; now the child has memories of memories, that is, she can remember that she remembers. With the advent of this capacity, multiple abilities emerge, in both the social-affective and the cognitive domains. In the latter, an appreciation of true causality enables the child to come to recognize means-ends relationships, and therefore to have what I have called objective intentions, as well as the ability to classify along dimensions not only realistic in nature, but abstract.[37]

———— • ————

By the end of the second year of life all three modes of self-knowledge have evolved. The sensorimotor-affective and the representational modes of knowing remain even as abstract knowledge develops. All modes of knowing continue to develop once they emerge. Affective knowledge about self continues to develop even as new emotions emerge. The same can be said of motor knowledge. The motor skills of children evolve across the life span. The middle-childhood child, for example, learns sports, and these new forms of physical activity allow her to know herself through more sophisticated motor behavior. In adolescence, puberty presents the adolescent with still other ways of knowing. A similar argument can be made concerning sensory knowledge. The sensory systems continue to develop and to change as we age. One grows to know oneself sensorially in different and changing ways over the life course, as any 50 year old with bifocals can report.

The other modes of knowing also change. Increased memory capacity, the result of elaboration of neural networks, means that the representations of which one is capable are likely to change. Representational memories grow more complex, and thereafter support new and more elaborate ways of knowing. Finally, abstractions continue to develop. Piaget has brilliantly demonstrated the development of thought from age 2 to the teenage years. Thus, for each mode of self-knowledge, there is a developmental path, each becoming more sophisticated over the course of development.

The adult forms of the three modes of self-knowledge correspond to the subjective and objective self that I have been discussing. The adult subjective self also is made up of reflexive and representational knowledge, which are likely to reside on some subcortical level (the limbic brain, for example). As we have seen, the subjective self is capable of bodily self-regulation as well as learned behavior. LeDoux's research on conditioning suggests that fairly complex learning can take place at this subjective self level.

Adult objective self-awareness corresponds to abstract self-knowledge, which is likely to reside in the neocortex, specifically in the frontal lobes, and is likely to be related to language. (See, for example, Pribram's research and the research on blindsightedness.) Objective self-awareness, necessary for experience of both ourselves and our bodily processes, allows for the consideration of the other modes, since the subjective self has no abstract ability.

The Causes of Self-Development

I have outlined the modes of self-awareness that culminate in objective self-awareness. Moreover, I have suggested that because these ways of knowing the self are nontransformable, all three modes are available to adults. Still to be addressed, however, is the question of how, from an ontogenetic point of view, these modes evolve, and the related question of how objective self-awareness may be stimulated in adults who more often use the other two modes. The first impetus to self-development has to do with the social world; the second is associated with maturational processes related to change in biological structures; and the third results from interaction between the social world and biological change.

Baldwin, Mead, and Cooley all focused on the social impetus. Although it is unclear whether Mead saw any maturational forces at work in the process of the development of objective self-awareness, he certainly argues for the child's involvement with its social world as the cause of its development. The child cannot develop a sense of the self, or objective self-awareness, alone. Mead uses the example of a boy running down a road. The boy has a rudimentary awareness of his body (subjective), but this awareness does not constitute a genuine self (objective). For Mead, the child's developmental task is to detach his awareness from within himself and assume an outside point of view. That is, individuals need to gain a vantage point external to themselves, and then look back at themselves. This ability to look back at oneself implies taking the role of another, as if the boy enters the head of the other and observes himself through the other's way of characterizing him. For Mead, the way others characterize one's self leads to objective self-awareness.

Caregivers, through their actions, have an impact on the child as the child moves through the various levels of self development. Poor caregiving, then, should logically result in disruptions of objective self-awareness. This view is held by almost all social theorists. While such a view is appealing, and on its face reasonable, closer examination reveals this view's flaws. Most important, except for the special classes of psychotic or autistic children, there is no evidence that poor caregiving results in the failure to develop objective self-awareness. While poor parenting has been shown to affect how children think of themselves (that is, whether they see themselves as good or bad people), to reduce their capacity for empathy, and to impair their ability to self-reflect, there is no support for the idea that poor parenting leads to the lack of objective self-awareness. Mahler's studies and theory grew out of her work with autistic children. Her explanations of individuation might be reasonable for this special category of children, but even here I have some doubt. Autism in children is now thought to be strongly biologically influenced. In some sense, then, the theory of the social origin of self-awareness remains in doubt. There is no doubt, however, that the qualities that we consider ourselves to possess, those aspects of our objective self, are influenced by social factors. Although we will discuss multiple personalities or multiple selves in chapter 9, I wish to emphasize now that almost all cases are caused by poor parenting, and especially by severe parental abuse. Even here, however, there is no failure at objective self-awareness: it is only that such children create multiple objective selves.[38]

The parent as mirror plays an important role in developing self-concept but not in developing objective self-awareness. Kenneth Kaye's interesting book on children's interactions with their parents argues that the meaning system attributed to the child by the parent is the causal agent in producing change.[39] Kaye theorizes that the adult's meaning system, as expressed in behavior toward the child, produces that which the parent thought the child already possessed. In a sense, the fact that parents believe that their children possess self-awareness serves as the mechanism by which children come to acquire self-awareness. This is a reasonable position from the standpoint of hermeneutics: meaning is not found within the individual but results from collective agreement as to meaning. The achievement of objective self-awareness should be no different from the achievement of other forms of meaning, since self-awareness is an idea we have about ourselves. The social cognitive theorists, and their position in terms of a looking glass, are extremely similar to the views of Kohut and Fairbairn, who argued for the development of knowledge through the social milieu.[40] Certainly, it appears that the acquisition of knowledge about the self and the various levels of self knowledge that children achieve are determined to some degree by the social environment. However, it seems unreasonable to assume that the particular biological makeup of humans has no role to play in the achievement of objective self-awareness.

In all of these theories, the relationship between children and their adult conspecifics constitutes the basis for children's knowledge about the social world and about others, including themselves. Nevertheless, answers to the questions of what agent propels objective self-awareness and how the social environment moves the child toward these different ways of knowing the self are still unclear. But common sense indicates that if we took a goldfish and treated it in the same fashion that we treat an infant, the goldfish would not develop objective self-awareness. Obviously, the human infant's genetic potential must allow and enable such development.

If the social environment by itself cannot account for the change, can genetically influenced maturation? Psychotic and autistic children often fail to show objective self-awareness if we use self-recognition as a measure of this capacity.[41] In fact, psychoanalyst Theodore Shapiro has suggested to me that the autistic children who show self-recognition are those most likely to recover. Failure to achieve objective self-recognition may be due to biochemical factors or may be related to failure in cognitive development.

Other support for a maturational explanation of the development of objective self-awareness comes from the data on mental age differences. Mental age is simply an attempt to estimate the capacities of children in regard to those of other children. It is a representation of the intellectual ability of the child at a particular point in time. In a series of studies conducted in our laboratory, we looked at children with mental handicaps and found that children need a mental age of approximately 15 to 20 months in order to be able to recognize themselves. We found that Down's syndrome children, for example, can recognize themselves if they have achieved a mental age of 18 months. If a 3-year-old Down's child only has a mental age of one year, it is unlikely to show self-recognition; however, a 30-month-old Down's child who has a mental age of 15 to 18 months will show self-recognition. It is clear that certain mental capacities are necessary for self-recognition, and therefore for achievement of objective self-awareness. Exactly what these capacities are is not yet clear. While the social environment may affect the mental age of children to some degree, in general, mental age is determined by the maturation of the child's nervous system.

As is usually the case, the combination of maturation and social context is most likely to account for objective-self awareness. Duval and Wicklund have suggested that at least three conditions need to be met if the child is to develop objective self-awareness: (1) there must be an entity who has a different point of view than the child; (2) the two different points of view must concern the same object; and (3) the child must be aware of these two different opinions simultaneously. They base their position on their belief that the objective self becomes differentiated from the subjective self. To begin with, the infant acts, perceives, and thinks but does not turn his attention on himself. The turning of attention on the self requires a conflict between the child's action and the action of others. This conflict enables the child to objectify his actions, thoughts, and feelings, and thus to develop objective self-awareness.

This conflict is most likely to occur in the social world. However, in order for this conflict to occur the child has to be able to compare two events simultaneously. Simultaneity requires that the child look at event *A* in space/time, have a memory of event *A,* and then look at event *B.* If the child is not able to retain a memory of *A* when it looks at *B, B* will be quite novel, and so no comparison will be possible. I have suggested that this ability to make comparisons requires memory capacity, and that memory capacity becomes sufficient for comparison somewhere around age 8 months. What is important here is that certain maturational capacities— namely, the growth of memory and, through this maturational capacity, the ability to make comparisons—are the prerequisites for consciousness. Another person with a differing point of view is only necessary to the extent that simultaneity of difference is an important feature in allowing the child to make a comparison, and the most simultaneous and discrepant events in the child's world are other social objects, especially parents. So, when the child starts to, let us say, reach for a toy, and the mother tells him not to, the desire and action pattern to reach for the toy is interrupted. This simultaneous comparison is what facilitates the objective self. As Duval and Wicklund have said:

> The interaction must generate an opposition between the child's own perception, thinking or doing at one point in time, and those same processes at another point in time. Accordingly, out of all the contacts the child has with the world, we are left with just two possibilities. One, the child could differ with a previous opinion. By examination of reality, he changes his opinion about some object and notes a contrast with the earlier. Two, the second possibility is disagreement with the perceptions of another. It now remains to be seen if both of these alternatives satisfy the requisite condition for activating the perceptual differentiating mechanism.[42]

By referring to Piaget's work on decentering, they reached the conclusion that, in fact, the parent-child relationship is likely to lead to this objectification. This occurs, in part, because interactions eliminate the time gap between the two perceptions, the child's own perception and the child's perception of the other as different than one's own.

It is the simultaneity of differing opinions and perceptions that is important. It is conflictual situations, ones in which there are punishments and negative prohibitions, that are likely to be the most effective in generating this perceptual difference.[43] Interestingly, this analysis bears a similarity to the psychoanalytic view of the emergence of secondary thought processes. The inability of the id to achieve its purpose in the world gives rise to ego mechanisms. Thus, wishing for something to eat gives rise to lawful planning in the world only to the degree that the environment is in some conflict with the id's desires.

To summarize: By the end of the second year of life children have developed an elaborate self system. While this system will undergo important changes over the life course, its fundamental features are now in place. These include three modes of self knowledge, with objective self-awareness being the last one to emerge. While all modes are used by adults (and children over the age of 2 years) it is the objective self-awareness mode that is associated with the emotions of shame, guilt, and pride.

4

Self Thoughts and Shame

W hen I first realized the extent of the shaming that occurs in everyday life, and wanted to explore others' views, I turned initially to the psychoanalytic literature. I did so especially because I thought Freud's distinction between superego, ego, and id would provide one source of understanding of this problem. But I discovered that neither Freud and proponents of classical psychoanalysis nor the object relations theorists considered the topic in detail. In fact, as Donald Nathanson has said, shame is conspicuously absent in Freud's writing and, until recently, in the psychoanalytic literature in general.[1]

Psychoanalysis and the Subject of Shame

In psychoanalytic theory, the origins and elicitation of shame are tied to the toilet situation. Fenichel, for example, pinpoints shame as being caused by toilet training, although he stresses urethral training rather than bowel training.[2] In his later writings Freud discusses the functions of guilt, but he says little about shame. Even in the discussion of guilt, Freud makes quite clear that he is not talking about shame. For Freud, the superego, the mechanism by which the standards of the parents are incorporated into the self, and specifically the child's fear of punishment by the parents for transgression by withdrawal of love or even by punishment, is the initial source of the feeling of guilt.[3]

Freud's discussion of guilt in relation to the superego is similar to his discussion of guilt in relation to the instinctual drives and their expression. For Freud, anxiety, or fear, is translatable directly into guilt. The two stages in the development of the sense of guilt related to the superego are, first, the fear of authority and, second, the fear of the superego itself once the authority's standards are incorporated. In the well-developed super-ego, the sense of guilt arises not only when a violation is committed but even when a violation is being anticipated. The guilt that Freud focuses on is not a guilt related to the whole self, but rather a guilt related to one's actions. Thus, in *Civilization and Its Discontents,* he says that once a transgression has occurred, the individual "searches his soul, acknowledges his sinfulness, heightens the claims on his conscience, imposes abstinence on himself or punishes himself with penance."[4] Thus, for Freud, guilt is a specific and focused response to a transgression that can be rectified by abstinence and penance.

Freud focuses upon guilt, not shame. If psychopathology is to be found, it is to be found in an overdeveloped sense of guilt, resulting from an overdeveloped superego. Within normal functioning the superego condemns the ego. This condemnation in turn gives rise to normal guilt. In *The Ego and the Id,* Freud does discuss the problem of an overly strong conscience or sense of guilt.[5] In such a situation the superego,

> displays particular severity, and often rages against the ego in a cruel fashion. The ego ideal in these two conditions, obsessional neuroses and melancholia, presents, alongside of the similarity, differences that are no less significant. In certain forms of obsessional neuroses, the sense of guilt is overly noisy, but cannot justify itself to the ego. Consequently, the patient's ego rebels against the imputation of guilt, and seeks the physician's support in repudiating it . . . In melancholia, the impression that the superego has obtained a hold upon consciousness is even stronger, but here the ego ventures no objection. It admits its guilt and submits to punishment.

When Freud does mention shame, he does so usually in the context of drives and impulses that require restriction. So, for example, in discussing the abandoned impulses having to do with the erogenous zones, he states that these impulses

> would seem in themselves to be perverse—that is to arise from erotogenic zones, and to derive their activity from instincts which, in view of the direction of the subject's development, can arouse only unpleasant feelings. They [the impulses] consequently evoke opposing mental forces [reacting impulses] which, in order to suppress this displeasure affectively, build up the mental dams of . . . disgust, shame and morality.[6]

Although Fenichel mentions four motives for defense, disgust, anxiety, shame, and guilt, Freud focused mainly on anxiety as a signal. Indeed, many since Freud, including Sullivan, Rank, and Horney, have used anxiety as a signal for defense.[7] It is clear that Freud and classical psychoanalytic thought focuses upon guilt and upon punishment as a retribution, rather than upon shame.

Erik Erikson does discuss shame, but he has no better time distinguishing between shame and guilt. Erikson returns more to the Darwinian view when he suggests that shame arises when "one is completely exposed and conscious of being looked at, in a word, self-conscious."[8] This self-consciousness is an undifferentiated state of being that subsumes shame, shyness, embarrassment, and guilt. Erikson tries to differentiate these terms, but is not completely successful. For example, he discusses visual shame versus auditory guilt, but does not develop this confusing concept. I imagine that the reference to visual shame is based on Darwin's theory that shame derives from being looked at, and that feeling shame one wishes to hide one's face and to disappear. Although Erikson holds to a more interactional view that involves the self and self-consciousness, he also indicates that the conditions necessary for feeling shame include being in an upright and exposed position. As he states, "Clinical observation leads me to believe that shame has much to do with a consciousness of having a front and a back, especially a 'behind.' "[9] Erikson believes that shame is related to specific bodily acts, in particular, the toilet functions. The developing child comes to view these functions as evil, shameful, and unsafe. Thus, as biological imperatives, the "backside" and its functions automatically provoke a shame experience. For Erikson, the shame experience also provides the opportunity for its counterpoint, that is, pride, certainty, initiative, and faith. Thus, the anal stage is connected with the emergence of both shame and pride.

Erikson's familiar theory of ego challenges offers the clearest differentiation between shame and guilt, their place in human life, and events likely to elicit them. Erikson's second challenge is autonomy versus shame and doubt. Autonomy is the attempt of the child to achieve, to do for itself, an attempt that is related to a developing sense of the self. Achieving muscular control, including control of the elimination of bodily waste, is the socialization and the developmental challenge for this life stage. Shame and doubt arise during this stage as the counterpoint to autonomy, the successful achievement. In other words, shame and doubt arise from the child's inability to fully control bodily functions. It is only after this basic ego task that the third ego task, initiative versus guilt, becomes significant. Here Erikson suggests that guilt has a reparative function. Erikson's developmental sequence indicates that he recognizes that shame and guilt are different emotions, that shame precedes guilt, and that they are associated in counterpoint with different ego tasks. Despite its significant differences from the psychoanalytical mainstream, Erikson's analysis remains imbedded in a biological imperative theory of body functions and the challenges they present. He does not posit a self theory. Erikson does not get past the traditional elicitors of shame and guilt: genital exposure and toilet training elicit shame, and failed achievement elicits regret and guilt.

Theorists in the classical analytical tradition have proposed a variety of shame-triggering causes: unacceptable impulses having to do with aggression and libidinal urges, for example, and reaction to the specific tasks and challenges that the developing ego is presented with as the child grows, especially muscular control waste elimination, and maintaining bodily cleanliness. Recently, within the psychoanalytic movement, there has been a growing recognition of the importance of shame. In the last decade, building on the work of H. B. Lewis, Piers and Singer, and Wurmser, a number of theoretically important analyses of shame, having to do with self psychology, have emerged, including the work of Broucek, Nathanson, and especially Morrison.[10]

I would like to offer two examples to clarify what I mean by shame.

A male student told me that he had recently had a big fight with his girlfriend. When he left her room, he could see that she was very upset. He did not stop to comfort her, but on the way back to his own room he began to think of her and her obvious suffering. He was so ashamed that he had left her feeling so miserable that he wanted to disappear.

Another student, a young woman, told me that in haste, without thinking, she had told her close friend that she did not look good in the dress she was wearing. She reported that her friend was obviously hurt by her thoughtless remark and that she, in turn, felt badly about what she had said. She then noted, "I must keep my mouth shut when Betty wears something horrible."

The second student's statement represents a totally different phenomenological experience from that of the first. In both examples the students committed a violation against some rule or standard to which they adhered. In the first case, that of the male student who ignored his girlfriend's emotional distress, the student had an intense negative response. He confessed that he wanted to disappear; thus, he focused on himself and on his own feelings. In the second case, the student likewise felt badly about what she had done, but she did not focus on herself. Instead, she focused on the feelings of Betty, her friend, and on what she herself could do to prevent hurting Betty in future situations. The first example provides us with a clear picture of shame, the second with a picture of guilt.

There is very little agreement as to the specific elicitors of shame. Many events are capable of eliciting shame or guilt. No particular stimulus has been identified or is likely to be identified as the trigger for shame and guilt.[11] It would be easier to understand shame if we could specify the class of external events likely to elicit it. If it were true that shame or guilt are similar to anxiety in that they reflect the subject's fear of uncontrollable impulses, then we could consider the causes of shame to be sexual or aggressive impulses. Alternatively, if we could prove that situations having to do with toilet or genital functions were likely to elicit shame, or if we could prove that the way we appeared physically or how we behaved in front of others would automatically elicit shame, we could then specify situations that would both help us to define shame and increase our understanding of its causes. But no such clear cause-and-effect pattern has been demonstrated. There is no simple class of events that precipitates shame. But we can say that shame is a feeling state that is associated with the activity of consciously paying attention to ourselves.

Clearly, we need a much more elaborated theory concerning the self-conscious emotions shame and guilt. Indeed, we need a theory concerning shame that also addresses and explains all the self-conscious emotions. To anticipate my argument, let me state its details broadly before going on. I propose that our success or failure in regard to abiding by standards, rules, and goals produces a signal to the self. This signal affects the organism and allows individuals to reflect upon themselves. This reflection is made on the basis of self-attribution. The self-attribution one makes determines the nature of the resulting emotion. Notice that the critical nature of the theory resides in three important factors. *First,* the model does not attempt to specify what constitutes success or failure or how the person goes about evaluating success or failure. *Second,* the model does not specify any particular standard, rule, or goal. In other words, it is not clear that there are any specific stimuli that uniquely contribute to shame or to any other self-conscious emotion. *Third,* the model assumes that self-attributions that lead to specific emotions are internal events that reside in people themselves.

Here I must state that although this model is based on a phenomenological and cognitive attributional approach, I do not mean to suggest that the self-conscious emotions are epiphenomenological or deserve "less status" than the cognitive attributional processes themselves. These emotions may have discrete and specific locations as well as specific processes that are themselves "bodily" in nature. What I propose is that the stimulus events for shame, guilt, and the other self-conscious emotions concern cognitive attributions. These cognitions serve simply as elicitors of specific emotions in the same way as do other stimuli, such as the social behavior of others or loud noises, sudden changes, or uncontrolled events in a person's physical surroundings. The important point here is that the eliciting of specific emotions can occur through a variety of attributions. The idea that cognitions can lead to emotions has been poorly received by some who believe that this idea implies that cognitions have real status while emotions are epiphenomenological.[12] I mean to give emotions the same status as cognitions. Just as cognitions lead to emotions, emotions can lead to cognitions. The theory implies no status difference. Specific to shame, the point I wish to make is that shame is not elicited by any event "out there." Rather, such external events lead to particular internal interpretations and attributions which, in turn, elicit shame.

Models that use a cognitive event as a stimulus to precipitate an emotional state are not rare or unusual. Specific stimuli—they just so happen to be a series of thought processes and interpretations—can produce a specific set of emotional responses. These emotional responses are real, of substance; that is, they have the potential to be observed as specific bodily actions measurable in unique ways, and to be phenomenologically experienced as different events. The behaviors associated with these different experiences are quite different. We therefore have no reason to assume that the emotion of shame is not substantial and that it is of a different substance than the emotion of guilt. Two features, the potential nonspecificability of the stimuli in terms of the individual's interpretation and attribution, and the fact that a class of events located in the thoughts, interpretations, and attributions of the person elicits these emotions, gives the theory its focus, and provides a way of bridging the various positions that have been held.[13]

A Cognitive Attributional Theory

The figure (p. 65) presents the structural model that I will use to define self-conscious emotions. The three subscripts, A, B, and C, represent cognitive processes that serve as stimuli for these cognitive emotions. I will use terms that are commonly used both in the literature and in everyday discussion. It may seem to some, at least at first, an idiosyncratic usage of the terms. However, as I already noted, one problem associated with the

A. STANDARDS AND RULES

B. EVALUATION

	SUCCESS	FAILURE	
GLOBAL	HUBRIS	SHAME	C. ATTRIBUTION OF SELF
SPECIFIC	PRIDE	GUILT/ REGRET	

study of the self-conscious emotions is the mixing of terms, for example, shame and guilt.

Standards, Rules, and Goals

The first feature of the model has to do with the standards, rules, and goals that govern our behavior. All of us have beliefs about what is acceptable for ourselves and for others in regard to these standards concerning actions, thoughts, and feelings. This set of standards, rules, and goals, or beliefs, is derived from the information one acquires through acculturation in a particular society. Standards (for simplicity, this term will serve as shorthand for standards, rules, and goals) differ across different societies, across groups within societies, across different time periods, and between individuals of different age, etc. The standards of our culture are varied and complex, yet each of us knows at least some of them. Moreover, each of us possesses a set of standards unique to ourselves. To become a member of any group requires that we learn the group's standards. I can think of no group that does not have such standards, nor of any group that does not employ negative sanctions to enforce their standards. These standards are acquired through a variety of processes. They always are associated with human behavior, including thinking, acting, and feeling. They are prescribed by the culture, which extends from the family group, through other social groups (peers, work groups, etc.), to the culture at large.[14]

Merely thinking about certain things can represent a violation of standards. Students who think about cheating, for example, are likely to know that they are thinking about violations of their standards and therefore might well be reluctant to disclose these thoughts, even to their intimates. Other inappropriate or taboo thoughts include thinking about one's neighbor's husband or wife in a sexual way, or elaborating a plot to kill someone, or even contemplating shoplifting an apple in a crowded grocery store. How we think and what we think of are modulated by standards.

Standards also modulate our feelings. Certain feeling states are appropriate and others inappropriate. We know what we ourselves or others are expected to feel in given situations. At funerals we know that laughing, expressing joy or happiness, or feeling glad that the person is dead is incompatible with the group's standards.[15] Relevant to this study of shame, there are many emotions that provoke shame. Here I can utilize instinctual drive analysis, where the feelings the child has—sexual and libidinal in nature—toward the mother or father constitute unacceptable feelings and therefore are repressed or, alternatively, produce anxiety, guilt, or shame.

Our prescribed actions and the standards associated with them are applied at the earliest of ages, at which time society carefully and deliberately teaches and regulates behaviors. For example, I myself have long been interested in the question of why women cry and men do not. Crying and the regulation of crying constitute a standard in which males are discouraged from crying under most circumstances, while females are allowed or even encouraged to cry.[16]

I think it is safe to claim that by the age of 1 year, children are beginning to learn the appropriate action patterns reflecting the standards of their culture. I would assume that within the second year of life children are beginning to learn both appropriate feelings and ways of thinking and things to think about that are appropriate and inappropriate in the culture. Standards are distributed differentially to members of a culture over time and status, but they begin to be transmitted to our children at an extremely early age. The process of acquisition of these standards is not completed within early life because they vary as a function of age within any culture: the process of acquisition is a never-ending one.

The evaluation of one's actions, thoughts, and feelings in terms of standards is the second cognitive evaluative process that serves as a stimulus for self-conscious emotions. There are two major aspects of this process. The first has to do with the internal and external aspects of evaluation. For my model to work in describing the process of eliciting emotions, internal evaluation, as opposed to either no evaluation or external evaluation, is necessary. Obviously, individuals differ in their characteristic evaluative response. Moreover, situations differ in the likelihood that they are internally caused. The second aspect of the evaluative process has to do with how individuals make a determination about success or failure in regard to any specific standard.

Evaluation of actions, thoughts, or feelings in terms of standards is an important feature of our ongoing behavior. I can think of no system that is oriented toward the achievement of some goal that lacks an evaluative component. In the same way that a person reaches out toward an object and, finding the object not there, readjusts the movement of his hand and arm, people set goals for themselves and evaluate their actions in relationship to achieving or failing to achieve these goals. As Lawrence Pervin has recently pointed out, goal setting is an important human activity.[17]

People create standards, rules, and goals from their internal needs as well as from the information gathered from the external environment. Skinner and his reinforcement paradigm emphasized the external environment.[18] In Skinner's view, people's behaviors, even the simplest of behaviors, are shaped and modified by external forces, including parents, peers, and other conspecifics. In his model organisms are compelled to action in specific ways by the differential rewards offered or punishments imposed by those around them.[19]

Goal setting can occur at many different levels. At the simplest level, it may involve physiological processes that order and stabilize our physical well-being. It seems reasonable to think about goal setting in terms of the homeostasis of the biological functions where our physiology is designed to achieve a certain goal, for example, the regulation of our thermal function. Put simply, the goal of the body is to readjust metabolic processes so as to maintain the correct temperature.

At the more complex levels, children, even at young ages, develop standards, rules, and goals. I recently observed a 1 year old as she moved across a playroom floor, going after an object she desired for play. It was clear to me that she had a goal in mind. Children do set themselves goals, and are able to do so at extremely early ages. The work of Hans Heckhausen or Deborah Stipek, as well as our own, seems to indicate that by the beginning of the third year of life children already have their own sets of standards, rules, and goals and seem to show distress when they violate them.[20] An example of this comes from our recent work on children's deceptive behavior.[21]

Children are placed in a room and told not to look at an attractive toy that has been placed behind them. After a few moments the experimenter leaves the room, first informing the children that they should not look at the toy while the experimenter is gone. For most of the 2½-year-old children, temptation is too great, and they turn toward the toy almost immediately.

When the experimenter reenters the room, the children are asked if they looked at the toy. At least 65% of these children report that they did not look at the toy. The children are videotaped before the experimenter leaves, while she is absent, and after her return. Examination of the children's expressions after the children look but before the experimenter returns reveals indications of guilt: a lowering of the eyes, no smile, and a certain tension in the body. By the time the experimenter reenters the room, the children no longer are exhibiting this facial expression. In fact, their facial expression might be described as neutral, innocent, or even "What? Me peek?"

These results indicate that by the beginning of the third year of life children become upset when they violate their own standards. The importance of these observations for the model is that the evaluation of our behavior in terms of our standards is a natural process independent of the nature of the standards themselves.

Some standards, rules, and goals are more valuable than others. For me, the goal of driving well is less valuable than the goal of helping a student or solving a problem. Thus, the evaluation of my behavior in relation to these two different standards should result in very different emotions. The violation of those more central to the definition of the self are more likely to lead to shame. What constitutes a more central or peripheral standard is defined by the individual as well as by the family, various intermediate groups, and the culture at large. Moreover, as new standards, rules, and goals are added to the individual's own set, their positions relative to the centrality of self differ. Thus, standards, rules, and goals and their importance change over the life course.

Internal Versus External Blame

The field of attributional studies has investigated another problem regarding evaluation, the problem of internal versus external attribution.[22] People violate standards, rules, and goals but often do not attribute the failure to themselves. Instead, they may explain their failure in terms of chance or the actions of others.[23]

A person might set a goal in business, but fail to achieve it. If he internalizes, he may say, "Yes, I am responsible. Had I only done such and such, I could have achieved my goal." The alternative is external attribution. Here the person attributes the failure to something outside the self. The businessman might say, "I shouldn't have bought the building because the real estate market turned sour. It was not my fault that the market collapsed. I lost money, but so did everyone else."

Internal and external evaluations are both situationally determined and a function of individual characteristics. There are people who are likely to blame themselves no matter what happens.

I have a friend for whom making money is very important. In fact, he embodies the prototypic good provider syndrome so common in American society, especially among men over 40. Being a good provider is a core goal for him. He internalizes any failure to make more money, even when he had no control over the events or situation that thwarted him. He would say, "It's my fault, I should have read the Wall Street Journal."

Carol Dweck and her associates carried out well-known studies in which young boys and girls were asked about the causes of their success and failure, especially within academic fields.[24] Many children blame their success or failure on external forces (some children, of course, also evaluate success and failure in terms of their own action). Interestingly, strong sex differences emerged. In academic achievement, boys are more apt to hold themselves responsible for their success and to blame others for their failure, whereas girls are apt to attribute their success to others and to blame themselves for failure.

To summarize: Sometimes when things go wrong a person will have rational reasons for blaming herself, and sometimes she will have rational reasons to blame others (or chance). Some situations are our fault, and some situations are not our fault. However, there are people who are prone to make internal attributions about success or failure, that is, they are likely to evaluate themselves in terms of standards, rules, and goals. They will do this evaluation, whether it is an evaluation marking success or marking failure, in terms of their own standards. On the other hand, there are individuals who are likely to blame others. Notice that in the latter case, these individuals are attempting to avoid blaming themselves. As we will see, I strongly suspect that individuals who characteristically blame others for failure and praise themselves for success suffer from narcissistic disorders, a topic we will return to in chapter 9.

Success or Failure

Another feature of evaluation has to do with the socialization of what constitutes success or failure. Having assumed responsibility (internal evaluation), how do we go about evaluating ourselves as succeeding or as failing? Perhaps an example will best illustrate what I mean.

A commercial real estate broker recently sold a rather large building. He received a handsome sales commission that should have made him happy. But he was anything but overjoyed at his seeming good fortune. When I asked him about the reason, he replied, "Yes, I sold it; but I know another real estate broker who sold a bigger building and made much more money."

While others, including myself, would have evaluated his business transaction as a great success, he regarded it as a failure. Such individual differences in evaluation are quite common.

I overheard two students talking. One was quite unhappy over the fact that she had only achieved a C on her organic chemistry examination. The other one turned to her friend and said, "You got a C, my God, I'd be overjoyed if I got a C!"

Here is an example of one individual who considers a C a success, while her friend considers a C a failure. Exactly how we come to evaluate our actions, thoughts, and feelings as success or failure is not well understood. As Figure 4.1 indicates the same standards, rules, and goals can result in radically different feelings, depending upon whether we attribute success or failure.

To begin with, the individual's evaluation of success or failure relative to standards can reflect an "accurate" interpretation, that is, his evaluation might be judged by an unbiased observer as normal, or as approximating the kind of evaluation a typical self would make in like situations. Alternatively, the individual's evaluation can reflect a unique interpretation. The unique interpretation could be a function of the consequences of establishing too high a standard. The student who sets his standards for school performance at a perfect score is likely to think of himself as a failure for receiving a grade of 90. Likewise, the student who sets too low a standard is likely to think himself a success just for achieving a barely passing grade. I should note that the inaccuracy of these students' interpretation of success and failure has to do with what other selves would conclude given the same situation.

An alternative reason for the inaccuracy of the interpretation has to do with misunderstanding. Take, for example, a student who thinks she knows the answer to a question presented in a test but, in fact, does not. From her point of view she did well, but from the point of view of the professor who created and grades the test, she did poorly. Here we have a case of misjudgment of success or failure relative to a standard.

Many factors are involved in producing inaccurate or unique evaluations of success or failure. These include early failures in the self system that lead to narcissistic disorders, harsh socialization experience, and high levels of reward for success or high levels of punishment for failure. When I discuss socialization factors in chapter 6, I will return to the possible causes related to the interpretation of success or failure of a standard. The evaluation of one's goal-directed behavior in terms of success and failure is a very important aspect of the organization of plans and the determination of new goals and new plans. Its importance in relation to the notion of interrupt is central. If, as I believe, the self-conscious emotions of shame and guilt serve as interrupt signals to inform us that the actions we have taken have failed, the interrupt clearly serves the biological function of enabling the organism to reconsider and alter its strategy. This process must be borne in mind when we start to consider what happens when we succeed (see Figure 4.1). Success results in positive affect such as joy, interest, excitement, and pride. The consequence here is to reward the self in terms of the action, thought, or feeling. In the negative as well as the positive evaluation of one's action, the consequence of evaluation is an affective discharge.

Attribution About Self

We now come to the final aspect of the cognitions needed to create the self-conscious emotions. Recall that in almost all of the models of self that describe the phenomenological experience of shame there appears to be some agreement as to the role of the self as object. H. B. Lewis, for example, speaks of shame as being more about the self, whereas guilt is more about the other. The phenomenology of these emotions suggests that the object of the self's orientation is quite different when we feel shame than when we feel guilt.

I want to suggest that shame is elicited when the self orients toward the self as a whole and involves an evaluation of the total self, whereas in guilt it is orientation of the self toward the actions of the self, either in terms of the actions of the self alone or in terms of the actions of the self as they have affected another. Consider the following example:

Robert, a patient of mine, says, "Last night I screwed my date even though she said she didn't want to. I felt terrible afterwards. Hell, why did I force her? What's wrong with me? I'm depressed. Didn't feel like getting out of bed this morning. I just lay there until John called."

Contrast Robert with Ted, another patient, who reports on an aggressive interchange with his girlfriend.

"Last night I visited Barbara [his girlfriend]. She wouldn't lower the sound on the tape recorder. I pushed her and pulled it off the table and broke it. Barbara started to cry. I was beside myself. All I could think about was my anger. I tried to tell her what I did was wrong and that I want to try real hard not to do that anymore. Since I broke her recorder, I gave her mine while I got hers fixed."

In both cases, these young men performed what they themselves interpret as morally inappropriate actions. In the first case, Robert focused on himself and his feelings of inadequacy, and revealed general feelings about how his self could be so bad. Ted's orientation, in contrast, was directed at the actions he had performed, trying to prevent that action from occurring again and seeking to rectify his bad action by repairing the damaged recorder. Notice that Robert does not focus on specific actions or upon the girl that he forced to have sex with him. He is uninterested in, or unable to focus upon, any other feature than the total self—and certainly not able to focus on the other.

Personality theory has drawn attention to an important feature of self-regard and evaluation of the self. Martin Seligman has discussed what he calls learned helplessness. Studies on depression, notably that of Aaron Beck, also have focused on individual differences in making self attributions.[25] *Global* and *specific* are terms used to specify the tendency of individuals to make evaluations about the self. Global refers to an individual's propensity to focus on the total self. Thus, for any particular behavior violation, some individuals, some of the time, are likely to focus on the totality of the self. These individuals use such evaluative phrases as "Because I did this, I am bad (or good)." Janoff-Bulman's distinction between characterological and behavioral self-blame is particularly relevant here.[26]

We can see how closely this idea agrees with the phenomenological experience of shame. In shame situations, the interrupt and focus is upon the self, both as object and as subject. The self becomes embroiled in the self because the evaluation of the self by the self is total. There is no way out. The focus is not upon the individual's behavior, but upon the total self. The individual who makes global attributions focuses upon herself, not upon her action. Focusing inward, such a person is unable to act, and is driven from the field of action into hiding or disappearing.

By specific attribution, I mean that in some situations, some of the time, some individuals have the propensity to focus on specific actions of the self. That is, their evaluation of their self is not global, but specific. It is not the total self that has done something wrong or right, bad or good: instead, specific behaviors are examined and judged. At such times as these, individuals will use such evaluative phrases as "What I did was wrong. I mustn't do it again." Notice that the individual's focus here is on the behavior of the self in interaction with objects or persons, and also on the individual's effect on other selves.

Global versus specific focus of the self may be a personality style.[27] Some individuals are likely to be stable in their global and specific evaluations. Under most conditions of success or failure, these subjects are likely to maintain a global or specific posture in regard to self attribution. In the attribution literature, as discussed by others, such dispositional factors have important consequences upon a variety of fixed "personality patterns." So, for example, depressed individuals are likely to make stable global attributions, whereas nondepressed individuals are less likely to be stable in their global attribution.

Dispositional factors have been found for gender. Data from a variety of sources, including Carol Dweck's work on sex differences in achievement and Aaron Beck's work on depression, suggest that females are more likely to make global attributions of failure than males. Whether this sex difference is general across all types of standard or goal failures remains to be seen. Nevertheless, in terms of school performance and academic achievement and in terms of interpersonal relationships, women, certainly in our culture, are more likely to make global attributions of failure than men.[28]

Before I conclude this section on global and specific attribution, it is important to mention one last group difference that may bear upon developmental theory. Again, although there is relatively little information on this topic, that which does exist suggests that younger children, as opposed to older ones, are more likely to make global than specific attributions. We will follow this developmental difference in considerable detail later; suffice it to say here that these differences in global and specific attribution as a function of age may have an important bearing on age differences in the emergence of shame and guilt and in differences between generations in terms of stimulus events likely to elicit shame.

While there may be dispositional factors in regard to specific or global attributions, there are likely to be situational constraints as well. Some have called these prototypic situations. That is, although there are dispositional factors, not all people all the time are involved in either global or specific attributions. Unfortunately, these situational factors have not been well studied. It seems reasonable to assume that certain classes of situation are more likely than others to elicit particular self focuses. But exactly what classes of stimuli are likely to elicit global or specific attributions remains unknown. Actions of the body are very difficult to divorce from the notion of total self.

I suggested to an adolescent patient that, while it is true that she is not physically beautiful, she is very bright, and that physical attractiveness is only one of many features of the self. It is surprising how resistant she is to these suggestions. Likewise, I have a middle-aged patient who has had a very vigorous physical life. However, because of disabilities, his participation in sports and other forms of physical activity have been severely curtailed. When he discusses his feelings with me, he often reports that this physical problem is like impotence and makes him feel ashamed. When I suggest that he might interpret his physical limitations as a specific failure, not a global failure, since he is successful in so many other aspects of his life, he reports that it is difficult for him to separate this physical feature of himself from his total self.

Such experiences raise the possibility that there may be prototypic standards that, when violated or achieved, are likely to result in global attribution. I will return to the issue of prototypicality.

Making Sense of the Model

Given these three sets of activities—(1) standards, rules, and goals, (2) the evaluation of success or failure of one's action in regard to these standards, and (3) the attribution of the self—it now is possible to observe the full set of self-conscious emotional states. Significantly, this model is symmetrical relative to positive and negative self-conscious emotions. Because of this symmetry, I will focus not only upon shame and guilt, but also upon the other side of the axis, hubris and pride. Throughout the discussion of these cognitive-evaluative processes, I have indicated that particular events may have unique eliciting properties. Nevertheless, it is the cognitive-evaluative process of the organism itself that elicits these states. The immediate elicitors of these self-conscious emotions are cognitive in nature.

In the model, I distinguish between four emotional states. Notice that shame is a consequence of a failure evaluation relative to the standards when the person makes a global evaluation of the self. Guilt is also the consequence of a failure; however, with guilt, the focus is on the self's action. A parallel exists as a consequence of success. When success is evaluated and the person makes a global attribution, hubris (pridefulness) is the resulting emotion; when success is evaluated and the person makes a specific attribution, pride is the resulting emotion.[29] I see hubris as the counterpoint to shame. The pride-shame axis has been described by others who have noticed the similarity between these two emotional states.[30]

Having outlined the situational features, I now can turn to specific definitions of these self-conscious emotions.

Shame

Shame is the product of a complex set of cognitive activities: the evaluation of an individual's actions in regard to her standards, rules, and goals, and her global evaluation of the self. The phenomenological experience of the person having shame is that of a wish to hide, disappear, or die. Shame is a highly negative and painful state that also results in the disruption of ongoing behavior, confusion in thought, and an inability to speak. The physical action accompanying shame includes a shrinking of the body, as though to disappear from the eye of the self or the other. This emotional state is so intense and has such a devastating effect on the self system that individuals presented with such a state must attempt to rid themselves of it. However, since shame represents a global attack on the self, people have great difficulty in dissipating this emotion. Individuals do take specific actions when shamed by which they try to undo the state. These actions will be discussed in chapters 7 and 8.

Notice that shame is not produced by any specific situation but rather by the individual's interpretation of a situation. Even more important, shame is not necessarily related to the public or private nature of the situation. While many hold that shame is a public failure, this need not be so. Failure, attributed to the whole self, can be either public or private. Let us consider an example of private shame:

Jeannette gave a lecture in which she presented some work that she had recently completed. The lecture was well received and her audience thought she had presented the material clearly. As she reported, "Their enthusiasm was extremely high and several people came up afterwards to tell me how well I did." Yet, she also reported that she felt she had failed and was

ashamed because "she didn't present her work as well as she might have."
Her shame derived from her failed internal standard of what she thought she
could have done, a standard independent of audience evaluation.

Shame is often public, but it is just as likely to be private. Each of us can think of private events when we said to ourselves "I'm ashamed for having done that." Shame can occur around moral action as well. Thus, when a person violates some moral standard, rule, or goal, they can experience shame. A friend recently told me of her shame because she had not given enough money for a charity she thought particularly important. When I asked her why she felt shame, not guilt, she replied "I should've known better," which I took to mean that she had made a global attribution about herself.

Guilt

The emotional state of guilt or regret is produced when individuals evaluate their behavior as failure but focus on the specific features of the self or on the self's action that led to the failure. Unlike shame, in which the focus is on the global self, with guilt the individual focuses on the self's actions and behaviors that are likely to repair the failure. From a phenomenological point of view, individuals are pained by their failure, but this pained feeling is directed to the cause of the failure or to the harmed object. Because the cognitive attributional process focuses on the action of the self rather than on the totality of the self, the feeling that is produced is not as intensely negative as shame and does not lead to confusion and to the loss of action. In fact, the emotion of guilt always has an associated corrective action, something that the individual can do—but does not necessarily actually do—to repair the failure. Rectification of the failure and preventing it from occurring again are the two possible corrective paths. Whereas in shame we see the body hunched over itself in an attempt to hide and disappear, in guilt we see individuals moving in space as if trying to repair their action. The postural differences that accompany shame and guilt are marked and are helpful both in distinguishing these emotions and in measuring individual differences. I might point to blushing as a measure also distinguishing shame from guilt; however, because of variability in the likelihood of individuals to blush, the use of blushing is not an accurate index.

Because in guilt the focus is on the specific, individuals who feel guilt have the capacity to rid themselves of this emotional state by means of corrective action. The corrective action can be directed toward the self as well as toward the other. Unlike shame, which is a melding of the self as subject and object, in guilt the self is differentiated from the object. As such, the emotion is less intense and more capable of dissipation.

Guilt can manifest itself at various levels, with the degree of severity tied to the ease or availability of corrective action. In some cases, corrective action may not be as readily available as in others. In all cases, however, there is an attempt at corrective action. Should the corrective action not be forthcoming, either in thought, feeling, or deed, it is possible that a guilt experience can be converted into one of shame. Here, then, is another difference between shame and guilt. We can be ashamed of our guilty action, but we cannot feel guilty about being ashamed—this reality suggests both a levels difference and a directional difference in the experiencing of these emotions. The emotion of guilt lacks the negative intensity of shame. It is not self destroying and, as such, can be viewed as a more useful emotion in motivating specific and corrective action. However, because it is less intense, it may not convey the motivation necessary for change or correction.

Another example of the difference between shame and guilt in terms of these evaluative processes and subsequent action might be helpful:

Consider the case of a colleague who has recently submitted a paper for publication in a journal. She learns that the paper has been rejected. Two types of evaluation are now possible. In the first, the scientist concludes that rejection is not her fault, but results from the "stupidity" of the reviewers. Thus, no evaluation of failure is made, and neither guilt nor shame occur. The second possibility is that the scientist assumes responsibility for the rejected paper. Now evaluation can occur. If the scientist evaluates the rejection as a reflection upon the totality of the self, as a sign that she is not a good scientist, she is likely to experience shame. Shame might cause the scientist to file her paper and make no attempt to improve it, or it might even cause her to destroy the paper. If, however, the scientist evaluates the rejection in terms of the specific criticisms leveled at it, she might well feel guilt. She might say to herself, "I failed to do the proper analysis." Notice that in the second case, the focus on the specific self allows the scientist a course of action. Under such a case, rather than removing the paper by either filing it or throwing it away, the scientist is likely to work on the paper and try to rectify its problems.[31]

Hubris

Hubris can be defined as exaggerated pride or self-confidence often resulting in retribution. It is an example of pridefulness, something dislikeable and to be avoided. Hubris is a consequence of an evaluation of success according to one's standards, rules, and goals where the focus is on the global self. In this emotion, the individual focuses on the total self as successful. In extreme cases, hubris is associated with grandiosity or with narcissism. Because of the global nature of this emotion, it is likely to be transient. To maintain this state, the individual must either alter standards or reevaluate what constitutes success. Unlike shame, hubris is highly positive and emotionally rewarding because the person feels "good" about herself.

Hubris is difficult to sustain because no specific action precipitates the feeling. Because hubris feelings are addictive, people prone to hubris derive little satisfaction from the emotion. Consequently, they seek out and invent situations likely to repeat this emotional state. This can be accomplished either by altering their standards, rules, and goals or by reevaluating what constitutes success according to their actions, thoughts, or feelings.

From the outside, other people observe the individual who feels hubris with some disdain. In fact, according to the dictionary definition, to be hubristic is to be insolent or contemptuous. Hubristic people have difficulty in their interpersonal relations since their own hubris is likely to interfere with the wishes, needs, and desires of others, thereby promoting interpersonal conflict. Moreover, given the contemptuousness associated with hubris, the other is likely to be shamed by the nature of the actions of the person having this emotion. The hubristic person faces three problems: (1) hubris is a transient but addictive emotion; (2) it is not related to a specific action and, therefore, requires altering patterns of goal setting or the evaluation of what constitutes success; and (3) it interferes with interpersonal relationships because of its contemptuous and insolent nature.

Pride

The emotion I label pride is the consequence of a successful evaluation of a specific action. The phenomenological experience might be described as joy over an action, thought, or feeling well done. Here, again, the focus of pleasure is specific and related to a particular behavior. In pride, just as in guilt, the self and object are separated. Unlike shame and hubris, where subject and object are fused, pride focuses the organism on its action. The organism is engrossed in the specific action that gives it pride. Some investigators have likened this state to achievement motivation,[32] an association that I believe is particularly apt. Because this positive state is associated with a particular action, individuals have available to themselves the means by which they can reproduce the state. Notice that, unlike hubris, pride's specific focus allows for action. Unfortunately, because of the use of the term pride to refer to both hubris and efficacy and satisfaction, the study of pride has received relatively little attention. Dweck and Leggett have approached pride through the use of individuals' implicit theories.[33] Like me, they see cognitive attributions as the stimuli for the elicitation of the self-conscious emotion of mastery.

Embarrassment and Shyness

In the discussion to this point, I have argued that one can differentiate, from a behavioral as well as a phenomenological point of view, shame and guilt. But there are two other emotions that tend to be confused with these two, embarrassment and shyness.

Izard and Tyson consider shyness to be sheepishness, bashfulness, a feeling of uneasiness or psychological discomfort in social situations; they suggest that shyness results from an oscillation between fear and interest or between avoidance and approach.[34] Notice that they relate shyness to fear and argue that it is a nonevaluative emotion that has its organization centered around the individual's discomfort response to others. I have had students tell me, "I am a very shy person. Please do not call upon me in class." I find that such students are not so much concerned with an evaluation of their performance vis-à-vis their standards as they are with the simple fact of observation. That is, their discomfort centers less around feelings of evaluation relative to their own standards, rules, and goals, and more around just being seen.

I have known a child of friends since her birth. She is painfully shy and fearful. She was quite fearful of strangers as early as age 3 months (stranger anxiety normally occurs in the last quarter of the first year) and by age 8 months her response to them was intense and prolonged. She was reticent about engaging in social contact and appeared to be asocial in orientation. However, once she got to know someone she was quite sociable.

Her shyness seems to be exhibited in situations in which she does not know other people. This case fits Arnold Buss's notion of shyness as an emotional response that is elicited by experiences of novelty or conspicuousness.[35] For Buss, shyness and fear are closely related and represent a fearfulness toward others. Shyness appears much earlier than either shame or guilt; this early emergence may provide an important clue to its distinct identity.

Such an approach to shyness seems reasonable because it fits with other notions relating the self to others, or to what we might call the social self. Eysenck, in particular, has characterized people as social and asocial by genetic disposition. Recently, Jerome Kagan and his associates have pointed out the physiological responses of children they call inhibited.[36] These inhibited or shy children are withdrawn, uncomfortable in social situations, and appear fearful. My own observations of very young children, those still in the first few months of life, also indicate that shyness may be a dispositional factor not related to self evaluation. Shyness may simply result from the discomfort of being in the company of other social objects.

In a series of studies, we have observed 3-month-old children interacting with their mothers. Two different types of children can be distinguished. The first group of children appeared to be socially oriented, even by 12 weeks of age. These children looked at, smiled at, and vocalized in interactive sequences with their mothers. Moreover, they preferred to play with their mothers rather than by themselves or with toys. We characterized these children as sociable children. The other group of children we characterized as asocial. They constitute about 20% of the population. Unlike the first group, these children preferred not to look at, smile at, and vocalize with their mothers—they did so significantly less than the first group. Even more surprisingly, these children preferred to play by themselves and with toys more than with their mothers.[37] This configuration of self-play and nonsocial interaction is in marked contrast to children who appear to be sociable.

We also noted that mothers of these two types of children behaved very differently toward them. Children who appeared asocial had mothers who repeatedly attempted to engage their children in interaction. At times it was almost painful to watch a mother of an asocial child try to initiate and to interact with her infant in an attempt to get it into social exchange. Thus, we could not account for these infant differences in terms of their maternal handling since the asocial children seem to have, for the most part, mothers eager for social exchange.

These asocial children were observed again at one or two years of age, and again we found them more asocial. While we have no direct data on their social interactions with others, we would expect them to be more shy than the other children. It seems clear to me that shyness is different from shame and embarrassment since it does not involve an evaluative component in regard to one's action in terms of standards, rules, and goals. Shyness is likely to be biological rather than psychological in origin.

———— • ————

For some, embarrassment is closely linked to shame.[38] The most notable difference between shame and embarrassment is the intensity level. While shame appears to be an intense and disruptive emotion, embarrassment is clearly less intense and does not involve the disruption of thought and language that shame does. In terms of body posture, people who are embarrassed do not assume the shame posture of one wishing to hide, disappear, or die. In fact, the bodies of the embarrassed reflect an ambivalent approach-and-avoidance posture. Typically, multiple looking and then looking away accompanied by smiling behavior index embarrassment.[39] Rarely in a shame situation do I see gaze aversion accompanied by smiling behavior. Thus, from a behavioral point of view, these two emotions appear to be different.

Phenomenologically, embarrassment is less differentiated from shame than from guilt. People often report that embarrassment is "a less intense experience of shame." Situations similar to those that invoke shame are found to invoke embarrassment. Again I must note that the intensity, duration, and disruptive quality of shame is not matched in embarrassment. To further distinguish shame from embarrassment, I wish to point to two types of embarrassment. These I will call embarrassment as self-consciousness and embarrassment as mild shame.

In the first type, embarrassment appears to be more similar to shyness than to shame. In certain situations of exposure, people become embarrassed. This type of embarrassment is not related to negative evaluation, as is shame. Perhaps the best example is the case of being complimented. One phenomenological experience of those who appear before audiences is that of embarrassment caused by the positive comments made during the introduction. Consider the moment when I am introduced. The person introducing me rises and, addressing the audience, extols my virtues. Surprisingly, this praise, rather than displeasure or negative evaluation, elicits embarrassment. Another example of this type of embarrassment can be seen in our reactions to public display. I have ofte. noticed that when people observe someone looking at them, they are apt to become self-conscious, to look away, and to touch or adjust their bodies. When the observed person is a woman, she will often adjust or touch her hair; an observed man is less likely to touch his hair but may adjust his clothes or change his body posture. In few cases do the observed people look sad. If anything, they appear pleased by the attention. This behavioral combination, typically signified by gaze turned away briefly, no frown, and nervous touching, looks like the type of embarrassment I will call self consciousness.

We often experience embarrassment when being complimented. Sometimes in class when I wish to demonstrate that embarrassment can be elicited just by exposure, I simply point to a student. My pointing invariably elicits embarrassment in the student pointed at. How, then, can embarrassment be likened to shame? In the case of shame, the experience is produced by the negative evaluation of the self in regard to standards, rules, and goals. This type of embarrassment is elicited by praise. Unless we construct a scenario in which the praise of individuals really is interpreted as a negative evaluation, it is difficult to imagine embarrassment as a less intense form of shame. Since praise cannot readily lead to an evaluation of failure, it is likely that embarrassment due to compliments has more to do with the exposure of the self than with evaluation. In other words, this type of embarrassment is related to self-consciousness. It is often associated with public exposure. Take, for example, the simple act of walking into a lecture hall a few minutes before the speaker has started to talk. The person who arrived on time may attract attention; as she notes the eyes of the already seated audience members turning toward her, she experiences embarrassment. One could say that this situation promotes a negative self-evaluation: "I should have been here earlier; I should have stayed at the back of the hall." I believe that the experience of embarrassment in this case is not elicited by negative self-evaluation, but simply by public exposure.

The second type of embarrassment, which I call embarrassment as less intense shame, seems to me to be related to a negative self-evaluation. The difference in intensity is likely due to the nature of the failed standard, rule, or goal. Recall that earlier I suggested that some standards are closely associated with the core of self, others less so; in one case, failure at driving a car is less important to one's sense of self than is failure at helping a student. I believe that failures associated with less important, less central standards, rules, and goals result in embarrassment rather than shame.[40]

It may well be that embarrassment is not the same as shame. Certainly, from a phenomenological stance, they appear very different. On the other hand, there is the possibility that embarrassment and shame are, in fact, related and that they only vary in intensity.

5

The Origins of Shame

Genesis and the Creation Myth

E very culture has its creation myth. Judeo-Christian Western society looks to the story of creation recounted in Genesis. I present part of this myth here because it bears directly on the subject of shame.

> And the Lord God planted a Garden in Eden . . . and caused to grow out of the ground every tree . . . and the tree of life in the midst of the garden, and the tree of knowledge of good and evil . . . God commanded the man, saying that, "Every tree of the garden thou mayest freely eat. But of the tree of the knowledge of good and evil, thou shalt not eat of it, for if on the day thou eatest thereof, thou shall surely die. . . ."
>
> And the serpent (to encourage evil, said), "Ye shall surely not die, for God doth know that, on the day ye eat thereof, your eyes will be opened, and ye will be as God, knowing good and evil . . ."
>
> She [Eve] took of its fruit, and did eat, and gave also unto her husband with her and he did eat. And the eyes of both of them were opened, and they felt that they were naked.
>
> And they hid from the Lord God and when he called to them they did not answer. And he said to them, "Why are you hiding from Me?" And they answered, *"Because we are naked."* And he knew, therefore, that they had eaten of the tree of knowledge.

In the Genesis story of creation, shame is the only emotion that is discussed at any length. The biblical version of the origin of shame has considerable significance for the Western mind. Moreover, the issue of shame as presented in the myth is particularly cogent for my view of the developmental process. Note that the Genesis version of the creation of the world and its inhabitants links the creation of man and woman with an almost immediate fall from grace. This Old Testament story provided theologians with the justification for the notion of original sin.[1] This sin, the violation of God's commandment, represents a particularly important and poignant story in the development of the human condition. For me, the Old Testament's story of Adam and Eve's creation, their freedom to obey or disobey God's injunction, their disobedience, judgment by God, and punishment signify the importance of shame.[2]

Shame is the focal emotion in the Genesis creation story. Shame behaviors, Adam and Eve's recognition of their own nakedness, their sense of exposure before God, and their attempt to hide their nakedness, are central to the story. There are three critical features to this story. Adam and Eve disobey God because they are curious, because they are tempted by the unknown. Their curiosity leads them to sample the fruit of the tree of knowledge: in other words, their curiosity leads to knowledge. This knowledge in turn leads to their sense of shame. To paraphrase what happens after they sin, God in effect says: "Ah! Since you know you are naked and are ashamed of your nakedness, you must have eaten the fruit of the tree of knowledge. You could not be ashamed unless you knew something, and the only way you could know something is through having eaten the forbidden fruit."

Here, then, is the core of the myth. Curiosity leads to knowledge, which leads to shame. The structure of this early creation story fits the ontogenetic development of shame for the child and describes the process of shame production for the human adult. In discussing shame and the other self-conscious emotions, I have already suggested that one has to have specific cognitions in order for them to occur: one has to know something about (1) standards, rules, and goals, (2) one's own behavior in regard to these standards, and (3) oneself. Only when these things are "known" can shame occur.

Another significant feature of the creation story is its portrayal of the differences between the sexes. Jewish and Christian theologians have traditionally made much of the fact that Eve, a woman, first breaks God's commandment and then convinces Adam to do likewise. It is the female, rather than the male, who commits the first violation. Adam sins but it was Eve's fault. The idea that women are more curious than men, more prone to temptation, and morally weaker has a long history in the West.[3] Freud, for one, accepted and developed these ideas, arguing that women were less moral than men.[4] This common theme was later elaborated by Lawrence Kohlberg in his theory of moral development.[5] Although the idea has been somewhat discredited by Carol Gilligan's work, the innate moral inferiority of women continues to be upheld by many religious traditions.[6] I will return to these sex differences later; here I simply wish to point out that the creation story informs us about historical beliefs held about human nature and about differences in males' and females' self-consciousness. For me, this theme provides a way of exploring ontogenic differences, something I take up below.

The Development of the Self-Conscious Emotions

The figure (p. 87) presents a schematic of the model of the development of shame. The model has five major features which account for the change over the first three years of life. The development of shame involves transformation and integration of structures and functions. It does not exist at birth, but instead develops. The first emotions to emerge are the primary emotions.[7]

Not all of these emotions appear at the same time. Bridges has described how the earliest two classes of emotion, positive emotion (joy/happiness) and distress, differentiate into the other emotions.[8] Disgust emerges from distress and is followed by anger, appearing somewhere between ages 2 and 4 months; fear emerges sometime later, at about 8 months. Likewise, surprise emerges early, perhaps emerging from the interest/joy axis. Somewhere around age 8 months these differentiated primary emotions are already evident. The socialization of these primary emotions within the interpersonal life of the child as well as maturation contribute to the next phase of development, the cognitive capacity of objective self-awareness.

Because I have already spent considerable time discussing objective self-awareness, I will only mention here that near the middle of the second year of life the child gains this capacity. When the Old Testament makes reference to Adam and Eve and the tree of knowledge, it offers a kind of metaphorical version of the emergence of objective self-awareness. The tree of knowledge provides Adam and Eve with two kinds of knowledge: knowledge of themselves, or what I call objective self-awareness, and knowledge about standards, rules, and goals. Following the development of objective self-awareness, the first class of self-conscious emotions emerges.

The Exposed Emotions

At the point when the child becomes objectively aware of herself, several emotions emerge that are related to this objectivity. These emotions are not evaluative in nature: they do not arise because of correct or incorrect thoughts, actions, or feelings. I can list three such emotions, embarrassment, empathy, and envy, but there may be others. These emotions, the consequence of self-objectification, make up the first set of emotions from the exposed self.

As I have already indicated, there are two kinds of embarrassment: one involves no evaluation and is related to exposure, while the other is related to evaluation. The kind of embarrassment I will treat here is the

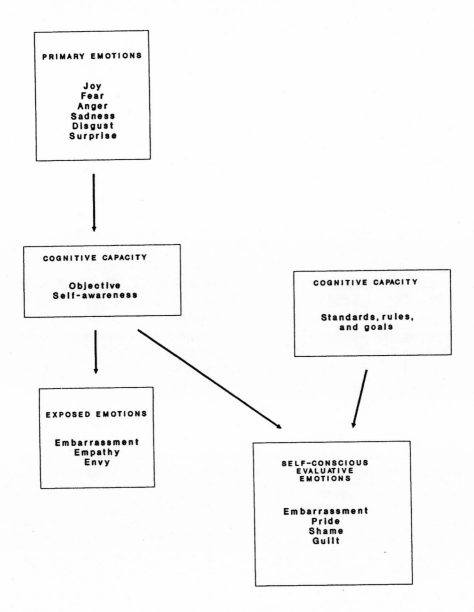

embarrassment caused by the objectification of the self or by exposure.

When the child becomes objectively aware of herself, embarrassment appears. Why should embarrassment emerge at the time when the self becomes differentiated and objectified? I suspect that there may be some evolutionary significance in the connection between self-objectification and this slightly negative, but intense, emotion. Embarrassment may provide protection against this emergent skill. Objective self-awareness is not always active in adults and may, at times, even be detrimental to the self's action. Focusing on the self may be costly because such a focus may result in a loss of performance. I can think of many situations in which focusing upon the self, that is, the self as object to the self, is harmful and interferes with ongoing behavior. If while giving a lecture you turn your attention to what you are saying or to how you look, you will interfere with your ability to continue giving the lecture. If a ballplayer in a hitting slump becomes too concerned about his lack of performance and spends his time and energy examining himself while at the plate, this concern itself can contribute to and prolong his slump. Sexual dysfunction provides another common example of the cost of attending to the self at the wrong time. It has often been pointed out that when one or both parties engaging in sexual behavior focus upon how they are doing rather than upon the stimulus sensation, that focus results in dysfunctional sexual behavior. The course of therapeutic treatment in such cases is to get the individuals to focus not upon themselves but on the set of genital stimuli.

I can also analyze the problem in terms of circular reactions and closed loops. The degree to which the self focuses upon the self is the degree to which the feedback reaction becomes a circular one: "I am thinking about thinking about thinking about thinking." A person can become trapped in an interminable regression in which he spends all of his time, thus preventing action. Organisms are designed to act in their world, by thinking, feeling, and behaving toward others, for example, so it is important that they do not spend all of their time thinking about themselves. Attention to the self is disruptive. The ability not to engage in objective self-awareness may be facilitated by an emotional concomitant that is intense and slightly aversive. I believe that the emergence of embarrassment, which appears to accompany the emergence of objectification, is designed to make objective self-awareness somewhat aversive and therefore allow the organism to break free from any circular reaction.[9]

My colleagues and I have been able to connect embarrassment with objective self-awareness. In a series of studies we have discovered that embarrassment does not appear until the child demonstrates objective self-awareness.[10] Some children show objective self-awareness by 15 to 18 months of age, and these children are also likely to show embarrassment at this point; other children of the same age who do not yet show objective self-awareness also do not show embarrassment.[11]

I have included empathy as an emotion, although many do not consider it to be so. But empathy is not only a form of knowledge, knowledge of what another may be feeling or thinking; it is also the actual feeling of the other's feeling. For this reason, I consider empathy an emotion.[12] Empathic behavior is the ability to put one's self in the place of the other. Empathic behavior or knowledge reflects an important class of knowing. I can imagine the pain of your headache by thinking about how I felt when I had a headache. We can read about the pain of a headache and we can observe another's behavior when she has a headache; however, we cannot *know* about another's headache if, by knowing, we mean actually experiencing it. At best, we can experience the other's headache by thinking about our own past headaches.

In order to carry out empathic behavior of this type, we need both the capacity to think about our own past headaches and the ability to put ourselves in the other's place. In other words, empathic behavior has both cognitive and affective aspects. No evidence indicates that the cognitive and affective aspects of adult empathic behavior are present in newborn or very young children. Indeed, I would argue that empathic behavior— putting the self in the place of the other—can not occur until objective self-awareness emerges. Therefore, I place empathy in the class of self-conscious emotions.

Nevertheless, there is some controversy regarding the timing of empathy's emergence since at least one study has shown that some newborns are apt to cry when another infant cries.[13] I am not prepared to call the cry of one child in response to the cry of another an empathic response, even though I might well call adult tears stimulated by the crying of another adult an empathic response. The same type of response does not always mean the same thing. I would prefer to use the term *empathic reflex* rather than the term *empathic response* for infants' crying behavior in the presence of other crying infants. This case is easy, so let me present a more difficult example. A mother playing with her 1-year-old child hurts her finger on a toy. She says, "Ouch! That hurts," makes a sad face, and holds her finger. The 1 year old is quite capable of making certain empathic-like responses. Under such conditions a child might well go to the mother and pat her on the back or hold her and try to comfort her. Such a response could be interpreted as empathic behavior.[14] Certainly, from the point of view of the mother, the child appears to demonstrate empathy. But is the child really experiencing empathy, or, in fact, is the child simply making a response that might be related to other processes? Given that the child, when distressed, has been held and patted by the mother, is it surprising that the child, in turn, utilizes these behaviors? What appears to be empathic behavior is really learned behavior. This analysis is supported by a study of children's emotional expressions when they are soothing their mothers. Their expressions do not reflect empathic behavior.

While some responses related to empathy appear early, they are not organized. Both the cognition and affect components of empathy are not organized until the second half of the second year of life. Miri Halperin has observed two classes of empathic behaviors, emotional and action.[15] In an experimental paradigm where the mother fakes injuring herself while trying to place a pin on the child, she says with a sad face, "Oh, I've hurt my finger!" While children tend to show empathic facial expression as early as 9 months of age, and while children also show behavior designed to repair the distress of their mothers, it is not until children have objective self-awareness that they show an organized response of action and face.

Adult empathic responses require that adults understand and sympathize with the other *because they are capable of placing themselves in the role of the other.* If this analysis of empathic behavior is correct, then empathy must await the emergence of an objective self-awareness. Prior to this emergence, organisms, whether they be young children or animals, are capable of learned responses or automatic reflexes, only a part of which represent empathic behavior.[16]

I have included envy, or the desire to get for the self what another has, as the third nonevaluative self-conscious emotion. Unfortunately, there has been very little research on this topic. Parental reports and my own observation indicate that children at about age 2 are likely to engage in behaviors, such as desire for another's toys, that are reminiscent of envy. At earlier ages children take objects that do not belong to them in the same way that they take any object. As they get older, this behavior undergoes some interesting developmental change. At the point of the emergence of objective self-awareness, children can be observed looking at objects belonging to other children and then, when the other is not looking, taking the desired objects for themselves.

In a series of studies looking at peer behavior in 1 and 2 year olds, we found that 1 year olds show no indication that objects are theirs. But by age 2 years, they appear to know which objects are "theirs" and which objects belong to other children. This knowledge of what is their own has been shown to occur around the time objective self-awareness appears, and has been used as another measure of this objectivity.[17]

It appears that a new set of emotions emerge at the time, or soon after, objective self-awareness emerges. These self-conscious emotions are not evaluative, but they do represent the emotional consequences of an exposed self. To summarize: The emergence of objectivity occurs somewhere around the middle of the second year of life and constitutes the final major structural feature of the self system. The emergence of objective self-awareness gives rise to sets of emotions that have to do with self-consciousness. The emergence of embarrassment, empathy, and, perhaps, envy represents a set of self-conscious emotions indicative of the process. By the second half of the second year of life, the human organism's metacognitions (memory of memories, knowledge of knowledge, feelings about feelings) provide the major milestone in the child's development of self-conscious emotions.

Origins of Shame

The emergence of shame and the other self-conscious emotions requires something more than objective self-awareness: the child must have certain other cognitive capacities. He must have standards, rules, and goals that, when accompanied by objective self-awareness, give rise to a new set of self-conscious emotions, the self-conscious *evaluative* emotions, including shame.

When does the emergence of standards, rules, and goals take place? From the moment the child enters into her social network, the rules, values, and standards of the primary caregiver, family, and culture start to be imposed. Certain behaviors are rewarded and others punished. Children are the recipients, both directly and indirectly, of standards and rules from the beginning of life. Why, then, characterize them as emerging at the 2-year mark? They are indicated at this point, not so much because the child does not know some rules, but because until objective self-awareness emerges, the child does not "own" these rules.

Let me explain what "to own" means. Standards and rules appear early in the child's life; in fact, they make up the material that helps to define the relationship of the child to the caregiver. When a child succeeds in meeting the other's standards, success results and the child shows joy. When the child fails, she may show fear, anxiety, or distress. The child's responses are determined by the anticipated rewards and punishments of the other. They are imposed on the child.

After the emergence of objective self-awareness, two events occur. First, emotions related to the exposed self, embarrassment, empathy, and envy, also emerge. Second, objective self-awareness allows for the incorporation of the standards of the other. This is what I mean by coming "to own" standards, rules, and goals. The acquisition and incorporation of standards is a two-stage process. In the beginning, the child passively accepts the standards of the other, since the child's emotional life is determined by following or failing to follow the rules established by the other. Later the child actually begins to incorporate these standards. The process determining this incorporation may be based on a backward observation. The child observes what makes her happy or sad and then generates the standards, rules, and goals without the other. This second learning allows for objectification of the standards and rules themselves.

Now it is not just the other who rewards or punishes the child. By incorporating the other's standards, the child becomes capable of rewarding and punishing herself. This capacity or ability to switch from the other's to the self's standards takes place only as a function of the emergence of an objective self. The "me" emerges in distinction from the "other." In the case of shame, it is the eye of the other in the me who beholds my transgression. This other within the self only can occur after there is an objective self into which it can be incorporated. At the point of objective self-awareness, when the parent's standards, rules, and goals have become the child's, the self-conscious evaluative emotions emerge. Because these self-conscious evaluative emotions require a more elaborate cognitive structure, they emerge after the self-evaluative emotions of embarrassment, empathy, and envy. Support for this timing comes from a variety of sources.

While Tomkins, for example, believes that shame, guilt, hubris, and pride exist in infancy, the evidence for their emergence after the first two years is impressive. Darwin's studies on blushing indicate that it does not occur before 2 1/2 years of age. Inge Bretherton's work on the child's acquisition of a theory of mind and my own work on embarrassment both point to the second to third year of life as the beginning of self-conscious emotions.[18] Work on the emergence of guilt and empathy also speaks to their emergence at this time period. Children's anxiety over their own failure occurs around age 2, a finding that supports the observation that evaluative processes emerge at the end of the second year of life.[19] Geppert and Kuster describe the reactions of young children when they were successful in a competitive task of tower stacking. The children who finished first and succeeded raised their eyes, smiled, and looked triumphantly at the losers. They also sat up straight, and some of them threw their arms up in the air, as if to inflate themselves. The children who failed exhibited body collapse, lowered heads, lack of eye contact with the winners, and hands that did not stray from their work. The developmental sequence of pride or failure indicates that the self related reactions are observed in children between 2 and 3 years of age.[20]

The psychoanalytic literature supports the same timing sequence. Freud first saw shame and guilt emerging quite early from unacceptable impulses of a sexual (or aggressive) nature. In his later elaboration of the emergence of a superego and identification, however, Freud placed the development of the self-conscious emotions around age 3. Erikson and Klein linked the emergence of the self-conscious emotions, in particular shame, to toilet training, which usually occurs at the end of the second year. It should be noted that Erikson saw the emergence of shame before guilt, and in his hierarchy of challenges he saw the shame challenge as occurring prior to the guilt and autonomy challenge.

How can some theorists maintain that these emotions emerge earlier? There is neither strong theoretical support nor empirical evidence for this idea, yet it remains a widely held view.[21] There are two possible explanations. The first has to do with attribution and anthropomorphizing. For example, Robert Emde asked mothers when they thought certain emotions emerged.[22] The great majority of mothers thought that interest, joy, surprise, anger, fear, and distress were present by 2 to 4 months, and significant percentages thought that sadness (38%), shyness (19%), disgust (27%), contempt (11%), and even guilt (3%) were present. What is amazing is that 11% thought contempt was present by 4 months and that 3% thought guilt was present. Thus, parents and, I suppose, scientists attribute a variety of abilities to the very young child.

The second explanation has been dealt with before but needs continued emphasis: earlier manifestations of later capacities do not necessarily represent adultlike modes. If we do not remember this simple rule, we must deny the very notion of development. We can see this truth using the emergence of pride as an example. At very early ages, infants show joy over particular forms of achievement. My associates and I have noted in a number of studies that children as young as 2 months exhibit positive affects when they succeed in a task.[23] But efficacy is not the same thing as pride, even though both appear around the same sorts of eliciting events. The 2-month-old child who can pull a string to get something to happen and the 5 year old who successfully solves a problem both show joy and pleasure over their competence. In the 5 year old, however, pride specifically makes reference to the achievement of an action that fulfills a requirement in regard to the standards, rules, and goals that the self knows. In like fashion, I would argue that failure in regard to the standards of the other leads to fear, anxiety, and sadness. After the development of an objective self-awareness, shame and guilt are added to sadness, anxiety, and fear. Given the same situations, it is understandable why the behaviors observed are often treated as the same. Only a developmental perspective allows for the growth of structures and processes.

Increasing evidence indicates that pride and shame are different from joy and sadness. Recently we conducted a study with 3-year-old children. They were given two types of tasks, easy ones that could be readily solved and more difficult ones. Several findings bear on this question of the timing of the emergence of evaluative emotions. When children succeeded in solving a problem they all showed joy; however, *when they succeeded with a difficult task they showed pride.* This finding suggests that pride is related to achievement on a task *the child himself evaluated as difficult to do.* Likewise, when the children failed a task they showed sadness; however, when they *failed an easy task they showed shame.* Both pride and shame were related to the children's evaluation of the task difficulty, but this was not the case for joy and sadness.[24]

Perhaps even more important is the recent work of Deborah Stipek and her colleagues.[25] In a series of studies looking at achievement-related self-evaluation, the following developmental sequence was observed. To begin with, children as young as 1 year experience joy in succeeding but "they lack the cognitive representational skill required for self-evaluation in a self-reflective sense." By 2 years of age children can anticipate adult reaction but their response is related to adults' behavior.[26] By about 3 years children remain concerned about disapproval from adults but "they may also react to failure more independently" as if they have a standard of their own.

The data from many sources indicates that self-evaluation and with it the self-evaluation emotions of shame, guilt, and pride emerge at around age 3, while self-reflected behavior and with it embarrassment emerges around 18 to 24 months. There is no longer doubt of a clear developmental sequence over the first 3 years of life.

Shame Versus Guilt: A Developmental Perspective

There are three possible models to describe the development of shame and guilt. In the first, shame emerges prior to guilt; in the second, guilt emerges prior to shame; and, in the third, both shame and guilt emerge at the same time. The first two models are predicated on the belief that one of these emotions is the major emotion and the other a subcategory of it. Although many would support either the first or second model, I believe that shame and guilt emerge at about the same time.

If shame is part of the same set as embarrassment and shyness, which have been shown to emerge early, I would be forced to admit that shame occurs earlier than guilt. Alternatively, it could be argued that guilt cannot emerge first because of the moral prerequisites necessary for its attainment: the child has to know right from wrong, and the child has to have a good sense of proper moral conduct for guilt to emerge. It has been assumed that moral behavior does not emerge until considerably after most people have observed shame or embarrassment. Blushing is reported by 2 1/2 years of age, but Piaget found that the emergence of a moral behavior is dependent upon cognitive capacities that do not occur prior to this age.[27] From this developmental point of view, shame appears to occur before moral standards and moral behavior, and guilt after; however, this developmental stance assumes that moral behavior and transgressions are the basis of guilt.

Shame may predate guilt, especially if my analysis of global versus specific attribution is correct. There are some who have argued that children's global attributions precede specific ones.[28] If this is the case, then shame should occur before guilt. Such a proposition seems reasonable to the degree to which global can be said to occur before specific attribution.

That guilt precedes shame is based upon a variety of beliefs. Typically, guilt rather than shame is the object of study. But no empirical data suggest that guilt occurs earlier than shame. A belief in the importance of guilt, as opposed to shame, could be used to support such a view, although, even here, it could be the case that guilt is considered to emerge later because it is more complex and differentiated than shame. That guilt is a higher form of a moral emotion is a widely held view.[29] Nonetheless, there is little reason to believe that guilt emerges earlier than shame. One could point to the fact that very young children deal only with specifics; the idea of classes is too intellectually advanced for them. From this fact, we might conclude that they can not produce global, but instead only specific, attributions. If this were so, guilt should precede shame.

The question remains as to whether these emotions emerge sequentially or at the same time. These emotions are dependent upon the particular self focus. The degree to which children are first able to make global attributions is the degree to which they are first likely to experience shame or hubris. The degree to which they are likely to focus on the action or the object of the action is the degree to which children are first likely to experience guilt or pride. Is there any indication that children are more likely to focus on one feature than the other? Some data do suggest that children are more likely to make global attributions early. But other data indicate that at about age 2 children show empathic behavior, that is, they are able to focus upon the feelings of others. Such findings would imply that children have some understanding of other selves and might be capable of orienting and focusing their concern on the other, a necessary feature for guilt. If this is so, then children are capable of showing guilt behavior at the same age they show shame.

This idea is supported by research that indicates that, after age 2, children show both shame and guilt in reaction to a transgression that they hold themselves responsible for. Recall that we gave children a toy to play with and, because of the way the toy was constructed, it fell apart after a moment. The behavior of the children in this situation seemed to reflect both shame and guilt. Some children avoided looking at the experimenter and telling that the doll was broken. They were unlikely to try to repair the doll, either by fixing it themselves or by getting the experimenter to fix it for them. But other children tried to repair the doll themselves or did show it to the experimenter and asked for help to repair it.[30] Children in the latter group did not avoid the adult, and they did not show the pattern of downcast eyes and shrunken body. If we interpret these behaviors in terms of our definitions of shame and guilt, we see that both shame and guilt are demonstrated in children of this age. From this type of evidence, it seems likely that both shame and guilt emerge at about the same time.

Exposed Versus Evaluative Self-Conscious Emotions

There is some possibility that my model needs further adjustment. One particular feature has to do with the relationship between the exposed self-conscious emotions and the evaluative self-conscious emotions. As I have indicated in Figure 5.1, it is the combination of objective self-awareness and standards that produces the evaluative emotions. While this may be true, it does not explain the developmental process itself.

I should like to propose that standards, rules, and goals and objective self-awareness interact with the exposed self-conscious emotions and transform them into the evaluative self-conscious emotions I have been discussing. This transformational process uses the exposure emotions, but in the developmental process these emotions are not destroyed. This transformation allows for the material of early structures to be utilized but not converted in the process. In this way *both* exposure and evaluative emotions appear at the next level. If this were the case, it would be appropriate to insert an arrow on Figure 5.1 from the exposure emotions to the evaluative emotions. In such a transformation, embarrassment becomes the material for shame, while empathy becomes the material for guilt. Let us see if there is a connection.

Empathy and guilt share a common process, namely, in both the person focuses on the other rather than on the self. Thus, it appears reasonable to assume that empathic behavior leads to guilt. The basis for this conversion from empathy to guilt is the use of both objective self-awareness and the application of the internalized standards. The structural similarity between them is apparent, and a connection has been proposed. The developmental sequence between them will become clearer when in chapter 6 I turn to socialization factors affecting the self-conscious emotions. Recently, June Tangney looked at the relationship between empathy, shame, and guilt and found, in adults, that empathy and guilt were highly positively correlated, whereas shame and empathy were negatively related.[31] People who showed a great deal of shame were less likely to show empathy. These data lend support for the processes underlying guilt and shame and highlight the fact that guilt and empathy involve the same processes: the ease with which one can focus on the other rather than oneself.

———— • ————

I have presented a developmental sequence that indicates the development of the self-conscious emotions by the end of the third year of life. At the broadest level, we can say that emotions give rise to thoughts about emotions that, in turn, give rise to the objectification of the self, and to the new self-conscious emotions. Although we exhibit self-conscious emotions by age 3, the process of differentiation and elaboration continues throughout life as new standards, rules, and goals are created and as new actions, thoughts, and feelings are expressed. Nevertheless, it is the early years, the preoedipal period, that are critical for our emotional and social growth and health.

6

The Socialization of Shame

From Parent to Child

In discussing my model I made reference to specific features that might be socialized in different ways, thus giving rise to individual differences in shame. Here I will consider how parents socialize the way children think and feel about themselves, paying strict attention to shame caused by humiliation, disgust, and love withdrawal.

How We Come to Think About Ourselves

Some adults set such high standards for their own behavior that they continually fail to succeed by their own measure. Failure relative to these internal standards leads to shame. Individual differences in the level of standards set should affect shame. Consider the student who receives a B grade. If he has a high standard, and hopes for and expects an A, the B grade will result in a sense of failure. In contrast, the student who sees a B as a measure of success will not respond to such a grade as a failure. Following a psychoanalytic perspective, we could say that such differences have to do with the severity of the superego. There have been attempts to explore the relationship between harsh socialization and strong superego, but they have produced mixed results. Severity of weaning or severity of toilet training, examples of harsh parental socialization, do not seem to be related to children's response to transgression.[1] Nevertheless, it seems reasonable to assume that early socialization of standards plays a role in shame induction.

Martin Hoffman's analysis of rigid and flexible guilt responses is relevant to the socialization of standards.[2] The rigid response reflects concern about the rule itself: the child focuses on the rule as a standard and his violation of this standard. The flexible response, sometimes called the humanistic or empathic response, reflects concern about harm done to others by means of the violation rather than on the violation itself. Love withdrawal or ego attacks, which are used to instill high standards through criticism and, perhaps, humiliation, lead to the rigid response. Whether this situation also has a bearing on shame is difficult to discern because Hoffman, like many others, does not differentiate between shame and guilt.

Individual differences in shame can be brought about by the differential socialization of standards, rules, and goals. I had a patient who told me that once when he received a 97 on a chemistry test, his father asked him "what happened to the 3 points?" The parent's question, "What happened to the 3 points?", indicates a situation in which high standards are made and demanded. Of course, the nature of demand in regard to the standard may be the critical factor. Although it is commonly believed that overburdened superegos lead to guilt, the real truth may be that the demand of a high standard itself is not at fault, but rather the punishment inflicted once the standard is not achieved. Consider two families, both of whom demand high standards. In the case of one, the parent's response to the child's failure is punitive or, perhaps, full of scorn, disgust, and humiliation. These children are humiliated and shamed by their parents when they do not achieve their standards. It is not the failure, but the punishment for failure, which causes the shame. Contrast such a family with a family equally insistent on high standards but who, instead of showing scorn or disgust or humiliation, explains to the child how she can do better.

Standards, rules, and goals always exist. The important feature may not be the imposition of high standards, but instead the response to their violation. I believe that, while standards are socialized, individual differences in standards are related to the *other's* response to their violation.

Differences in individuals' standards will lead to differences in situations likely to produce shame. Thus, for example, some families value academic performance more than others. Within these families, failure in academic subjects is more likely to lead to shame for their children than for the children of other families who do not hold to a high standard of academic excellence. Likewise, a family that values physical activity, sports, and risk taking may socialize their children to feel shame over a failure in such situations, while children in families that pay little attention to physical activities are less likely to be ashamed over this type of failure.[3]

The role of different standards, rules, and goals may contribute to sex differences. Some parents socialize male and female children differently:

females are commonly oriented toward standards related to interpersonal relationships, while males are oriented toward standards related to efficacy and mastery of objects and things. Socialization differences in such standards could lead to differences in the elicitation of shame around particular behaviors. For example, aggressive behavior in interpersonal exchanges is often socialized differently according to the sex of the aggressor. When a female child shows anger, parents use a variety of techniques, including direct punishment and love withdrawal, to inhibit her behavior. But when a male child exhibits aggressive behavior, his parents make little or no effort to inhibit his behavior; indeed, they may even actively encourage such behavior.

School achievement is another arena where different goals may be socialized. Academic achievement appears to be more a goal sought by males than by females. While equal numbers of males and females go to college, a disproportionately low number of females attend graduate or professional schools, even today. The differences around standards clearly need more exploration. What is clear is that parents who hold high standards are likely to have children who also will have them. When such children fail to achieve desired goals, they feel badly. Whether these feelings of failure lead to differences in shame is dependent upon other factors, yet it seems reasonable to assume a significant linkage between high standards, failure to achieve these standards, and a propensity for shame.

Internal and External Attributions

Setting standards, rules, and goals is one aspect of the attributional system that involves the self and that leads to shame. A second aspect has to do with the subject's evaluation of the self. This attribution can be specific, focusing on the self's action, or global, focusing on the total self. I have already suggested that shame results only when people make an internal evaluation, that is, when they see themselves as responsible for the particular failure. But they can also make an external evaluation, that is, they can attribute the failure to someone else or to chance. Thus, one source of individual differences is the likelihood that a person will make an internal attribution.

The woman who cleans my office recently won a small amount of money in a lottery. I congratulated her on her good luck and she replied, "No, it wasn't luck. I knew that if I bet on my daughter's birth date I would win." This woman habitually makes internal attributions. She attributed

*her success in the lottery to something that she did—for her, chance had no
part in her win.*

Blame can also be internally attributed. The best examples of this are
people whose family member has had a serious illness.

*A student of mine felt that it was his fault that his father suffered a
coronary. This student said to me, "If only I had gone home [for the
holidays] instead of going to Florida, I might have prevented him from
having his coronary."*

Such ideation reflects an unreasonable individual demand on the self as a
causal agent to an event over which one has no control. Another person
might have attributed his father's heart attack to overweight, heavy
smoking, lack of exercise, stress at work, the aging process, genetic
propensity, mere bad luck, or any number of external causes. But my
student had a propensity to make internal attributions, and so he blamed
himself for his father's illness: "If only I had gone home . . ." This may be
the same process that makes holocaust survivors so upset. They somehow
hold themselves responsible for the deaths of the others.

Work concerning children of depressed parents bears on the socialization of internal attribution. Very young children of sick parents are apt to
internalize blame.[4] This can come about in several ways. These children
may feel unrealistically that they should be able to discover some means to
help their parents. After all, since parents are able to help children, should
not children be able to help their parents? But because the children cannot
help their parents, they assume some of the blame for their parents' illness.
Alternatively, sick parents themselves can convince their children that they
are responsible for the parents' illness.

*I had a patient whose mother had serious high blood pressure. The mother
suffered terrible headaches and had to lie down to relieve them. If the child
made any noise, his mother would say, "Be quiet, you're hurting my
head." Since it was almost impossible for the child to be completely quiet
for lengthy periods, he was often told he was the cause of his mother's
headaches. Eventually, he blamed himself because his mother had
headaches.*

Young children appear to be more susceptible to internalization than older
children. For example, the death of a parent earlier rather than later in a
child's life is more apt to lead to shame because younger children are more

likely to blame themselves for the death and therefore are more susceptible to shame. Individual differences in the socialization of this attribution have received minimal attention; it has been noted, however, that children of depressed parents appear to internalize the blame for their parents' illness.

Whether an individual internalizes or externalizes blame will be important in determining whether she is shamed by a failure.[5] The more one can blame an external source, the more likely one will avoid feeling shame. Steve Alessandri and I looked at what parents say to young children when they are involved in an achievement task. Our data indicate that some parents tend to attribute the child's success or failure to forces outside the child. When the task was to toss a ball into a net, one parent said of a 3-year-old child's failure: "The ring [of the basket] is too small; you can't get the ball in." Such statements inform children that their failure is not related to what they try to do but rather to the nature of the task itself. Other parents made remarks such as "You have to practice more get the ball into the basket" or "You're not trying; try harder and you'll do it." These parents cause their children to focus on their own efforts to achieve success. Parents' behavior informs the child about internal or external self-attributions.

Internal or external attribution can be a function of a particular situation or an individual characteristic. Some people make a consistent attribution, whether internal or external. Other people make either internal or external attributions depending on the particular task. A switching from internal to external attribution and vice versa according to the task is the typical form of behavior; the tendency to make only one type of attribution is often associated with pathology. Moreover, individuals vary in their internal or external attributions as a function of whether they succeed or fail at the task. All possible combinations exist. Some people are apt to credit themselves when they succeed at a task but to blame others (or chance) when they fail. The opposite case is also possible: some people attribute success at a task to others, but blame themselves for failure.

The narcissistic personality type, as described by Morrison and others, attributes success to his own efforts even when, as with winning the lottery, the individual has no logical reason to claim credit; but at the same time is unwilling to blame himself for any failure.[6] As we will see, such personality types are prone to make global attributions of failure. If they internalize their failure, they will be shamed; thus they try, at all costs, to avoid this feeling.

Looking at individual differences in internal and external attribution as a function of success and failure reveals some interesting sex differences.

Women are likely to make internal attribution for their failures and external attribution for their successes, whereas men are likely to do the reverse. Differences in parental and teacher behavior with male children versus female children have been linked to children's attribution styles although these differences interact with the nature of the task. With interpersonal relationships as well as academic success, women are likely to show this pattern of internalization of failure and externalization of success.

We have the most data for this sex difference as it shows up in academic performance. Women are socialized to blame themselves for their failures, but not to reward themselves for their successes; the reverse is true for men. Our study of parents' response to their children's task performance revealed that both mothers and fathers made significantly more positive attributions to boys than to girls. They would say, "That's a good way of getting the piece [of the puzzle] in the box" or "You place your left foot forward, that's how to throw the ball [into the hoop]." These positive specific attributions were higher for 3-year-old boys than they were for 3-year-old girls; however, negative specific attributions were higher for the girls. Such differences in socialization suggest that many differences we see in school-aged children, as well as the differences we see among adults in general, are caused by this unique socialization pattern. Similar findings in young children have been reported by others. Seligman and his colleagues, for example, reported that mothers who attributed bad events internally had children with similar self-attribution patterns.[7]

Such differences between individuals in internal and external attributional style determine whether an individual is likely to enter into a system where self-evaluative emotions occur. For individuals who do not blame themselves for failure and/or do not credit themselves for success, the evaluative emotions of shame, guilt, hubris, and pride are not likely to appear. Only those people who make internal attributions are likely to experience shame as one consequence of their failures.

Specific and Global Attributions

The third attributional feature of the model involves the global or specific self orientation. Global and specific self orientation interact with internal and external attribution, thus giving us four cells. Global versus specific attribution represents a concept that is called by a variety of terms, including self characteristic versus self action, entity versus incremental, or self focus on performance versus self focus on learning.[8] However named, the concept can be defined as focus on the total self versus focus on the action of the self.

> *Some time ago, a student complained to me about a problem she had studying. She told me that she was too anxious to study because she was concerned about the grade she was going to get. When I asked her if she was at all interested in the subject, she replied, "I'm very much interested [in the subject] but I can't pay attention, I'm too concerned about how well I'll do."*

Here is an example of a person focusing on her performance rather than on her learning. She could only see course work in relation to her performance and her evaluation as a person rather than as a task that would lead to learning something.

Although data concerning the acquisition of global versus specific self attribution and individual differences would be very useful, relatively little work has been done in this area. Most of the work involves looking at sex differences, so we must turn to these differences to study the process. It is important to remember that individuals who show global attribution to failure are not necessarily those who show global attribution to success. This must be taken into account when considering global attributions as a personality characteristic.

Biological Factors in Global Attribution

Attributional styles such as global and specific might be genetic in origin. Such a possibility was considered by Herman Witkin, working in the area of field dependence. Field dependency has to do with analytic and perceptual ability: the ability to keep an object within perception in the context in which it is embedded.[9] A standard test used to determine such analytic capacity measures the individual's ability to maintain a rod in a vertical position relative to the floor. The task is made more difficult by presenting the rod in a tilted frame. In a series of studies described by Witkin, stable individual differences were observed. Witkin believed that this ability is a biological disposition. H. B. Lewis claimed that global attribution, especially of failure, was associated with field dependence.[10,11] Except in this work, the genetic differences in self attribution along the dimension of global and specific have not received attention. However, there may be some relationship to temperament.

Some people have been characterized as having a difficult temperament: these people are more irritable and tend to be highly somatic. They complain about minor pain, and they seem to have difficulty in coping with internal bodily sensations. These difficult temperament people focus on the stimuli emanating from their own bodies. Because they spend more time self-focused than non-difficult-temperament people, they may be more likely to make global, as opposed to specific, attributions. Recently, working in my laboratory, Rose DiBiase was able to show that difficult temperament children are more likely to be those who are easily embarrassed at age 2.[12] We have been able to extend this finding to show that these difficult temperament children are likely to show more shame during failure on tasks at age 3. Difficult temperament may predispose the child toward global attributions of failure, but it is likely that such differences are not a major factor.

Socialization Factors in Global Attribution

Early trauma. There is a large literature on the socialization of guilt. This literature could have bearing on global versus specific attribution since the authors may be discussing shame as well as guilt.

A moderate relationship between the nature of socialization and the amount of guilt (or shame) expressed has been reported. Perhaps more important, the climate of the home seems to have a substantial influence on the child's guilt development. One finding is of particular importance in affecting self attribution: depressed mothers are likely to blame themselves for their problems, and these women tend to make global evaluations of failure about themselves and about their children. Moreover, the children of depressed mothers receive more love withdrawal punishment and are likely to assume blame for their parents' problems. The depression of the mother is interpreted by the children to be their fault; thus, they show more concern for their parents' well-being than do children who do not have depressed parents.[13]

We can generalize from these findings and conclude that parents with difficulties—which could include alcoholism, drug addiction, parental fighting or strife, etc.—may initially produce more empathic-like behavior in their children because their children try to help them. Moreover, since the children are unlikely to succeed in helping their parents, their failure is likely to be blamed globally on themselves. Children in a family environment characterized by parental distress are likely to make global attributions about themselves as a cause of the problem. Under such circumstances, this global attribution may be carried into later childhood and adult life.

Strong negative events that occur in young children's lives may be likely, by their intensity, to force children into making global attributions about themselves. The intensity and the power of the negative event creates global attribution of failure because the child finds it too difficult to construct a thought about specific attribution under such conditions. Thus, one form of early socialization likely to lead to global rather than specific attribution of failure concerns the intensity of negative events that occur in the child's life. Unfortunately, the class of these negative events remains somewhat vague. My analysis indicates that these events need to satisfy the conditions of intensity and negativeness. Whether they have to do with parents directly or with others in the immediate family, or whether they have to do with general calamities that occur to the family (as well as others), remains open. It is likely that a house fire in which all the family's possessions have been destroyed may be a sufficiently negative condition to generate a global self attribution of failure. Clearly, more work in this area should be conducted, since it may allow us to understand why early traumatic events have such profound effects on children's lives. I suggest that trauma is mediated by the attributional style imposed by the events themselves. Global attributional style of failure, which plays a role in other disorders, is created in the cauldron of stress.

Adult use of global attribution. The tendency to make global or specific attributions about our failure can be learned from those around us. How our parents or teachers describe our action is likely to contribute to this style. For example, if a mother says of her daughter's failure, "You're not smart," she likely is blaming her daughter for the failure (an internal attribution) and, at the same time, making a global self statement. Under such conditions, the child also is likely to make such attributions. These attributions can be learned. While we have relatively little data on the topic of parental use of attribution, we do possess some information from teacher behavior as related to achievement, specifically in regard to sex differences.

Studies in school-aged children's achievement behavior provide evidence for differences in global and specific attribution associated with failure. Girls tend to attribute their failures to factors such as lack of ability, while boys tend to attribute failure to specific factors, including teachers' attitudes.[14] Moreover, girls avoid situations in which failure is likely, whereas boys approach such situations as a challenge, indicating that failure differentially affects self-esteem (shame). Females who fail, for example, are likely to think that they generally are no good, a global attribution, and, consequently, are likely to experience a loss of self-esteem. Males are likely not to think that they are the cause of their own failure, and therefore are not likely to suffer loss of self-esteem. In my terms, boys do not make an internal attribution; they tend to tell themselves "It's not my fault that I failed."

During the elementary school years, one of the primary agents of evaluation, and one that is likely to exert considerable influence on attributional style and achievement behavior, is the child's teacher. Differential treatment by teachers of boys and girls has been documented.[15] Most of the criticism that teachers direct at boys concerns specific instances of misbehavior or lack of motivation rather than general academic failings. There is no global attribution. Girls have fewer behavioral problems and, overall, are harder working and more conscientious in their academic work than boys. Despite the fact that girls, on average, do better in elementary school than boys do, girls are more likely to attribute failure to their general lack of ability. This general lack of ability is what I have been talking about in terms of global attribution. Dweck and Leggett see the teachers' use of evaluative feedback as a direct cause of learned helplessness or mastery orientation in children. They found that teachers' criticisms of girls almost always indicated that they lacked general competence and did not understand the work (global attributions), whereas criticism of boys often referred to specific and nonintellectual aspects of failure.

There are almost no studies on parental attribution as a function of the child's sex. Since, prior to school, children are socialized in the family with parents serving as the primary agents of evaluation, it may be that attributional differences have their origin in the preschool years. To study this problem, Steve Alessandri and I looked at mothers and fathers of 3-year-old children, both when the parents played with the children and when they gave them problems to solve. We examined mothers' and fathers' statements regarding their children playing with toys to observe the nature of their attributional style. We scored parents' statements for global attribution, that is, statements that had to do with some aspect of the children themselves: "You're really good," for example, or "You're smart." We also scored specific self attributions. These were statements that had to do with a particular action of the children, usually around the task. Both positive and negative global and specific attributions were scored.

Our findings bear on individual differences as well as on sex differences. We found that parents have a wide range of attributional styles. Mothers and fathers showed only moderate consistency, that is, some mothers used more specific attribution than global, while others used more global attribution than specific. The same held true for fathers. In general, we found large parental differences in self attribution toward their children. Unfortunately, these children were only 3 years old, so it was not possible to obtain a self attribution score for the children themselves. We were, however, able to score pride and shame responses to the success and failure on the task. We found a relation between the use of global attribution by the parents and the amount of shame the children exhibited when they failed the task. Such findings indicate that individual differences in global and specific attributions exist and that these differences appear to be related to early social experiences.

Attributional style was different for fathers than for mothers, and fathers made more specific attributions than mothers. Mothers and fathers both made more specific attributions to boys than girls. When the task was focused, fathers' specific achievement comments, such as "That's a good job" or "That's the way to do it," were greater for sons than for daughters. Fathers appeared to differentiate their own behavior depending on the sex of the child. Mothers also made more of these types of specific self attributions to sons than to daughters. Fathers with their sons used the most specific self attributions, and mothers with their daughters used the least specific self attributions. Mothers with their daughters were often observed saying such things as "You're really good" or "What a good girl!" We are impressed with the intergenerational effect between gender and the use of specific self attribution; males receive more as children and use more as adults.

We observed very few negative specific self attributions, in part because parents knew they were being videotaped during the study. Nevertheless, there were enough negative self attribution comments of parents to reach some conclusions. Both mothers and fathers used more negatives for girls than for boys. This finding may be related to why girls are more likely to blame themselves for failures than boys and less likely to claim success globally than boys. These findings support my belief that some of the sex differences in global and specific attribution are likely to be related to the nature of the socialization experience of the child. At the moment, the evidence suggests that females are more likely to make global self attributions of failure than men.

In the model that I have articulated, the causes of shame can be located in the evaluation of standards, rules, and goals, and in global and specific attributions. Individual and sex differences in both of these aspects have been found, suggesting that individual differences in shame are likely to stem, in part, from socialization differences as they relate to these two processes. How parents (and teachers) treat their children and the amount of stress within the family both contribute to the differences in these attributions.

The Roles of Disgust, Contempt, Humiliation, and Love Withdrawal in the Production of Shame

Up until now, I have suggested that socialization experiences operate on the formation of attributions by direct action. Parents or teachers say things that are global or specific in nature. While this is true, other factors also are likely to play a role in the creation of these attributions. As will become clearer as we proceed, the humiliation and shame children receive, or even the withdrawal of love, may contribute to these attributions. Heinz Kohut touches on this problem when he discusses self-esteem.[16]

> The most intense experiences of shame and the most violent forms of narcissistic rage arise in those individuals for whom a sense of absolute control in an archaic environment is indispensable because the maintenance of self-esteem and indeed of the self depends on the unconditional availability of the approving mirror functions of an admiring self-object or on the ever present opportunity of the merger with an ideal one.

As Andrew Morrison, in his book on narcissism, points out, Kohut sees rectification through psychoanalytic treatment as "either reparation of the self's nuclear defect through repeated transmuting internalizations (within the analytic context, through transference to the mostly-empathic analyst as a responsive self object); or through modification of the compensatory structures, by establishing more flexible and realistic ambitions, goals, and ideals."[17] One can view the "compensatory" action in relation to shame as either (1) altering the standards, rules, or goals, or (2) altering one's attribution of success and failure, or (3) altering one's self attribution. For example, I can (1) decide that achieving a good grade is not important or (2) I can decide that a C grade is a success not a failure, or (3) I can decide that getting a C does not indicate that "I am stupid" (a general evaluation of self), but instead reflects my lack of study (a specific self action). Patients in cognitive therapy are encouraged to apply one or another of these thoughts as a means of altering their attributions.

The analysis of individual differences in attribution usually focuses on statements and behaviors that directly relate to these attributions. While these behaviors are likely to affect people's attributions and feelings of shame, other causes can be cited. Kohut's emphasis on the parent as a mirror draws us more to this consideration. My own data also contribute to it. As I have reported, parental statements about global and specific are related to shame. However, I have also found that shame is more related to how the children are generally treated. Harsh and negative behavior, including humiliation, is related to shame. Parents socialize through the use of reasoning, shaming, and love withdrawal. These techniques may be of equal importance to the use of attribution in the development of individual differences in shame.

Parents, especially middle-class parents, see themselves as benign socializers of their children. However, Freud and psychoanalytic theory gave us a model of socialization as a struggle. The young child, full of drives and needs, enters into battle with parents whose task is to socialize the child, transforming her into an adult who possesses the same values, goals, and cognitive structures. The methods that we employ in this struggle, although appearing benign, may not be so. Indeed, Alice Miller contends that the socialization process is full of humiliation and shame.[18] Many children develop within a context of humiliation and shame. Miller quotes from Hermann Hesse's *A Child's Heart*: "Would not God find a way out, some superior deception such as the grownups and the powerful contrived, producing one more trump card at the last moment, shaming me after all, not taking me seriously, humiliating me under the damnable mask of kindness?"[19]

Miller wants us to examine how we shame and humiliate children. You might ask, how can it be possible that concerned parents in the twentieth century shame and humiliate their children? Yet, examination of children's and parents' behavior indicates that this may be more true than we think. I would like to talk about two methods of socialization, shame/humiliation and love withdrawal.

Disgust, Contempt, and Humiliation

Recall the young man mentioned in Chapter 1 who was repeatedly shamed and humiliated by his father. He was often the butt of sarcasm and was frequently humiliated. Such cases are common. Parents, and others, deny the impact of humiliation by using the term "teasing" or a synonym such as "ranking." People recognize the aggressive nature of teasing, but they do not perceive it as an engine for humiliation and shame. I would contend that many instances of teasing really constitute acts of humiliation or shaming. Instances of humiliating or shaming can be seen in everyday life.[20]

In my observations, one of the most painful personal experiences is the display of disgust by another toward one's actions, thoughts, or feelings. Most people would be surprised to learn that a disgusted face is widely used in the socialization of children. After all, the middle class is not supposed to be punitive toward their children. How, then, do middle-class parents get their children to do what they want them to do? A variety of techniques are used, including reasoning, power assertion, physical punishment, love withdrawal, and humiliation/shame.[21] In fact, the use of the last two techniques is widespread. Imagine a disgusted face. Think of eating something that tastes terrible, so bad that you spit it out. The upper lip and nose are raised, the teeth often show, the tongue sticks out, the nostrils flare. If you look in a mirror and make such an expression, one of the things you will notice is that, if you bare your teeth further by drawing your lips back, the disgusted face becomes similar to an angry/rage face. Moreover, if you reduce the intensity of the muscle movement and do not stick out your tongue, the face now looks like contempt. The similarity of the disgust, contempt, and rage faces has been alluded to by others.

I have frequently observed parents who use the disgusted face when the child does something of which the parent disapproves. Mothers will say, "Oh, don't touch that," raising their nostrils and upper lip, flashing a disgusted face. This expression might appear only briefly, but children do perceive it. When they see a disgusted face they turn sharply away and seem inhibited for a moment. It is likely that such behavior reflects shame. The disgusted face is effective in socialization through shaming as well as informing the child not to repeat that action.

Parents use a variety of socializing techniques. If a parent fails to use reasoning and finds it inappropriate or inadmissable to yell or punish, the use of the disgusted/contemptuous face is an ideal solution. It is ideal because it serves to inhibit the action that the parent does not wish the child to perform. It is all the more effective because it is secretive. The disgusted face is made very quickly, and parents can deny that they made it; or, if they admit to it, they can deny that it was detected by the child. Parents are often unaware that they are producing these faces. When I have pointed out their use of the disgusted face, they often are shocked to discover this action. Even more important, parents are usually unaware that their use of the disgusted face is a shaming device.

My observation of parents and their children in normal circumstances reveals that disgusted/contemptuous or rage faces that are accompanied by verbal prohibitions occupy at least 40% of codable facial expression in parents' behavior. My colleagues and I have seen far too many parent-child relationships that we think are in danger because of the overuse of the disgusted/contemptuous face. One case in particular comes to mind.

A mother and her 3-year-old daughter were playing in the playroom. The child was asked by the mother not to play with the Playdough because it

*would mess her dress. The child persisted. The mother now raised the ante.
She looked at the child, showed a disgusted/contemptuous face, and said
"Yuck! You're making yourself dirty." The little girl looked at her, turned
away, and then proceeded to pick up the Playdough and throw it angrily on
the ground.*

This show of anger was a response to being shamed. In this case, the
mother often used this shaming technique in dealing with her child.

I cannot help but think that shame plays a significant role in socialization. The task of parents is to teach their children to internalize values and
to motivate their children, in the absence of the parents, not to violate these
standards, rules, and goals. What better way to prevent the child from
doing this than by producing a strong emotion? The production of shame,
even at normal levels, is an ideal device for instilling internalized values. I
will return to this topic in chapter 11 because of its importance in cultural
differences. Let it suffice for now to remember that parents, teachers, and
peers all use the disgust/contempt expression to produce shame and
humiliation in children as well as in other adults.

The use of disgusted/contemptuous faces in the interpersonal behavior of adults is readily observable. I will discuss interpersonal relationships and the environment of shame in detail in chapter 10. It will suffice for now to suggest that adults use disgusted/contemptuous faces to
elicit shame in one another. But the use of shame is not as widespread
between two adults as it is between parents and children. This is due to
the likelihood that such a face will elicit rage in the receiver. For this reason adults, fearing the rage of other adults, exercise more restraint in
its use.

How does disgust/contempt elicit shame in another? It is not necessary
for us to leave the attributional framework to understand the process.
Disgust/contempt marks for the other a failure in regard to some standard.
The disgust/contempt of another also forces us into a global attribution. It
is very difficult to envision someone making a specific attribution in the
face of another's disgusted/contemptuous look because the look says, "You
disgust me." Thus, shame is likely to be produced in the child by the
disgusted/contemptuous look of the mother through the mechanisms
already stated.

While such an analysis is reasonable, one might prefer a view in which
the child witnesses disgust/contempt and models this behavior. Such an
explanation may well apply in situations in which the adult feels shamed.
As I have noted, people are likely to feel shame over the shame of another.
Empathic shame has been discussed by others, and is familiar to

us—think of Paul and his father as described in chapter 1. When their parents are shamed, children are likely to learn to experience shame through empathic shame induction. Simply being with a parent who is shame-prone is likely to lead to shame in children. Such shame production in children should take place as a function of modeling, and only later would features such as blame and global attributions appear. But modeling shame only explains the instigation of this emotion. The self-generation of shame under other conditions should follow the same rules that I have articulated earlier. In an environment of shame, individuals will experience more shame than others not so embedded. A shame-filled environment for any child is comparable to a stress-filled environment. In this way, the shame-filled environment has the same impact on the child's disposition toward shame as the death of a parent or serious distress. As we have seen, such stress environments are likely to cause the child to take a self-blame global stance. If the child is in a shame-filled environment, he will empathically feel shamed. This in turn will lead to attributions that will maintain the feeling.

While individual differences are apparent, the question of sex differences in the use of the disgusted/contemptuous face remains to be explored. There are no direct data to support the fact that mothers are likely to use these techniques more on girls than on boys, although we do possess suggestive data. For example, the socialization literature indicates that mothers tend to be more punitive toward their daughters than their sons, but that they use more physical punishment with their sons. I think that this data on mothers' punitive behavior reflects their use of disgust/contempt more with their daughters than with sons. If mothers punish daughters more than sons, but employ physical punishments less frequently for girls than for boys, mothers must use other forms of punishment, including more shame, on daughters than on sons. The special relationship that seems to bond mothers and daughters may have as one of its components the use and transmission of shame for behavioral modification. Moreover, the lack of similarity in the shame experience between mother and son, as a reflection of the difference between males and females, may find its origin in maternal differential use of disgust/contempt.

———— • ————

What is interesting about the socialization practice of humiliation/disgust/contempt is that it usually occurs around specific events, for example, when the child cries, bodily function disputes, genital play, and eating rules. It is not surprising that disgust/contempt and shame are associated with such bodily functions as toilet training and genital play. The psychoanalytic observation of children's shame around bodily functions may be related to parents' high disgust and humiliation behavior in these situations. Children's shame is created by their parents' disgust with these functions. For me then, the association of these functions with shame has little to do with the nature of the activity, but is instead based on the disgust/contempt/humiliation component of the parents' reaction which leads to children's self attributions.

How are we to understand the socialization of shame through the use of disgust/contempt? Clearly its use has positive virtues, namely, that the parent can avoid yelling, other kinds of public display, and physical punishment. Moreover, parental disgust is likely to be effective. Disgust/contempt is used frequently, often without conscious intent. Indeed, the disgust technique is used too often. Alice Miller's work is an attempt not only to alert us to the use of the technique in socialization practice but to point to its pathological use by some parents.

Various other types of socializing techniques, specifically, power assertion, love withdrawal, and reasoning, need to be considered in regard to shame. Power assertion is said to lead to guilt as well as to anxiety and fear. Exactly how power assertion is related to shame is unclear. There is good reason to believe that power assertion itself may be shame producing because the intensity of the stimulus forces children away from thinking about the content of the message. This makes children incapable of reparation since they cannot pay attention to the message of harm or fault that has been given.

Reasoning is likely to lead to guilt. Induction consists mainly of reasoning with children about the cause of their problem. Reasoning leads children to examine their action and to initiate reparation, thus producing internal specific attribution. Moreover, because induction is a less intense message, children are more apt to attend to the message and therefore to adhere to the prescription being offered.

Love Withdrawal

The use of love withdrawal as a technique in socialization has been discussed by many investigators.[22] Although love withdrawal is usually linked to guilt, I believe that most people confuse guilt with shame or treat these two different emotions as equivalents. Love withdrawal, by its nature, is intense, thus making it difficult for the person affected to attend to the reason why the love was withdrawn. Love withdrawal leads to internal attributions of blame, and since it refers to the whole self—"I don't love you"—it also leads to global attribution of failure.[23] Love withdrawal produces shame through the same attributional processes I have mentioned before.

The withdrawal of love as a precipitating event for interpersonal difficulties has been discussed by object relations and attachment theorists. Their emphasis is on the failure of interpersonal relationships. I think we can understand psychopathology by viewing love withdrawal as provoking shame and shame as leading to poor interpersonal relationships. Clearly, the biological helplessness of the infant requires the child's care by another; and through this care, the caregiver becomes a significant other. From a sociobiological point of view, the withdrawal of love and attention by the other is likely to lead to death or at least to serious consequences for the child. The attachment theorists, John Bowlby in particular, have pointed out the biological significance of the mother-child relationship.[24] Love withdrawal represents a serious biological loss for the infant and even for the young child. As children get older, they are able to form models of this relationship. These models have an impact on the child's life in terms of affecting other social relationships. These working models of the child involve not only representing the mother but also representing the self, since the representation of the mother involves the self. For example, Bowlby states that "the model of the attachment figure and the model of the self are likely to develop so as to be complementary and mutually confirming. Thus an unwanted child is likely not only to feel unwanted by his parents but to believe that he is essentially unwantable."[25] Notice that the model describes the child's attribution that he or she is "unwanted." This is a global attribution created by the unloving parent. In the same way, the withdrawal of love of the parent must generate a very powerful internal global attribution of failure, the essential ingredients for shame![26]

This analysis confirms for me the idea that the withdrawal of love of a significant other plays an important part in the child's development. I prefer to view the significance from the point of view of the development of emotion and the development of self—in particular, the differences in children's susceptibility to shame. The fundamental underlying construct that unites me with the more traditional object relations theorists is my belief that the failure in the parent-child relationship leads to pathology through a disposition to shame. Such an analysis is difficult to test directly in very young children; however, our work with adults, both students and patients, and couples makes it clear that love withdrawal is a precipitant of shame.

Prototypicality of Stimuli That Produce Shame

In order to study the topic of prototypicality of events that lead to shame, we explore what situations people think cause shame. In the last two years I have asked a large number of people, usually in audiences, to tell me by show of hands whether they have felt shame in the last 24 hours or whether they have experienced shame in the past week. Because the definition of shame is open to so much interpretation, I have asked the question in this fashion: "Can you tell me if you've had a failure experience of one sort or another where you felt like hiding or disappearing?" I use such a description of shame in order to try to differentiate it from guilt or other emotions that have been confused with it. Of perhaps a thousand people who have been asked this question, easily 20% have reported shame experiences in the last 24 hours, and well over 50% have reported shame in the past week—this in a public forum.

I have asked the same question in a classroom of 15 graduate students over the age of 25. First I asked them whether they had experienced shame in the last 24 hours, and then to estimate the number of times they had experienced shame in the past week. The results indicated wide variability in the experience of shame. Three students reported no shame experiences in the past week; three students reported as many as ten or more in the past week; the remainder varied between these two extremes. Since these students were well versed in the distinction between shame, guilt, and embarrassment, their responses were particularly interesting.

They were asked to write down a number of shame experiences and situations likely to be eliciting causes. The variety of responses to the eliciting situations were consistent with Arnold Buss's five types of embarrassment (which I take for measures of shame) and to the Modigliani list.[27] They included:

Impropriety or doing something inappropriate, for example, walking into an occupied bathroom
Lack of competence, or the failure of some skill deemed to be important
Simple conspicuousness, such as belching or making a loud bodily sound
Breaches of privacy—one girl felt ashamed about talking too loudly
Failure in interpersonal relationships, such as a fight with one's boyfriend or girlfriend
Empathic shame—one student mentioned feeling shame because a friend of hers was shamed in front of her

———— • ————

Clearly, this list of situations likely to produce shame indicates that it is varied and idiosyncratic in nature. However, all of the situations appear to have similar features: the violation of some rule or standard and the evaluation of one's self as globally inadequate or no good.

Recently June Tangney asked a large number of undergraduates to briefly describe three shame and three guilt experiences.[28] The results indicated that the situations that elicited the most shame were, in order: failure at work, failure at sports, failure at school, and lying to someone.[29] Lawrence Pervin also asked students for situations that were likely to produce shame and received such diverse answers as "my rent check bouncing," "being caught lying about where I was," "trying to look good in front of a woman and failing," "my girlfriend's parents note that she was late to work the morning that we spent the night together," and "getting off the bus, falling on my butt, and hearing people laugh."[30]

It is apparent that individuals differ both in terms of situations likely to elicit their shame, and in the frequency of occasions in which shame is likely to be a consequence. I have no difficulty understanding the reason why different situations for different people are likely to elicit shame: any situation in which one interprets one's self as responsible for failure, regardless of the nature of failure, and in which one makes a global attribution can lead to shame. Although any situation can lead to shame, those situations that do not involve core capacities are more likely to lead to a less intense feeling of shame, or what I have called embarrassment.

Thus, by prototypicality (see chapter 4) I mean that given a particular event, people have no choice but to make an internal and global attribution of self failure. Prototypicality does not involve the elimination of the attributional process; rather it is likely that for all people certain events lead to these particular attributions and therefore to shame. In its most general form, it is based on my belief in the idea that all stimulus events elicit emotion through some cognitive process.

Throughout this discussion of shame and its possible causes, the lack of prototypicality in shame-inducing events has been mentioned as I stressed that events only produce shame if they induce self attributions of global self failure. Nevertheless, my analysis does point to the fact that there may be certain situations that are more likely to lead to those attributions associated with shame. Thus, for example, impotence in a male is likely to lead to such attributions. This event is prototypic since impotence and a sense of shame seem to be linked. To avoid shame, a man would have to be able to say something like "Well, my penis doesn't work, but my brain works fine." Such ideation is possible; indeed, we know that older men are capable of such attribution. However, even here shame may be likely. The same prototypicality may exist for women in regard to attractiveness. While I could imagine attributions around such events that would not result in shame, it is hard to do so.

Most of the candidates for prototypicality that have been suggested, such as toilet training and playing with the genitals, probably have more to do with parental attitudes than with their own likelihood to lead to attributions. The same is not true for love withdrawal by the significant other. I nominate this for prototypicality for several reasons: first, for the adaptive significance of being loved by another when we are children, and second, for the adaptive significance of love and affection of others for reproductive success as adults. From an attributional standpoint, love involves the whole self, and thus must lead to a global ideation. Because of this, it seems reasonable to assume that for the young child, as for the adult, the withdrawal of the love of another constitutes a prototypic situation of shame. While one can externalize the cause of the withdrawal of love, by blaming it on some fault of the other or by pointing to circumstances beyond one's control, such withdrawal is still likely first to elicit internalization and global attribution of failure. For these reasons, it seems to me that withdrawal of love serves as the most likely candidate for prototypicality and is likely to lead to shame.

7

Reacting to Our Feelings

Felt and Unfelt Shame

S hame is like an atomic particle: we often know where it is only by the
trace it leaves, by the effects it causes. Donald Nathanson has said of
shame, "What the therapist sees is not shame, the symptom, but shame,
the shaper of symptoms."[1] I have no doubt that this is the case. H. B.
Lewis made this point eloquently over two decades ago. Although I find
some fault with her statements and construction, I certainly share her
belief that shame, like other intense emotions, when repressed, denied, or
otherwise not dealt with, is likely to lead to symptom formation. In Lewis's
final book, she once again made this point by entitling her volume *The Role
of Shame in Symptom Formation*.[2] Here she challenges and expands the
traditional psychoanalytic notion of repression of libidinal drive by adding
the repression of shame as an important feature in explaining why people
become sick. In her discussion of this phenomenon, Lewis used the term
"bypassed shame." I will borrow this nomenclature and use it to talk
about two aspects of shame: felt and unfelt, or bypassed, shame. In this
chapter and the next I intend to explore how felt and bypassed shame
affect our lives. Before considering how shame, a frequently occurring
emotion, is dealt with, I will contrast felt and bypassed shame. I begin by
considering H. B. Lewis's definition of bypassed shame and then explore
how such a notion can be broadened to induce a wide array of topics.

Felt and Bypassed Shame

H. B. Lewis articulated a theory of shame that spoke to the occurrence of
shame within the normal life course of an individual. Because she was an

analyst, she focused upon shame and guilt in neurosis. The theory she evolved was based on her work with patients whom she saw and treated. Her discoveries about shame and guilt took place within the context of their occurrence in the lives of people having real difficulties. Like any theory that grows out of clinical work, Lewis's work reveals the risk of viewing a phenomenon solely from a pathological viewpoint. Indeed, most of her writings, references, and considerations grew out of her concern for psychopathological conditions and how they might arise. The theory that I have been articulating places shame within a more normal context. I view individual differences in shame in everyday life not from a pathological point of view but from an affective cognitive view.

When we look at shame in the psychic life of the individual we need to focus on a set of parallel questions that grow out of the role of shame as both a felt feeling and an unacknowledged or bypassed event. Much of the effect of shame in our lives occurs because of unacknowledged shame. Indeed, it may well be the case that the major portion of shame within our lives is unacknowledged or bypassed. Nevertheless, some portion of shame in our lives is felt and acknowledged. Shame that is overtly expressed and shame that is unacknowledged or bypassed affect our lives in different ways. Individuals do experience their shame and acknowledge it. How do we deal with acknowledged shame? There are three possibilities which I will discuss later. These have to do with forgetting, humor, and confession. Now, however, I want to focus on unacknowledged shame which has to do with denial and its many manifestations, including depression, rage, narcissism, and multiple personality disorders.

Unacknowledged, denied, repressed, or bypassed shame exerts its detrimental force in two ways within our intrapsychic life. The first has to do with the problem of not understanding what is happening in our lives, namely, that unacknowledged shame causes behavior that we cannot readily account for, and therefore leads us into trouble in terms of its effect. The second difficulty concerns the problem inherent in all strong emotions that are repressed or denied. It was Freud's original notion that repressed aspects of the psyche are not resolved, and that this acts in a metaphorical sense as an irritant. The idea of repression leading to psychic irritation is in keeping with H. B. Lewis's idea distilled from traditional psychoanalysis: repressed events cause psychopathology.

For me, the problem with unacknowledged or bypassed shame is less that it is an irritant and more that it is unavailable as an explanation, for individuals attempting to account for their behavior either to themselves or to others with whom they interact.

According to Lewis, with bypassed shame, "The affective component of the shame reaction is expressed as a wince or jolt, or a wordless shock in feeling, followed by an ideation about the self from the other's viewpoint."[3] Notice that her definition includes two features. First, there is an expression or indication that shame has occurred, what Lewis calls a "wince, jolt or a wordless shock." Second, for some reason, perhaps because of the individual's particular difficulty with accepting shame, the person next engages in an ideation about the self from the other's viewpoint. By this she seems to mean that the self, first, tries to rid itself of shame's affective component—the wince, jolt, or shock—and, second, uses ideation to distance the self from the emotion of shame.

Lewis utilizes the concept of bypassed shame in many ways, but I will mention only a few. In one case, the patient sees herself as guilty, not as shamed. Guilt is used to bypass shame, since it is a less acute emotion. I accept Lewis's idea that under some circumstances shame is transformed to guilt. I also accept the idea that one is likely to begin by choosing one or the other. That the patient bypasses shame and goes to guilt simply means that one possible transformation of shame is guilt. However, guilt is secondary to shame. According to my model, this would mean that individuals who are unwilling to experience shame deny their shame through the mechanism of focusing on their action rather than on their entire self. In other words, they practice specific, as opposed to global, attribution. Guilt can also exist in its own right.[4] I think it is reasonable to think that shame can be bypassed and transformed into guilt. But the opposite transformation, from guilt to shame, is not likely to occur, again reflecting the intensity difference between the two.

Individuals also attempt to deal with a shameful experience through the use of a variety of forms of ideation. These ideations allow the patient to shift the self into the position of the other and thus to move away from being the one experiencing the shame. This method of bypassing shame often manifests itself through laughter or confession, two attempts to move away from the shamed self by assuming the role of other. Ideation as an escape from shame is central to my analysis of narcissism and multiple personality disorders, topics discussed in chapter 9.[5] Another reaction to bypassed shame is the loss of self, not as in psychosis or multiple personality disorder, but as a result of a loss of memory. Shame can cause memory loss.[6] Lewis also talks about bypassed shame and the ego ideal and retaliatory hostility.

Lewis saw bypassed shame, at least in her original conception, as an attempt by the individual to distance the self from the emotion of shame. We have much to be thankful for in her analysis. However, the concept of bypassed shame needs further articulation and analysis. As she said, "The notion of a phenomenology of bypassed shame is almost a contradiction in terms."[7] Her recognition of the contradiction inherent to the concept of bypassed shame directs us to consider it in more detail. In discussing bypassed shame, we need to accept two basic ideas: thoughts and feelings can be repressed, and their repression, acting as an irritant, causes psychic difficulties that are expressed in symptoms. These symptoms, in turn, alert us to repression and conversion.

To accept the idea that shame can be repressed and converted into something else, that is, bypassed, we have to accept the concepts of unconscious conversion of shame as the result of repression.[8] While repression may be a useful construct, bypassed shame, or what I prefer to call unacknowledged (or unowned) shame, can be explained in other ways. Thomas Scheff suggests that unacknowledged shame involves excessive thought or speech but little feeling.[9] He also suggests that the reverse is true for overt shame, which involves lots of feeling but very little thought. Although Scheff equivocates regarding whether there is any feeling in bypassed shame, it seems reasonable to assume that there is some feeling involved: "Bypassed shame unanalyzed is manifested by a brief moment of painful feeling followed by a lengthy episode of obsessive thought or speech." It seems clear to me that in unacknowledged shame the question is not whether shame has occurred but whether it is acknowledged as having occurred. From a clinical perspective, almost everyone would agree that some form of registration occurs: the wince, jolt, or shock indicates the occurrence of shame.

Scheff's analysis is useful, although it, too, may beg the issue. For him, unacknowledged shame does not involve much feeling. Should we then conclude that shame, itself a feeling, can have little feeling? I think not. Then what happens to the feeling? Scheff does not specify. "Bypassed shame usually is manifested as a brief moment of powerful feeling, followed by a lengthy episode of obsessive thought or speech. . . . One might experience a very brief jab of painful feeling . . . followed immediately by a compulsive replaying of the scene."[10] The question remains, what happens to the wince or jab, the feeling of shame? For Lewis, it is repressed. But if we do not wish to use repression, what mechanism becomes available?

I suggest the focus of attention hypothesis that I presented earlier when discussing the self. Objective self-awareness is just one aspect of the self system. The system can operate without paying objective attention to states or even to goals. This does not mean the state is not operating, quite the opposite. You may be in an angry state and act accordingly, yet not be objectively aware of your emotional state or actions. Likewise for the shame state. You may be in the state of shame, which requires initial objective awareness, but choose not to remain attending to that state. You remove yourself from attending to the feeling, but the state itself remains. Overt feelings of shame simply indicate that you have not removed your objective focus or attention from the state you are in, and that you are trying one of a variety of procedures—already outlined above—to dissipate the negative state. In unacknowledged shame, you have removed your objective focus or attention from the negative state. You can do so immediately upon its creation; thus, all the observer would see is the "wince, jolt, or shock." Alternatively, you can remove your objective focus more slowly, through such a process as forgetting.

The conversion of the repression of shame can be handled in a similar fashion. We may wish to accept the notion of conversion, as yet undefined, where stored up energy acts as an irritant and gets expressed in terms of symptoms. It is an appealing idea; although how such a conversion comes about is difficult to specify. An alternative position is suggested by the work of those interested in multiple personality disorders.[11] This alternative centers around the concept of disassociation which, in turn, involves the unity of the self. I will discuss this theory in more detail later.

We now can understand unacknowledged shame as the existence of the emotion, caused by objective self-awareness, but unacknowledged because *it is not chosen as a focus.* The problems that become associated with this unacknowledged shame do not have to do with conversion but with the problems produced when people are in a state but do not wish to pay objective attention to that state. There are three areas of difficulty in the use of this psychic strategy: (1) physical actions, (2) thinking of other states, and (3) interpersonal exchanges.

First, the unacknowledged state is produced by some external events and *has some physical consequences.* We have not been terribly successful in specifying the physical concomitants to all the emotions, but we have made some progress in regard to shame. People experiencing shame may blush, their bodily action changes (a collapse of their posture and gaze avert), they have difficulty thinking, and they feel uncomfortable and pained. Not to acknowledge the state does not mean that these physical characteristics have not occurred. In fact, from our observations of people who have unacknowledged shame, we can see the physical change in the jolt or wince before it disappears.

Moreover, there are precipitating events that have caused our internal attribution. These may be unacknowledged or may be given new meaning so as to help us not acknowledge the shame. The difficulty here is that unacknowledged physical states do not allow us to take action to relieve them. They also may be contradictory to the new states we have or wish to have. As such, we have a conflict between different levels of self caused by focused objective awareness which excludes important bodily information.

If the shame remains unacknowledged, a person may decide to *focus on another emotional state*. I call this an act of emotional substitution. Emotional substitution is quite common for many different emotions. Earlier I spoke about John, a patient who was saddened by the death of his aunt. He chose to focus on his fatigue rather than on his sadness. Emotional substitution can take many forms. In John's case, a simple example, he chose to focus on a specific feature of the feeling state rather than the whole state. In the case of shame, it is possible to focus on a specific feature. For example, we could focus on the blushing aspect. Since blushing takes place in any situation of exposure, even those *without* evaluation, we can tell ourselves "I am blushing because I feel so embarrassed" instead of "I am blushing because I feel so ashamed." Indeed, we often use the term "embarrassing" to avoid acknowledging shame. Alternatively, we might focus on the mental confusion aspect of shame and say to ourselves "I just don't understand what's happened." Or we can focus on some feature of the negative feeling state that accompanies shame. We can easily "somatize" by thinking that this feeling has something to do with our physical well-being. We might even connect our negative feeling state with some previous physical or health difficulty in a type of process known as backward conditioning. Again, by focusing on only a single feature of the entire state, we avoid acknowledging shame as shame. The difficulty for the person here is that this explanation is inconsistent with what really is happening. Again, intrapsychic conflict has to result.

Another form of substitution involves the acknowledgment of an entirely new emotion. This can take the form of an emotion not at all relevant to the situation, or it can take the form of an emotion likely to be associated with the situation. In the former case, individuals are shamed but do not acknowledge shame. Instead, they become manic and start to talk compulsively.

I have a colleague who is readily shamed. Indeed, he is shame-prone; he treats any criticism as a global statement of failure. I always can tell when he is shamed because, immediately after the shame event, he shows an unhappy smile (his wince) and then starts a nonstop conversation. It is not clear to me why his unacknowledged shame is associated with a state similar to extreme happiness, except that it appears to block his acknowledging the shame.

Specific substitution principles may exist. Lewis has suggested some. I think that these principles may be based upon the hierarchy of possible emotions available to the person and available under the given situation. Alternatively, early learning may provide the mechanisms. This early learning acts to provide ready habit strengths when substitution is called for.

The emotions relevant to unacknowledged shame are those associated with elicitors and responses. The two major emotions that fit this requirement are sadness and anger. Since we will explore this topic in detail later, I will only offer a brief summary here. Sadness occurs around unacknowledged shame for a variety of reasons. Shame's emotional tone is negative and aversive, and the object is the self. "To feel bad"—that is, to be sad—is an emotional substitution not too removed from the shame state.[12] Moreover, the attributions of sadness are very similar to those that elicit shame: global and self-blame. Sadness may be a natural substitution because shame is often produced in the company of others or by the cause of others. That these others have caused the shame emotion you are feeling can lead naturally to sadness since someone you know has caused you harm. In this last case of sadness, the shamed individual focuses on the social embeddedness of the harmful situation and/or the elicitors of the emotion rather than on the shame itself. Sadness probably is more comfortable to experience than shame; thus, we may be more than willing to substitute it for the more painful shame.

Anger as a substitute emotion also has multiple causes. Again, from a phenomenological point of view, when we feel shame we also notice that we are feeling pain. To be in pain implies a cause, and anger is an appropriate emotion in order to overcome a painful cause. It has been noticed that a pain expression bears some similarity to an anger expression and that an anger expression often accompanies physical pain.[13] Past learning may be associated with anger over any physical or social pain. Thus, anger has a high place in the emotional response repertoire to shame. The substitution of anger for shame is more likely for men than for women.

Instead of directing anger outward, to the cause of our shame pain, we may become angry with ourselves for the "stupid thing I did." The "stupid thing" done was the cause of the attribution in the first place, and thus the cause of the shame. By focusing on the cause, we can avoid the feeling itself. The anger directed at our action allows us to bypass the shame feeling and, at the same time, to correct the events likely to lead to shame again.

Finally, as a third possible use for anger as a shame substitute, we may focus on the social aspects of causes. Shame often takes place in a social context. Thus, a shamed person, unwilling to acknowledge the feeling of shame, can become angry with someone else, making this other a kind of scapegoat for self-blame. This kind of anger allows us to externalize blame, thereby reducing our own part in the shame experience. This use of anger does not allow us to rectify our mistakes but only to dissociate ourselves from blame. Anger, like sadness, is more comfortable (or less uncomfortable) to experience than shame.

The use of substitution in all its varieties carries with it the intrapsychic cost of being objectively unaware of the emotion state that is currently present. By not focusing on this state but instead attending to other aspects or other emotions, we lose the opportunity to understand the forces at work around us and within us. This lack of focus may be adaptive, at least in part, since it protects the psyche from an intense and painful emotional experience. However, it is not totally beneficial, since the emotional state exists and is present, affecting our behavior, even if we are not attending to it. Substitution is a form of self-deception: it relieves the pain and discomfort but does not alter the state, at least not immediately.

The adaptive significance, or its lack, associated with unacknowledged shame is best seen in its *socially interactive significance*. In my earlier discussion of emotions, I pointed out that emotions are not only states within individuals, they are communicative signals that serve as part of the material of social exchanges and relationships. Unacknowledged emotional states of any kind are, by necessity, disruptive of social interactions. Recall the example of my patient and the car mechanic. My patient was angry, but he did not acknowledge his anger. As I already have indicated, a state exists whether or not it is objectified. The patient was in a state of anger, even though unacknowledged, and he therefore acted angry, an action that included facial, bodily, and language behavior. The auto mechanic read this message and responded with anger in turn. Because my patient did not acknowledge his own anger, he was surprised when his own behavior prompted the mechanic's anger. Conflicts and confusion result from action and emotion states that are unacknowledged.

This general truth applies even more in the case of shame. I say even more because shame is so powerful an emotion that the behaviors associated with its state are likely to be highly signaled. Unfortunately, since the shame states of others can cause shame in ourselves, these states may go unnoticed by both the sender and the receiver of the message. In the first kind of faulty message sending, the person is shamed but does not acknowledge it. The person's behavior does not agree with the stated or acknowledged state, and the other receives a "mixed" message, a mix of overt and covert forms of different emotions. Such a mixed mess: to lead to interpersonal difficulties.

Take, for example, a patient who is shamed by his father's comments to him. He does not acknowledge the shame but, instead, becomes tired. His girlfriend witnesses this interaction between father and son and feels badly for her boyfriend. She says, "I'm sorry your father said those things to you. He was wrong. He had no right to say those things." But the boy responds, "What are you talking about? It's nothing; I'm just sleepy."

His girlfriend does not know what to do since her attempt to comfort him has been denied. But she feels badly and wants to help. She does not understand that the patient has unacknowledged shame. He prefers to feel tired rather than shamed. When she acts appropriately to deal with the shame emotion she senses he must be feeling, she forces him to acknowledge the shame. Since he does not want to do this, he avoids her comfort.[14]

The second kind of faulty message sending involves emotional substitution. In this type of situation the shamed person expresses another emotion. As noted above, the two most common substitutes are sadness and anger. These substitutes cause all sorts of message problems. For example, recall the case of the couple who does not understand that they are shaming each other, with the male feeling angry and the female feeling sad and withdrawn. Because this topic carries me toward the consideration of interpersonal conflicts, I prefer to hold off complete discussion for chapters 8 and 10. However, let me preview my theory here, that coping with the emotional life of each individual is the major task of relationships. This task is made more difficult by the hidden emotion of shame which itself provides much of the material for conflict.

Owning Shame: How to Get Rid of It

What do people do when they have overt or felt shame? Their attributions have led them to shame and now they need to deal with this feeling. Because of shame's intensity and pain, the individual experiences a strong need to get rid of the feeling. At the same time, again because of its intensity and pain, and also because of its disruptive nature, the individual finds coping with shame very difficult. The simplest method to cope is to "own it" and allow shame to dissipate with time. People do this by removing themselves from the shaming situation, if and when they can, and then allowing shame to dissipate by itself. Like all intense events, shame eventually fades, to be replaced by other emotions and cognitions. No emotion lasts forever. But there are at least three other methods people use to help rid themselves of shame: denial/forgetting, laughter, and confession.

Denial and Forgetting

Denial can act upon the shame phenomenon in many ways. Suppose a shame experience has occurred and the person wishes to dissipate the shame. Shame has been experienced and acknowledged but, because of its intensity and its adverse characteristics, the person wants to rid himself of the shame feeling. Each of us can remember a shame occurrence and perhaps what we did to rid ourselves of it. My colleague, who takes her paper, rejected by a journal, and puts it in a drawer never to be seen again, uses a lack of focus procedure in order to forget about the shame experience that she acknowledges. Hiding her paper, she denies its existence, and thereby denies the shame experience caused by its rejection. Although denial is an adequate term to describe this action, I prefer the term forgetting. Shame in this kind of case is not really denied: it is still available to the person as shame, but it simply is not focused on.

> In the case of my colleague, she recognizes her shame in the failure to have her paper accepted. She simply says, in effect, "I don't want to think about it. I want to forget it, to get it out of my head." She does so by moving it to a place where it will cease to be a stimulus for her memory. By putting it in a drawer and going on to other work, she has the opportunity to forget.

The use of forgetting, simply dismissing something from active consideration, is a way of separating the self from the feeling. However, forgetting differs from denial in that with forgetting shame is a recognized feeling, one that is acknowledged. A student told me a story that illustrates this point.

> Her seminar professor asked her to prepare a review of a theory discussed by a certain Professor X. She got up in class and presented the theory of Professor X, only to discover that Professor X was sitting in on the seminar. At one point in her presentation she reported that Professor X had made a particular statement. Then she noticed Professor X shake her head, indicating that she was not offering an accurate view of Professor X's thoughts. The student reported to me that she thought that she would die: all she wanted to do was to hide and disappear. She was able to finish her

presentation, but, as soon as it was over, she gathered her things, excused herself, and left the seminar room.

She acknowledged her shame both directly, through saying "I was mortified," and by her action, which was to disappear by leaving the classroom and avoiding Professor X. Two days went by and she could not return to the seminar because she still remembered the event. She was unable to forget the shaming experience. Eventually, of course, she was able to forget her shame and return to the seminar. But her shame was not fully dissipated until she was able to complete a paper for the course. The use of forgetting clearly is one way to dissipate the shame experience. It allows us to distance and remove ourselves from the experience, once acknowledged.

Denial can act to prevent shame from occurring. Denial is not the same as forgetting. Thus, for example, a patient might say, "I didn't violate the rule, so there's no reason for me to blame myself." Alternatively, one could deny even having a standard or goal. Comments such as "I didn't want it anyway" may be an attempt to eliminate a goal or standard from consideration so that the entire attributional cycle leading to shame does not take place. If no standard has been violated, then one has no reason to worry about shame. We all feel, and rightly so, that many of these types of denial are "after-the-fact" denials, that is, they do not reflect ideation *prior* to the shame experience but *after it.* This ideation represents an attempt to move the self away from the shame through denial that anything bad has occurred. In general, I suspect that denial is usually used as a means of bypassing shame rather than as a method of not experiencing shame in the first place.[15]

But it may be true that denial sometimes operates prior to the shame experience, preventing it from occurring, as well as after the shame experience, as a way of bypassing the feeling. More work on this problem is needed. Perhaps the use of the wince, jolt, or shock as a marker of the occurrence of shame allows us to differentiate denial as bypassing shame from denial as preventing shame from occurring. If we could accurately measure this registration of shame, then we would know if the denial was after the fact or not.

Denial manifests itself in other ways. For example, we can use denial to prevent the internal attribution of blame. If a person prevents such attribution, then no shame will occur, as the following case demonstrates.

An adolescent in one of our longitudinal studies, when asked about why he was unsuccessful in completing a simple task that he had had five minutes

to complete, commented, "I couldn't finish it because of the noise that I
heard next door." It was true that some construction was going on and that
the adolescent may have been distracted by the noise. But many other
children had been placed in the same circumstances and were able to finish
the task or, if unable, did not blame lack of success on the noise outside.
This child's failure was attributed to some external event. From his facial
and bodily action it seemed to me that his not blaming himself for the
failure was a form of denial after the fact.

Laughter

Laughter also is a mechanism by which acknowledged shame can be
reduced or eliminated. The use of laughter involves a large number of
different mechanisms. First, laughing at one's self serves to distance one's
self from the emotional experience. Because laughter is such a powerful
stimulus, it allows us to focus on another emotion, and thereby enables us
to defocus the shame.

Second, laughter, especially laughter around one's transgression as
it occurs in a social context, provides the opportunity for the transgress-
ing person to join others in viewing the self. In this way, the self metaphorically moves from the site of the shame to the site of observing the
shame with the other. Consider the example of a person who slips on
her own scarf and falls. Others around her laugh at her clumsy behavior.
This laughter serves to humiliate the woman and she immediately feels
shame; however, by laughing at herself, she joins the others; now, rather
than being the object of others' laughter, she joins, in part, with the
others, becoming one who laughs at the misfortune of another. It is as
if the self moves from the position of being shamed, of having others'
eyes on one, to a position where one is with the others, the observing
eyes. Such a movement allows for identification with the observer rather
than identification as the observed, and has a very similar mechanism
to the movement Freud reported as identification with the aggressor.
By laughing, the person identifies with the observer rather than with
the observed; with those laughing at the one shamed, not the one
shamed.

A third feature of laughter is its social significance. I have noted that
experiencing someone's shame is shameful. Sensitive, empathic observers, seeing the woman trip, producing and hearing laughter, and registering her shame, are in turn shamed. There is a contagious effect: the
woman who feels shamed because she tripped causes those watching to

become shamed for her. This spiral of shame can be broken by means of the laughter of the one initially shamed. It is as if the woman says to the observers, "See, I'm not really shamed, so there's no reason for you to be shamed by my shame." In other words, laughter can be used to break the spiral of the observer and the observed shame exchange.[16]

Suzanne Retzinger observed the shame/laughter phenomenon in a rather clever study of videotapes recording couples in what she calls a shame-rage spiral.[17] She observed that laughter has the effect of terminating a shame spiral of the type I have just described. Freud reported a strong association between jokes and shame. For example, he reported that jokes that caused the most laughter were associated with incidents of humiliation.[18]

Laughter may have still another effect. Laughter itself is likely to be physiologically antagonistic to shame. The use of laughter as tension reduction for the self seems, phenomenologically, a reasonable ideal.[19] Moreover, Norman Cousins's celebrated "cure" for his cancer suggested the use of laughter as an antagonistic response to stress and illness. Certainly, there are physiological correlates that are likely to be antithetical to the physiology of shame. Unfortunately, the physiology of both shame and laughter is still relatively undefined; until such time as we have a better understanding of it, I only can conjecture as to the actual mechanisms that make laughter antagonistic to shame.

Laughter is a good example of how acknowledged shame can be reduced. Its use appears to be in its social function, although its physiological function may be greater than we know.

Confession

Confession, like laughter and forgetting, is an attempt to deal with acknowledged shame once it occurs. In confession, we go to others and tell them about an event that has shamed us. This public acknowledgment of the transgression and the shame that accompanies it appears to be a successful way of dealing with shame. Certainly, the use of confession by certain religions for hundreds of years is an indication of its success in dealing with shame.

But the process of confession does not require some assigned religious leader. Secular confessors can be just as effective if capable of understanding, appreciating, and, as we will see, forgiving us for our transgression.

Let me explore how confession works. In a sense, confession is like laughter. The degree to which people confess their transgressions to others is the degree to which they join in with the others in observing themselves. This allows the self to move from the self, that is, from the source of the shame, to the other. This, in turn, allows the self as the "confessee" to look upon the self as the object rather than the subject.

I once interviewed a man who told me of an experience that had recently occurred to him. After an interval of almost 10 years he met with an old girlfriend. They had gone together for 4 or 5 years, and had intended to marry. However, their relationship was often quite stormy. Eventually, she became quite angry with him and broke off the engagement. They drifted apart. He had not seen, spoken with, or written to her—nor she to him—for over a decade. By the time they met again he already had married, as had she. During the course of their conversation she talked about how unpleasant a person he had been. He told me that he did not feel upset about her continued anger—in fact, he was quite pleased that she still had strong feelings for him. When I inquired how he felt about the criticism she had leveled against him, he reported "It had happened so long ago, it didn't seem that she was talking about me." He went on to talk about how he had listened to her, and how he had been able to disarm her ongoing anger at him by agreeing with her about the person he had been. It was, he said, "As if we were talking about someone else. It was as if we both were looking at me from a distance."

Using that mechanism, he was able to disengage himself and to shift himself into the position of the other. Because of this shift, he reported, although he could see that he had been wrong, as he had since come to realize, he did not feel any shame because the past him was not really him. A similar shift of the self to the position of the other is exactly what occurs during confession. By admitting to a past error, the person is able to move from the site of the observed to the site of the observer.

Confession also has another role.[20] If one feels shame about a global self, to confess to this shame somehow is a virtue that allows some relief in terms of one's global evaluation. Such ideation might take the form of "Well, I'm not good, but at least I can own up to my faults." Such an ideation allows one to dissipate some of the intensity of the devalued self through regaining value by a positive action. This role may appear surprising, in light of the fact that I have designated shame as the result of a global self attribution that does not allow for consideration of specific action. Thus, the attempt to dissipate a global attribution through the positive act of confession appears, on its face, unreasonable. But the technique does appear to work.

I think I can show how and why. The sexual dysfunction literature offers evidence that confession of sexual difficulty relieves some of the shame associated with that dysfunction. Consider the case of a female who cannot reach orgasm without prolonged manual stimulation. Let us assume that she is ashamed because she has to ask her partner to provide this type of stimulation. Because of her shame, the patient avoids heterosexual activity because she knows such activity will likely lead to a shame occurrence as well as activate a shame reaction toward past experiences. Even if she attempts a heterosexual activity, she will be terribly anxious. The therapeutic literature suggests that to "own" her need serves as a way of distancing herself from the problem itself. The act of "owning" her special sexual need will reduce the anxiety associated with the potential occurrence of a subsequent shame experience. The clinical data from such cases suggest that confession is an effective technique for reducing shame.

One could conclude that her confession of difficulty has the consequence of reducing the shame associated with it which, in turn, may reduce her sexual problem. It may be, however, that the sexual difficulty does not have to do solely with the shame associated with past failures but with the anxiety associated with future shame. The confession serves to reduce the anxiety over being shamed, thus facilitating sexual feelings by reducing tension. Notice here that even if confession leads to a reduction of anxiety, it is the reduction of an anxiety associated with potential shame. That confession can act to reduce the anxiety of shame also must mean that it can act to prevent shame. After confessing her sexual problem and discussing it with the therapist, she can say to the other, "You see, I was right. I told you I couldn't do it—I need manual stimulation." Notice here that the shame may be dissipated through confession by moving the self away from the self ashamed.

Confession is associated with the concepts of forgiveness and love. We can best understand this feature of confession if we return to its original place within Catholic doctrine. Recall that Christ suffers and dies for the sins of mankind. The priest, the confessor, through his relationship to Christ, is capable of delivering God's forgiveness and love. Confession serves as a way of dissipating shame through the act of redemption. Notice that this feature of confession requires that the confessor possess those features that allow for forgiveness and love. Not every person can offer forgiveness and love to every other person under all conditions. Within the formal structure of religion, such as Catholicism, the priest, through his special relationship to God, is given such powers. The degree to which the individual believes that the priest possesses these powers is the degree to which confession is a successful medium for reducing shame.

Other individuals, besides religious figures, are capable of assuming such a role. For example, if your shame is caused by some behavior that you have done to another, the other person possesses the ability to forgive you.

> *A patient of mine had a sexual encounter with someone outside of her marriage. She told me that this encounter had occurred several years earlier and that she had felt terribly ashamed. She saw herself as violating the family unit and, because of this shame, found herself so unhappy that she finally confessed her transgression to her husband. It is important to note what she reported she felt after she finally confessed. She said, "After I told him, and he said that he understood and still loved me, I felt as if a weight had been lifted from me." In other words, confession had redeemed her, since she could confess to the one whom she had transgressed against and who forgave her.*

Individuals are capable of forgiving us to the degree to which we assign them this social role, usually through some religious belief, or they are the ones against whom we have transgressed. A third group of people is also capable of serving as confessors. These we might call *people of status,* people whom society has endowed with a special authority by reason of their profession, wealth, power, etc. People in the healing professions, for example, are often treated as confessors. Colleagues at the medical school report to me that their patients confess things to them that are totally irrelevant to their treatment. For example, an internist colleague reported that several of his patients had told him details about their lives that appeared to have nothing to do with their treatment. One case in particular stands out.

> *The internist had been examining a young university student for a normal physical. He was going to spend the summer at a camp and needed to have a general examination. The doctor had taken his pulse, listened to his heart rate, and was doing an EKG examination. The student suddenly told him that he recently had taken an examination and had, as he said, "Used an exam from last year that someone gave him." The internist could not understand why he had told him about this transgression and, as he reported to me, all he could think of saying was, "I don't think that's honest." I*

asked him what the patient's reaction was: he reported that he was unsure, but the student did not speak much to him after that.

My own interpretation is that the student was confessing to him as an authority figure, as one with high status; the doctor's nonsympathetic or unforgiving response reinduced shame and led to the student's silence.

Apparently, individuals assigned high status in a society, through their social role, gain some right to hear confession and to dispense forgiveness. It is not clear to me exactly why this should be the case. Perhaps shame, confession, and authority figures are linked from childhood: the child experiences relief after confessing to the parent, and thereafter associates relief with confession to authority figures. Since the "confessee" seeks forgiveness, we may be witnessing the reenactment of the original shame-inducing events. Remember that the socialization of shame involves accepting the standards, rules, and goals of the other, as well as their evaluation of one's success or failure. It is an incorporation and internalization of the other's view that, of course, becomes our own. To the extent that the confession reenacts the parent-child relationship, the confession will be able to reduce shame through forgiveness and love. If, as I believe, prototypic shame is caused by the withdrawal of love, which is caused by violation of standards, then love through confession banishes the shame. Confession, then, is a reenactment of the original source of shame. Through it, we are able to dissipate our shame and restore our intrapsychic life to balance.

I need to mention two cautions in regard to confession. The first has to do with confession to the person against whom one has transgressed. When we confess to the one transgressed against we may dissipate the shame, but at a certain cost to the other and to our relationship with the other. People who hear the news that their mate has been unfaithful and wishes forgiveness are caught in an intolerable bind. They have to forgive because they love and care for the other and because the other's desire for forgiveness, through contrition, indicates sorrow. Unfortunately, the confession often hurts and angers the person confessed to, who, because of the role assigned, is not allowed to express hurt or anger. The "confessee" may feel relieved, but the confessor is now saddled with heavy emotional baggage. Indeed, for the "confessee" to demand this role of the injured party may itself be an aggressive act, one that seeks both narcissistic satisfaction—namely the reduction of one's own shame—and the prevention of anger being directed against the self by the other, since the other is forced into the role of the person being confessed to. The use of confession for shame reduction in this interpersonal dynamic sense is likely to play an important role in interpsychic difficulties. This can be seen in the following example.

A man confesses to his wife that he has been having an affair with another woman. He claims that he is confessing to her because he really loves her, his wife, and wants to improve their relationship. He indicates that the best way to achieve a closer relationship and greater intimacy is to confess so that there will be no secrets between them.

His confession, presented in this way, seems to him to be a statement of love, sharing and renewed commitment. His wife, however, is injured twice: once by his act of unfaithfulness and again by his report of his unfaithfulness. She is angry and hurt, but prevented from expressing these emotions. Because he has confessed and because he sees this act as a renewal of their relationship, she finds it difficult to express her shame at being rejected and her anger over his transgression. By relieving his shame, he may shame her and make her unable to express her feelings.

The second point I want to mention has to do with the effect of confession upon the production of shame-proneness. When we give the confessor the power to relieve the shame through forgiveness of the self, we may actually increase the likelihood of promoting further shame. Notice that shame reduction-through-confession takes place because the other is able, through love, to forgive the whole self. Since both love and forgiveness have as their focus the whole self, the transgressor remains, through this process, likely to make global attributions. The forgiveness and love of the whole self serve to unite the individual with the confessor, since it is only the confessor who can forgive the whole self. However, in the forgiving of the whole self, the whole self remains the focus of the individual. Thus, any new transgression is likely to be globally ascribed, and therefore likely to need a new confession. In a very real sense, a system that promotes forgiveness of a global self also promotes the self as a focus of attention. Confession can be addictive, for it promotes global attribution and, at the same time, provides an opportunity for the reduction of shame. Because of this, confession can be a very powerful mechanism by which people are maintained within a social order.

While confession can create new problems, I do not view it as a negative method for dealing with shame, at least in most cases. The confessor's role is a very positive role that we give to select people in a society. The loss of such role assignment within a society is likely to have serious implications for many people, especially those suffering from narcissistic disorders. If shame cannot be forgiven because no social structure exists within the culture that allows it to be forgiven, the experience of shame becomes especially dangerous and people will seek to avoid it. To this extent, the role of confession within a society is significant; indeed, its loss (associated with the decline of religion) is likely to be related to the rise of narcissistic disorders.

By means of forgetting, laughter, and confession shamed individuals attempt to dissipate their feelings through a variety of techniques. Because shame, like all emotions, has a transient character and is likely to dissipate on its own, these techniques serve a useful function in facilitating the process. In all these cases the shame is owned first and then reduced.

8

Prolonged Reactions to
Shame

Humiliation, Depression, and Rage

When we discuss what happens when we feel shame, either acknowledged or not, we cannot keep the discussion within the bounds of the individual. People are, by their nature, social. Our evolutionary history in regard to cognition, perception, motivation, emotions, and social behavior is designed around their adaptive significance for a species that is social in nature. Born helpless, we need others to help us survive. Sexually dimorphic, we need others to perpetuate our kind. As Levi-Strauss has said, even our language is an agreed-upon system. When a person's language use is so idiosyncratic that it fails to communicate, we recognize that psychopathology is likely.[1] Although individuals can experience (objectify) their shame in the absence of others, the standards, rules, and goals that we have are acquired from others and generally fit with the standards of others. Thus, even these standards are social. Moreover, objectification itself must be, at least in part, related to the actions of others.[2] Our evaluations of success or failure are derived in part from the values and goals of our families, friends, and parents. The totality of our emotional life, including the experience of shame, takes place in a social nexus.

Much of the discussion of intrapsychic events related to shame involved interpersonal behavior. It could not be otherwise, since children and adults exist in a social environment and the attributions that they make are made in the context of these interpersonal situations. Moreover, individuals behave toward others in such ways as to produce specific emotions—in this case, shame—through a variety of techniques. Thus, parents who use humiliation as a socializing technique are likely to induce shame in their children either directly, through certain classes of behavior, or indirectly, by provoking certain attributions in their children. In the case of humiliation, as in the attribution case, individuals come to recognize and feel shame through their commerce with their environment.

While I do not feel that another need be present for us to experience shame, and I have suggested that individuals are not always embedded in a nexus, it is clear that to understand shame, we need to see it in the context of others.[3] This is especially true since there are those who would argue that shame, unlike guilt, must involve the presence of another. Think of Darwin's example of giving money to a beggar. Embarrassment only occurs if we imagine God watching us. Of course, even Darwin recognized that the actual presence of the other was not necessary: the mere thought of the other is often sufficient. The problem of the need for the other is readily solved by talking about the other as part of the individual's internalized standards, rules, and goals, and part of the attribution of success or failure. It is the eye within us. As Cooley and Mead indicated, we only can come to view ourselves through the eyes of those who view us. Since objectification occurs in early childhood, the eyes of the other(s) usually are those of our parents—but they can also be other adults, depending on whether we know them well during this time. Our social nature can lay claim to much of what causes shame. Nevertheless, once shame is created, it can be objectively experienced in the silence of the empty room. As this example demonstrates, shame can occur without the presence of the other.

> *A teacher colleague recently gave a lecture. Everyone who heard the lecture thought it was wonderful: scholarly, coherent, and full of information. The teacher herself, however, knew that she had failed to mention an important exception. While she knew that no one else would know about this exception, she still went home feeling shamed. She said to me, "It didn't matter what they all thought, I knew I had failed."*

In talking about shame from an intrapsychic perspective, I looked at how shame, once elicited, is dealt with by individuals. If shame is acknowledged, attempts can be made to eliminate it. These include forgetting/denial, laughter, and confession. Even here, the self attempts to separate itself from the shame. In each case, the person moves away from the shamed self. Denial and forgetting require a refocusing, removing attention from the events that caused the shame or from the shaming experience itself. Laughter serves, in part, as a physiological block to the shame emotion, and also has the function of removing the self from the shamed self. By laughing at our shame, we become an observer of the self—we enact a form of dissociation. In confession, we again give up the self, this time to another person capable of forgiving us. In all cases, people attempt to rid themselves of the unpleasant shame feeling. The critical feature of all forms of dealing with acknowledged shame is that the sufferer must first "own it" before giving it away.

In situations of unacknowledged shame, the individual works to avoid "owning" shame. This is done using the same basic process used in the case of acknowledged shame: the individual attempts to separate the self from the shamed self. The methods used to effect this process involve emotional substitution in its various forms. Note that I avoid the use of the concept of conversion which, while descriptive, does not aid in understanding of the process itself. The two emotional substitutes for which we possess the most information are depression and rage. You may have noticed that in the last chapter I used the terms sadness and anger, not depression and rage. There was an important reason for this usage: sadness and anger are the normal forms of emotions whose psychopathological forms are depression and rage.

As I have pointed out, the study of emotions in general, and shame in particular, often has been carried out in a clinical context. Our understanding of the shame process, then, comes from working with psychopathology. While it is possible to generalize to broad normal, developmental, and individual differences from the pathological, we often run some risk in doing so. Besides the fact that normal processes may differ in significant ways from pathological ones, the major problem is rooted in the view of the topic. Specifically, shame is not a pathological condition.[4] It is a normal emotion, if by normal we mean that all of us are capable of feeling it and do so on some occasions. Indeed, not to have experienced shame, being incapable of feeling shame is the pathological condition. I have tried to indicate this idea throughout this book. No one likes to experience shame and we all try to dissipate the shame feeling once it occurs. Emotional substitution for shame, within limits, is an absolutely normal process. To feel sad or angry when you are shamed is a defensive process. From an adaptive point of view, however, it is important that we own at least some of our shame for at least some of the time. I point to this because shame serves a moral function, and perhaps others as well. Things that shame us should not be done, at least from our particular perspective. The intensity of the aversive experience serves to ensure that the thoughts, actions, or feelings that led to shame do not recur.

I have often been amazed as to why certain actions that have a high likelihood of producing shame are not done even when it is clear that no direct harm can result if we actually do them. Perhaps an example can illustrate the point.

A female friend had to get to the airport early, so she was on the road by 5:00 A.M. The small road from her house led to a larger one with a stoplight on the corner. The light turned red just as she arrived. Worried about being late, she moved the car slightly forward to see if the road was empty. It was deserted. Knowing it was a long light, not in her favor, and also knowing that there was no traffic, she thought about going through the light. She did so, and was not stopped by hidden police, nor crushed by an unseen oncoming truck. Nevertheless, for a while, she felt terrible. I asked her how she felt, and she reported that she felt badly about herself. I do not know her full attribution, and therefore do not know if she was feeling shame or guilt. But my question concerning the adaptive function of shame and guilt was answered. We need to own our shame so that we will know what we should or should not feel, think, or do.

From this example, it seems reasonable to assume that the consistent refusal or inability to own shame, and thereby never (or almost never) experience it, probably is maladaptive. This being so, the consistent use of substitution or any other process that does not allow us to own shame, at least for a time, must be admitted as pathological. Some people do not feel shame, but do feel guilt. If it is true that people often substitute emotional terms but not the feelings, then guilt without shame would be another example of pathology. Imagine someone who says that she feels all emotions except sadness. If she were speaking the truth, you would agree with me that this would be a peculiar situation, perhaps even pathological. The same is true for shame.

In the case of emotional substitution, especially for sadness and anger, we have the opportunity to look at patterns of substitution over time and in interactions. Single instances of shame can lead to sadness or anger as substitute emotions. However, during prolonged instances and interactions, in which sadness or anger are consistently substituted for shame, sadness turns to depression and anger to rage. Because H. B. Lewis was examining pathological rather than normal processes, she observed depression and rage. These pathological conditions arise from prolonged histories of shame, either because individuals are shame-prone or because they are trapped in interpersonal environments in which they are consistently shamed. The pathological condition known as the shame-depression or shame-rage axis has been discussed by others.[5] I now intend to treat shame as a trait, with the understanding that while some people possess this trait more than others, they can do so for two very different reasons. In the first case, it is part of their personality: they possess too strong an evaluative mechanism for success and failure or they suffered a humiliating childhood that led to global evaluations. The second case has to do with the nature of their social relationships. In this case, people are subjected to being shamed by others. While the first is a trait located in the individual, the second is a trait located in the social nexus.

This analysis forces me to return to a most compelling proposition: if individuals deal with shame by emotional substitution then they remain at the mercy of their focus and concern. Likewise, from a therapeutic point of view, the therapist, focusing upon the symptoms of depression or aggression, is likely to miss the underlying stimulus event, namely, the global, internal attribution of failure associated with being shamed. This is a point first mentioned by H. B. Lewis nearly 20 years ago and is just now beginning to be accepted by the therapeutic community.[6] Recently Morrison made this same point: "because depression is so observable whereas shame so frequently remains hidden, this relationship has not been emphasized, and the elements of shame frequently have remained unexplored."[7]

To understand interpersonal issues around shame we have to deal with the basic assumption that the shame experience is not acknowledged by either or by both members of the dyad—or by the family, if we are dealing with units larger than two people. Because emotional substitution is the most likely reaction to prolonged shame experiences, these two axes, the shame-depression and the shame-rage, must be considered in more detail.

The question remains: How does this substitution take place? This question has just begun to receive some attention.[8] Concerning the shame-depression and shame-rage axes, another question arises: Are these two substitutions governed by the same processes? They well might be, if depression and rage are related, and there is some evidence that they are.

Freud, in *Mourning and Melancholia,* suggests that depression arises out of hostility turned toward the self under the press of guilt.[9] I believe that the press of shame produces a similar outcome. Assume that depression is aggression turned inward, an explanation that would unite the depression or anger substitution. How might this retroflexed hostility work? Shame can lead to anger. The earlier discussion explains the process of substitution: unacknowledged shame at times elicits anger because the self has been injured. Anger is easily substituted for unacknowledged shame because of the latter's aversive quality and the inhibition of activity associated with it. If inhibition of ongoing behavior is frustrating, the frustration-anger connection would be an easy substitution for shame.

Given that anger is substituted for unacknowledged shame, the anger has to be retroflexed so that it now becomes anger at self. The process starts with unacknowledged shame leading to anger, and continues with anger leading to depression. While such a process is possible, its complicated set of substitutions and conversions makes it unwieldy. There are alternatives to the theory of depression as hostility turned inward that allow us to consider depression as a direct consequence of unacknowledged shame.

Shame, Depression, and Interpersonal Life

As I have already explained, unacknowledged shame can be transformed into sadness. Since sadness is an emotion that normally is produced on occasion while depression is an ongoing personality characteristic or trait, the discussion of the connection between shame and depression requires reconsideration. We need to consider the possibility that the association between shame and depression is based upon repeated instances of shame. What is the clinical association between these two emotional states?

The information that we have on the association between shame and depression grows out of clinical observations and the research on depression.[10] Freud's idea about depression reflects an object-libidinal orientation, suggesting that depression is aggression turned inward.[11] Since my viewpoint of emotional life centers around the self system, I find Bibring and Bowlby's analyses more appealing.[12] Bibring preferred to view depression as the consequence of the lowering of self-esteem due to the failure to succeed in meeting the person's narcissistic aspirations. Bibring's view is consistent with the more prevalent notion of depression stemming from issues having to do with self-esteem, in particular, with the current attributional work associated with Aaron Beck, Martin Seligman, and Bernard Weiner. All these theorists suggest that depression results from attributions of failure that are internal, having to do with the self's fault; global, having to do with the whole self; and stable, consistent over time. The attributional and self psychologies are on common ground in their analysis of depression. Interestingly, this depression-through-attribution literature closely parallels my analysis of shame! The consequence of certain situations is shame and/or depression. It would appear, then, that depression is not a conversion of shame but an accompanying emotion. From my point of view, depression, rather than shame, is focused upon by the person.

From a self psychology or attributional theory perspective, shame and sadness share a common cause and exhibit behavioral similarities. Our studies of shame indicate that when individuals experience shame in a particular situation, they show behaviors characteristic of a sad person. They gaze avert, hunch their shoulders up, push their bodies inward, become inhibited, and show problems in thinking. From an expressive point of view, these people appear to be sad.

I have suggested that emotional substitution or particular objective self focus is what allows for sadness or shame. The same is true for the shame-depression connection. It appears that individuals who undergo repeated shame experiences experience depression rather than sadness. Given this connectiveness, why do individuals who are repeatedly shamed (either because they are shame-prone or because they live in a shame environment) focus on the depression rather than the shame? The question to be answered is, Is there any choice, given repeated shame, but to be depressed? I have suggested that other emotion substitutes are possible, for example, rage. The previous question leads to another one: Is it possible to see a patient who is continuously shamed and who acknowledges this shame? In my own experience, I have not found such a case except for borderline or psychotic patients. Nor have I discovered references to such cases in the literature. Here, the shame becomes so intolerable that instead of employing a defensive emotional substitution, the self disintegrates. When I discuss the issues of multiple personality disorders in chapter 9, I will return to the topic of multiple selves. Here it is sufficient to mention that a self, shamed repeatedly or prone to shame, unable to move toward emotional substitution, is likely to become disorganized and disruptive. Loss of self, as seen in affect disorders such as schizophrenia or borderline psychosis, is the likely consequence. If this analysis is correct, and some clinical work does support it, then we can explain depressive symptomatology as an attempt, perhaps more successful than others, of guarding the integrity of the self against assault.[13]

I have not addressed the specific question of why repeated shame or shame-proneness should be expressed in depressive symptomatology rather than aggressive behavior. Here I want to turn to socialization. Depressive symptomatology, at least in adults, is more likely to appear in women than in men. This association may help us understand the socialization mechanism responsible. Given that an individual experiences repeated shame, there are multiple choices available for dealing with this problem. I have already mentioned some, such as forgetfulness, denial, laughter, confession, and the like; however, these are available for single instances of shame, not for repeated experiences. Repeated shame experiences are too overwhelming for these mechanisms to work. Emotional substitution symptoms are likely to manifest themselves as the person attempts to prevent the disintegration of the self system.[14]

Given that women, as opposed to men in our culture, are not allowed to act aggressively and are actively socialized not to be aggressive, females are more likely, as a substitution, to turn toward the depressive symptomatology as a way of warding off the disintegration of the self.

Other factors may also be relevant. Dispositional factors, genetic in origin, may move one to adopt different emotional substitutions. Individuals may differ in their disposition toward depression. If placed in shame-inducing situations, some people may be more likely than others to use depression rather than rage as an emotional substitution.

I suspect that depression, rather than aggression, which is seriously frowned upon by society, is used as an emotional substitute for shame when the self system is threatened by breakdown. If this is the case, there are important clinical implications. We must be prepared to treat individuals with depressive symptomatology, which may reflect underlying shame, with care, since the removal of the depressive symptomatology will uncover the shame, and without any defense the shame may promote more serious disorders, such as schizophrenia.[15]

I have recently been involved in two situations that seem to highlight this dynamic.

The first case involved a friend of one of my students. She arrived at my office well dressed. She told me that her problem was that she was depressed, but she did not know why. Her family was supportive, she did well in school, she had several good relationships with friends, and she was currently going with a senior whom she had been seeing for over a year. Their sexual life was good, but she was not sure if the relationship would last once he graduated.

The more she talked about the boyfriend, the clearer it became that he was the cause of her depression. From what she said, her boyfriend was very bright, but quite arrogant. He was contemptuous of her sloppy thinking and "always was putting her down [intellectually]." She reported that she got angry at his behavior but, because he was so smart, she also believed he must be right. Moreover, she felt "terribly about fighting." "Was it her own stupidity and sensitivity which was causing the trouble?" I suggested therapy but she refused because her boyfriend thought the idea foolish and a waste of effort.

I did not treat her, but I do think that this young woman's difficulties were of the type we have been considering. She was in a relationship in which her partner consistently shamed her. He was contemptuous toward her and "always put her down." Since she valued the relationship and did not want to leave it, she was trapped in a shaming environment. As a consequence, she suffered depression and self-deprecation. It is interesting to note that she appears to have accepted her boyfriend's belief that her problems are her own fault. Even when she becomes angry over being shamed, she feels that she is at fault for disrupting the relationship which, in turn, makes her more ashamed.

The second case involves an abused wife who was referred to the mental health center because of depression. A colleague related that the patient had been beaten by her husband and now was depressed. From the reports of the therapist, it seemed to me that the woman might be ashamed of being beaten and abused. It was the shame that was causing her patient's depression, not the beating. In exploring this possibility with her patient, the therapist reported that the woman did believe that she was the cause of the beating. This attribution contributed to her shame. The therapist also reported that the wife was humiliated by the beating itself. The public display of being beaten was humiliating for her and she hid in her house, ashamed to go out where others could witness the signs of her physical abuse. This shame over her abuse contributed to her isolation.

This report about the abused wife seems consistent with other clinical data in regard to physical abuse. The person abused is shamed for several reasons, including (1) the belief that they are the causal agent of the abuse, (2) the feeling of being no good, and (3) the humiliation associated with the display of the abuse.

These studies are consistent with the work of others who point to the relationship between depression and shame.[16] What is clear is that depression is likely to accompany the feelings of low self-esteem or shame. Because interpersonal relationships are particularly important for women, more so than for men, these relationships are likely to be a strong source of feelings of shame and depression. Even when women are abused, either psychologically or physically, they are likely to blame themselves for the failure of the relationship and for their own abuse. This ideation constitutes a trap from which the victim cannot escape. This analysis points to why the victims of abuse most often express depression.

The axis between shame, depression, and rage will become clear when we explore the shame-rage problem. Before doing so, however, I would like to turn to a particular shame depression problem: the loss of the parent through death.

Over the last two decades I have gathered data on three adolescents who lost their mothers at early ages, all before they were 10 years old. Of particular interest was the fact that only one of them appeared to be depressed. Given the association between early parental loss and depression, I have been curious as to why they were not all depressed, or at least depression-prone. Studies by Brown and colleagues have been able to show a strong connection between early loss of the mother and depression.[17] Nevertheless, there are children, as these cases attest, who do not show depression to loss of the parent. Brown et al. postulated that the underlying cause of the depression is shame, shame caused by the death itself and sometimes also by the deficient care the children received after the parent's death. This is consistent with my three cases.

All three adolescents expressed the pain associated with being different. One of them said to me, "You know, I was always ashamed not having a mother. All the kids had mothers, I was so different."

While all three of the children had lost their mothers at an early age, only one seemed depressed. The second child, who was not depressed, seemed ashamed, so that the connection between shame and depression was not automatic. This adolescent expressed some degree of anger; in fact, he entered therapy because of his fighting. We worked on the anger but I do not feel we made much progress. As I now view the situation, his shame manifested itself in rage rather than depression. Because we focused on the rage and not the underlying cause, we made little progress.

The third child was the most interesting. He appeared at my office because of school problems. Although he, too, had lost his mother early and felt different than the other children, he showed neither depressive nor aggressive symptoms. He described to me a now understandable event that occurred soon after his mother's death. He remembered being in his room and thinking about the causes of her death. He thought that she died either because she was bad, he was bad, or God was bad. He could not think of anything that his mother had done that was so bad that she would die nor could he think of anything he did which was so bad. Therefore, he remembered feeling that it must be God who is bad. At that point he ceased to believe in God.

I think that this case represents an important example of attributional styles at work. Notice that the third child remembers that he concluded that he was not bad, and therefore could not have caused his mother's death. The attribution he made was external, that is, there was no self-blame and, because of this, there could be no evaluative process leading to shame.

These three cases with three outcomes, all due to parental loss, point to an important aspect of the connection between parental death, depression, and shame. I would suggest that, in general, people, especially young children, are likely to make an internal attribution of self-blame when a parent dies (perhaps also when the parent is sick or incapable). Moreover, children are likely to make a global attribution, and therefore experience shame. If the child does not make such an internal attribution, if he concludes "It's not my fault but God's" or focuses on some other external cause, shame will not occur. This does not mean the child will not experience sadness over the loss, but depression is not likely. If children do make an internal attribution, shame, depression, or rage may result.

These studies bear on object relations theory as they relate to depression. The withdrawal of the mother or failure of the mother to supply appropriate care subjects the child to the potential of depression through the loss of the love object.[18] In its broad form, I might state the proposition as follows: Given that children need the care and love of an adult, and given their biological disposition to form attachments, children who form attachments with objects who are lost are likely to become depressed. The loss of the love object can take place either through the unavailability of the love object, caused by death, illness, or separation, or because the love object is incapable of delivering the affection that the child needs. In all of these cases, the net consequence is the likelihood of depression. Within object relations theory, the loss of the love object is more directly associated with depression. This might be the case, except that we do not always see depression. Rather than conceptualizing the loss of the love object, for whatever reason, as directly leading to depression, I propose that the loss of the love object leads to the loss of self-esteem or shame, which, in turn, *can* lead to depression. This modification involves the patient's shame as the intermediate variable between the loss of love and depression. To the degree that shame does not occur or to the degree that shame leads to rage, we will not see depression as a result of loss. Since it is rare that loss does not lead to shame through self-blame, it is likely that we will see either depression or rage. It is understandable that the direct association is made, although I suspect the process is more complicated.

———— • ————

The connection between shame and depression is complex. On the one hand, some evidence suggests that from a structural point of view they are quite similar. Therefore, we might suspect that shame automatically evokes depression. On the other hand, we have seen that emotional substitution is a likely consequence of unacknowledged shame and that the nature of the substitution is dependent upon socialization rules. Both processes are possible. Alternatively, it may be the case that they are both needed to explain the phenomenon. Consider that depression always is evoked in unacknowledged shame (proposition one); however, emotional substitution is determined by socialization rules (proposition two). In that case, females are allowed the depressive response but males are encouraged to substitute rage for depression. We may be better able to answer this puzzle after we explore the shame-rage axis.

Anger, Rage, and Shame

We need to draw a distinction between shame and anger versus shame and rage. I see shame-anger as a consequence of a particular event of shaming.

I witnessed a 4 year old who was criticized by his mother in the waiting room of my laboratory. They entered the room and she told the child to play with the toys that already were taken out. The child started to play with those toys, but he soon saw some other toys on a shelf and went to them. His mother said, "Jonathan, I told you not to do that. Why are you always so bad?" She said this with a disgusted facial expression and a contemptuous tone. Jonathan did not move away, but he stopped all action for a moment before he began to noisily bang two of the forbidden toys together. My observation of Jonathan indicated that he was shamed and that anger was his response. I see this particular event as more than an example of frustration resulting in anger. This mother's verbal statement, "Why are you always so bad?," was a global evaluation of his failure. So was her facial response of disgust. Jonathan's behavior, the initial freezing, characteristic of the wince, marks the initial shame response. But he then used anger as a substitute for his shame.

Anger here was the consequence of a particular event. Rage, in contrast, is the response to prolonged shaming.[19]

As I tried to point out earlier when examining the shame-sadness/depression axis, anger and rage also are emotional substitutes for shame. There are a variety of causes for such a substitution. One has to do with the pain associated with shame and with the anger for having that pain. We are all familiar with people who get angry with themselves for doing really stupid things.

> *I have a student who came into my office and told me that she was terribly embarrassed that she had forgotten to do her assignment. She went on to say, "When I remembered I didn't do it, I was really pissed." This behavior belongs to the general class of events that are expressed by the statement, "I could kick myself for being so stupid."*

This simple example illustrates that shame can be dissipated by becoming angry at oneself. People can first own their shame (it has to be acknowledged) and then become angry with themselves for shaming themselves in the same way that people can become angry with themselves for any number of painful experiences they cause. Usually, however, anger is an emotional substitute for unacknowledged shame. Substituting anger for shame helps the self avoid the shame, and being angry may also have some adaptive significance, especially if the person's culture allows for anger. In American culture, the substitution of anger for shame is more adaptive for men than it is for women.

Anger and rage can also be directed at another. Again, we start with unacknowledged shame. This time the anger substitute is expressed outwardly, either to the person causing the shame or, in the case where the expression of anger or rage at this target is dangerous, at another person.

> *Recently, I was talking to a couple. The wife related an experience that had just occurred while they were driving to my office. The husband failed to stop for a traffic light as the yellow turned to red. This error was compounded by the fact that a policeman saw him go through the light. He was stopped by the officer, who lectured him about his failure to stop in time. He, in his wife's terms, was humiliated by the policeman's attitude and by the fact that he was given a ticket. After the policeman left, his wife reported that he turned toward her, red-faced, and said angrily, "Why didn't you warn me there was a policeman?" The husband had been shamed and humiliated by the policeman. He did not own the shame; instead, he expressed anger. Since it was dangerous to express anger to the policeman, he directed this feeling toward his wife.*

This example demonstrates that directing anger/rage toward another rather than toward the self is an attempt to ward off the shame, and, in some way, also an attempt to undo the shame through a reinterpretation of the blame from an internal to an external cause. Such behavior often speaks to a shame-prone personality and is consistent with narcissistic disorders.

If the husband were capable of blaming his wife prior to his evaluation, he would not have been shamed at all. However, as the situation unfolded, he did appear ashamed and, subsequently, admitted it by talking about how the policeman humiliated him. In our therapy session he was able to see that his anger toward his wife was an attempt to ward off the feelings of shame that he had. He agreed that it would be better to admit that he was shamed rather than to become angry.

I can think of other examples where a shame/rage situation is likely to occur. Again, one might argue that the rage is not a substitute for the unacknowledged shame but rather anger/rage directed toward the identified source of the shame. It is my experience that the shame is not really acknowledged, that is, it is possible to know that the other is shaming you without owning the shame the other caused. Consider another couple.

The husband, Jerry, has continuously shamed his wife, Lynn, for more than 10 years. Not only does he blame her for things for which she clearly is not responsible, but, because of his own needs, he finds many occasions to ridicule, shame, and humiliate her. Lynn's presenting symptom is extreme anger toward Jerry. Within the first hour of our session, she takes the opportunity at least five times to express her rage at him. Lynn's posture, facial expression, and verbalizations are all consistent with rage, controlled rage, but rage nonetheless. During the course of our hours together she confesses that she has "lost all of my self-esteem and Jerry's responsible for it." Although she admits loss of self-esteem, she has not accepted her shame. Her case reflects Scheff's idea that bypassed shame involves excessive thought and or speech, but little feeling.[20]

People who are continuously shamed by others can develop rage. This rage may be expressed toward those causing them shame or displayed to others for a variety of reasons: the other may be too powerful, the other may pose a physical threat, the other may be someone for whom the shamed person feels strong positive emotions, and therefore with whom rage would be incompatible with other feelings, etc. In addition, the rage may be deflected because the other is needed.

Many examples of displaced rage or the suppression of rage can be seen in everyday life, especially in families. The young child, humiliated by her parents, is unable to express anger toward them, because to do so endangers the child, so the child yells at the pet dog or hits it. The employee, shamed by her boss, realizes she could lose her job if she rages at her boss, and so she displaces her anger on her innocent secretary. Recall the case of the Puerto Rican boy in chapter 1. He was shamed by the police and then became angry. His anger could not be expressed to the police, so it was displaced to smashing garbage cans. Rage against inanimate objects is highly likely, especially in people who feel powerless.

H. B. Lewis discussed the shame-rage axis; however, in her analysis, shame that led to rage subsequently led to guilt. She believed that rage was an unacceptable impulse and the checking of the unacceptable impulse was associated with guilt, an idea reminiscent of the guilt associated with id impulses. Scheff suggests that the shame-rage axis does not need to involve guilt, although it might. What should be noted is that the shame-rage connection can lead to a spiral in which the rage itself becomes a new source of shame. The shame-rage-shame-rage spiral is important for understanding a variety of interpersonal conflicts.

Keep in mind that a spiral can take place within the individual as well as between people in interpersonal interactions. In the former kind of spiral, for example, a person shamed becomes enraged and smashes his favorite object which, in turn, shames him, which again leads to rage and, again, destruction of another object, and so on. This type of spiral usually leads upward toward increasing violence and destruction which becomes ever more difficult to self-regulate. Termination of the spiral results either from exhaustion or from the intercession of another who calms the raging person. In the interpersonal spiral, at least two people interact to keep the shame-rage oscillation active. A man rages at his wife, who becomes sad. The man feels shame because he has caused his wife's distress, but he does not own his shame—instead, he displaces it to anger at his wife, etc. It could also be the case that the man's shame-rage leads to his wife's shame-rage which, in turn, leads to more shame-rage in him. I will return to these problems shortly.

Before proceeding to discuss interpersonal behavior around shame, we need to make sure the distinction between anger and rage is understood. Anger is a primary emotion, a response designed to overcome an obstacle or frustration. The anger response consists of a particular neuromuscular facial expression and body activity designed to overcome the source of the frustration. The connection between frustration and anger has long been recognized. Anger is a natural and normal occurrence in organisms, including humans, in their daily attempts to overcome barriers. Some have likened it to will.[21]

Rage, in contrast, is more intense and less related to overcoming an obstacle. Rage is anger out of control. Rage is associated with a serious, intense wounding of the self. Kohut's discussion of narcissistic rage is very helpful, though this phrase may be redundant: all rage is narcissistic.[22] I think the following distinction is useful: anger is a response to a frustration of our action, while rage is a response to an injury to the self. This distinction suggests that anger is a response that enables us in overcoming an obstacle, and rage is a response to shame.[23]

This conceptualization has recently been presented by Suzanne Retzinger.[24] In her studies of the shame-rage spiral, she has drawn a distinction that she calls "shame-rage response versus the rage response." From my perspective, she is making a distinction between rage and anger, although she calls one "normal rage" and the other "rage/shame/rage." Even so, her analysis is helpful in distinguishing between anger and rage. According to Retzinger, normal rage, or what I call anger, is different from rage in nine ways. Anger is a simple bodily response, whereas rage is a process, moving from shame to rage in alternative spiral fashion. Anger feels justified, whereas in rage one feels powerless. Injury is recognized in anger, but injury is denied in rage. Anger is conscious, whereas rage, based on shame substitution, is pushed from awareness. While anger may be easily resolved, rage, initiated by shame, sets up a feeling trap in which shame leads to rage which, in turn, leads to shame, etc. Anger is not displaced, whereas rage is. Anger focuses on the actual cause, whereas rage is a generalized response. Anger is an individual phenomenon, rage is a social phenomenon. Anger results in few negative consequences, and rage results in many. As these differences suggest, anger is a restricted, focused response while rage is not; and anger has a specific object, while rage tends to be diffused both in terms of its occurrence and in terms of its object. Finally, anger appears bounded, that is, there is a way to resolve it; whereas rage itself may be unbounded.

In the same way that I have chosen to speak of shame-depression, I will use the shame-rage axis when talking about traits. When I talk about particular situations, I will employ the expressions shame-sadness or shame-anger. We now will turn to specific classes of interpersonal difficulties that are best seen in the context of shame spirals. Although I will consider mostly shame-rage, shame-depression also is part of these interpersonal exchanges and will be presented when appropriate. In what follows, I will try to show that such diverse phenomena as child abuse, crimes of passion, minority and underclass crime, as well as a set of adult and parent-child interactions, are shame dependent.

Uncovering Shame in Interpersonal Relationships

Child Abuse

*I recently was in a department store, where I witnessed a mother with her
young child, a boy about 5 years old. The mother wanted to shop and the
child was crawling around under some garments. She told the child to stop,
but he continued to play. She then grabbed him and picked him up, at which
point he began to cry loudly. She looked around and saw another woman
looking at her. She appeared to be shamed by her child's loud crying. To get
him to quiet, she hit him. This only made him cry more and drew more
attention to her. She hit him again to get him to stop. He only cried more.
She was about to hit the child again, when a saleswoman came over and
gave the child a lollipop to quiet him.*

What happened here? This was a shame-rage spiral. The child's
behavior, crying in public after being stopped from crawling on the floor,
made the mother ashamed; the mother's unacknowledged shame led to
rage and her hitting the child, which, in turn, led to more shame which led
to more rage. This progression, or spiral, is likely to be the cause of many
forms of violence. While this mother-child interaction did not embody the
kind of child abuse we read about in the papers, it did have the same basic
structure as those more serious cases.

The study of child abuse has revealed some interesting facts relevant to
my hypothesis. Abused children are often characterized by some difficulty.
Low-birthweight, premature children are more likely to be physically
abused than other children, for example, and evidence suggests that
children with difficult temperament—that is, children who are not readily
soothable—are also more likely to be abused. Can such a difference and
the shame-rage spiral inform us about abuse?

Consider this particular scenario. The caregiver attempts to quiet a
distressed baby. The baby does not quiet readily because of its characteristics. The caregiver's attempt at mothering does not seem to work. As a
consequence, the caregiver feels shame over her (or his) failure to soothe
the child. Shame turns to rage. Because the source of the shame is the child
and her crying, the caregiver strikes out and smacks it. The child, of
course, does not quiet. The caregiver's abusive act precipitates increased
shame, which leads to further rage. This spiraling effect of shame/rage/
shame results in child abuse. John Reid, in studying the punishment
patterns of abusing and nonabusing parents, found that the punishing

bouts varied in length.[25] Abusing parents' abusive chain was three times as long as an abusive chain for a nonabusing parent! This indicates that once abusing parents start to punish they have trouble stopping. I suggest that their shame-rage spiral is out of control. Because of this spiraling effect, what with another parent would be simple punishment of the child becomes, in effect, child abuse, resulting in serious injury or even death to the child.

Parental Shame in the Middle Class:
My Child Doesn't Love Me

It appears to be the case that the start of an abusing sequence occurs when there is a perceived failure in parenting. The caregiver tries to get the child to behave in a certain way. If the child does not behave in the desired way, the caregiver registers failure as a parent, and this failure leads to a sense of shame. My observation of parents and children has presented me with countless examples of the following sequence: Mother or father says to the child, "You cannot do this." "This" refers to something that the child wants to do. The child either starts to cry, or protests, or might even be sad and distressed from being prohibited from carrying out the action. The child's behavior, especially the protest and sad behavior, serves as a stimulus to evoke shame in the parents.

This shame may arise from several causes. The parents may feel that they have let the child down. The child's upset may cause the parent to worry that the child is withdrawing love from them. Interestingly, the loss of love from one's child can evoke shame in the same way that the loss of love from another adult can. Rage follows and the parent may strike out, physically or verbally, at the child for protesting the parent's refusal to let him do what he wants. In effect, the parent is saying to the child, "Not only can you not do what you want to do, but you cannot be unhappy about not being able to do it."

Until I understood the role of shame in this interaction, it was a mystery to me why parents could not appreciate the fact that children might acquiesce to their request but did not have to be happy about it. Isn't it obvious that it is too much to expect children to be happy about being told not to do something they want to do? Why, then, should parents be so upset over the fact that children are unhappy over being told not to do something? The reason, of course, resides in the shame-rage connection. A child's protest, unhappiness, and distress can trigger parental shame and result in rage. Discussing this sequence with parents, we found that they immediately understand and agree that shame may be at work, since there is no logical reason why they should be angry because a child is upset at not being able to do something he wants to do. Thus, even in more normal circumstances the shame-rage spiral appears at work.

Crimes of Passion

A police detective told me something interesting about murders: forensic experts can give the police some idea as to the likely identity of the murderer just by examining the extent and nature of the physical injury that led to the person's death. Homicides come in two types. There are those in which the victim is killed in a rather simple and direct fashion: shot, stabbed, or strangled. Others involve a multitude of wounds and destructive forces: the victim is shot 10 times, stabbed repeatedly, or murdered by a combination of stabbing, shooting, and mutilation. These brutal murders are quite different than the single-wound murders. Although all murders are likely to be committed by someone the person knows, brutal murders are likely to be caused by someone the victim knows well, usually a family member.[26] I asked the detective why this should be the case. He responded, "Clearly, in every murder, there is anger and perhaps even rage, although some murders are done for financial gain in which there may be no rage [a contract killing, for example]. In simple murders, the person is injured sufficiently to kill them. In the brutal murders, someone in effect is murdered 10 times over. Those murders are likely to be murders of rage. Murders of rage are most likely to be caused by someone who knows the victim."

I have puzzled over his statement for quite some time. It seems to me that the shame-rage spiral fits the phenomenon the police detective described. A brutal murder is likely to be caused by someone the person knows well because it is likely to be caused by the shame-rage of the murderer. The victim, either knowingly or not, shames the murderer, who becomes enraged over the shame and commits multiple violence against the victim.

I was asked to testify, as an expert witness, in a case in which a husband was accused of murdering his wife. Although I did not have the opportunity to examine the murderer, I was asked to examine their 2-year-old child. I was told by the husband's lawyer that the reason he committed the murder was because he came downstairs early one morning and saw his wife at the back door kissing her lover. The husband described his experience as humiliating and then reported going white with rage. He proceeded to pick up an iron bar and strike her many times, crushing her skull and killing her instantly. Psychiatric testimony, on his behalf, indicated the personality of a man who was, in general, easily offended by others and who often engaged in physical violence when he thought he had been offended.

This idea of being offended reflects the person's feeling of being humiliated or shamed through the action of another. In this particular case, his wife's infidelity was sufficiently humiliating to him that he was shamed and enraged, resulting in her brutal murder. Shame and humiliation can lead to rage. Such findings are supported by Katz's studies that indicate that humiliation underlies violent family quarrels and often leads to homicide.[27] Moreover, Lansky, in studying marital relationships, found that relationships involving spousal abuse are rampant with shame as stimuli for these specific emotions.[28]

Crime, Criminals, and Racism

Rage can take the form of violence, both against individuals and against property. If we walk through any large city in the United States, we are struck by the amount of violence against property that we can identify: telephones ripped out of public phone booths, buildings vandalized, monuments and statues defaced with graffiti. All of these bear witness to a destructive element on the part of some segment of the citizenry against the superstructure of the society in which they live. While such action against the structures of cities can be found in other countries, it clearly seems to be more extensive here than in Europe or Asia.

How are we to understand the violence against property that we see in this country? Might it not be the case that the poor, the black, the disenfranchised are continuously shamed? I think we can apply the shame-rage spiral to much of the antisocial action that we see around us.[29]

The *New York Times* magazine section for 20 August 1989 included an article entitled *Willie Horton and Me*, written by Anthony Walton. Mr. Walton is a writer and filmmaker, a successful, black, middle-class professional. He related how one night a temporary doorman at his Greenwich Village highrise refused to let him pass into the building because he was black: he assumed that a black man could not live in such a building. He went on to relate another instance of discrimination: "A friend's landlord in Brooklyn asked if I was living in his apartment. We had been working on a screenplay, under deadline, and I was there several days in a row. The landlord said that she didn't mind, but neighbors . . ." The neighbors would not like a black man living there. He also described waiting 30 minutes for a taxicab and finally realizing that no taxicab driver was going to stop and pick him up because he was a black man. Walton went on to say, "I am recognizing my veil of double consciousness, my American self and my black self. I must battle, like all humans, to see myself. I must also battle, because I am black, to see myself as others see me."

It seems to me that this black man is telling us that, even as a middle-class, successful human being, he continues to be humiliated and shamed because of his skin color. His realization that he is humiliated and shamed because he is black leads him increasingly toward a dissatisfaction, which, in turn, leads him "to despise the White Dragon, instead of the Dragon of Racism." Notice the term "despise." Walton also talked about how his best friends probably would not understand why "I was ready to start World War III over perceived slights at an American Express office." This articulate, sensitive human being is crying out for the need to recognize how white society treats blacks and how the shame inflicted by whites upon blacks must be faced and owned up to because that humiliation and shame carries with it the potential for black rage and violence.

I mention this article, in part, to drive home the point that the consequences of poverty and of minority status include not only the powerlessness that derives from such conditions, but also shame. If my analysis of the shame-rage spiral makes sense, we must recognize its applicability to the social as well as to the individual level. The illogical ravaging of our cities and their infrastructure must be related to the intrapsychic phenomenon of shame. I suggest that poor, black males, in particular, are shamed in many ways by the culture in which they live. They are shamed by how they are treated as students in our school systems; they are shamed by the inability to find jobs; they are shamed by the police; they are shamed by their mere identity as a black minority in a white majority society. All these causes of shame—and many, many more I have not enumerated—are likely to produce rage.

Poverty, school failure, and delinquency continue to plague our society. These associated problems are usually considered by evaluating the capacity of the delinquent child. Multiple problems associated with overall mental ability and specific capacities usually are considered.[30] For example, Michael Chandler found that aggressive boys were deficient in role-taking skills, and others have found that aggressive boys have problems generating alternative solutions to social problems.[31] Ample evidence indicates that juvenile delinquents do poorly in school. The meaning of the association between delinquency and school failure, however, remains unclear. It may be that school failure and delinquency are related to the same general problem. The assumption here is that low ability results in both types of problems.

The cause of the delinquency can be found in the characteristics of the child: a not very bright child may be prone to delinquent behavior. This certainly is the general belief. But other possibilities, including the shame-rage spiral, need to be considered. A child who can neither read nor write is going to be a problem in school, and so he drops out; having too much free time and little to do, he gets into trouble. This analysis, related to the old adage that idle hands make for devil's play, may be correct. This interpretation avoids the possibility of shame. Imagine yourself, however, in a school situation in which you repeatedly are informed about your inadequacy. Day after day you fail in the tasks you are given. Children who fail in school are likely to be shamed and humiliated by their failure. Thus, the connection between school failure and delinquency may not be due to intellectual weakness as many would have us believe; rather, it is more likely to be due to the shame produced by failure and the rage that follows. This rage is both self directed and other directed. Not only the incidence of delinquency but the incidence of suicide is very high among the poor and disadvantaged. Crime is not committed just because the criminal is dull. Crime obviously also results from the rage part of the shame spiral. The connection between school failure and delinquency is real, but I believe this connection is causal rather than related to the intellectual characteristics of the children. Application of the shame-rage spiral suggests a program of prevention and possible cure. If we could increase these children's positive feelings about themselves, we should be able to eliminate many social problems. Putting delinquent or potentially delinquent children into situations of success and helping them to build self-esteem is more likely to prevent antisocial behavior than further punitive action. This same analysis can be applied to rage responses that are turned inward and result in suicide or drug addiction. The solution I propose is a cognitive-affective program designed to reduce shame.

The association between events likely to cause shame and antisocial outcomes is obvious, if one accepts this perspective. I recently read a research report from the University of Stockholm, part of a longitudinal study exploring the problems of delinquency. Stattin and Klachenberg-Larsson, the authors, note a connection between delinquency and parents' preference for their child's gender.[32] The results showed the prevalence for delinquency to be about twice as high for children whose parents wanted a child of the opposite sex as it was for children whose sex was consistent with the parents' preference. This finding supports the connection between delinquency and shame. Desired less, loved less, and, perhaps, even rejected and humiliated because of its gender, the child becomes a candidate for the shame-rage spiral.

Such studies, linking aggression and delinquency to a lowered self-esteem or shame, are not unique. Slaby and Guerra, in a study of male and female adolescents incarcerated for antisocial aggressive offenses, found other evidence to support the connection.[33] They found that antisocial and aggressive individuals believed that their use of aggression was a legitimate response and, in particular, that it *increased self-esteem* and helped avoid a negative image. The finding that aggressive behavior facilitates an increase in self-esteem and helps to avoid a negative image supports my argument that the shame-rage spiral may be useful in understanding antisocial behavior.

Repeatedly, we find evidence that a weak sense of self (low self-esteem or shame) contributes to aggression. Toch, speaking of prisoners, said "that they invariably respond with violence to defend themselves against belittlement."[34] He also found in his work with prisoners that those who feel worthless seek violent encounters to convince others that they are fearless. Thus, not only does low self-esteem lead to aggressive behavior, but that aggressive behavior itself may facilitate self-esteem. In the work of Norma Feshbach and Seymour Feshbach, the relationship between self-concept and aggression are correlated such that low self-esteem leads to aggression.[35] Otto Rank, in his theory of efficacy and power, was perhaps the first to bring to our attention the role of loss of esteem or self-worth and its relationship to aggression.[36]

A teacher in a prison for adolescent delinquent males reported to me that the males would often be physically violent toward one another for the least provocative of situations. One, in particular, struck her as rather unusual.

She told me that when a boy in a classroom passed wind, often the boy sitting next to him would become angered and would get up and punch him in the face. I asked her what she thought was the cause of this rather violent outbreak over such a mild provocation. She replied to me that she thought that the wind pass (the fart) was an embarrassment to the person sitting close to it. Perhaps such a situation is, in some unanalyzed way, related to shame. Perhaps people with low self-esteem confuse being in the presence of someone who farts with the different situation of actually being farted upon. To be deliberately farted upon, obviously, is a humiliating and shameful event for most people. In this case, shame and rage are provoked by an innocent act that shames.

Suicide: Depression or Shame?

Suicide usually is thought of as the ultimate measure of depression. The destruction of the self is used to index this state. However, Melvin Lansky, in his work on families and suicide, states, "But it is unlikely that suicidality results from depression itself as opposed to the patient's shame over his or her depressive preoccupations."[37] Suicide is likely to be the result of shame associated with rage directed inward. Durkheim, in his classical study of the problem, noted that suicide is related to shame. In fact, there are cultural differences in suicide related to shame. In prewar Japan, shame was associated with suicide. Indeed, suicide was an expected and appropriate response to being shamed. As murder is the outward manifestation of the shame-rage spiral, suicide is its inward manifestation. Lansky suggests that suicidal patients are shame-prone and are "exquisitely sensitive to both overregulation and abandonment by supportive persons" and are "flooded with shame if a less than optimal distance is maintained."[38]

When I was a boy, I had a friend, Gerald, who committed suicide. I could never understand his reason until its relationship to shame became clear. One day he had an argument with his dad, the person he was most attached to. In the course of the argument, he pushed his father down. The father was stunned for a minute or two and Gerald yelled, "I killed him," upon which he ran to the nearest subway station and threw himself in front of a train.

I always thought that he might have been frightened, even horrified, at what he thought he did, but such self-violence did not make sense. That he was overwhelmed by shame for striking his father makes more sense. In fact, what this example points to is a rage/shame/rage spiral. For whatever reason, he was enraged at his father and struck him, producing shame which, in turn, produced rage turned toward himself.

———— • ————

Much of our interpersonal life revolves around the shame-rage axis. Families and friends need to cope with this unresolved dilemma. Because of the likely sex differences in its use, it characterizes men's more than women's behavior. This only exaggerates the male-female struggle. If the analysis I have presented here is correct, the only way to meet the societal problems of rage is to reduce shame. Retribution and punishment may not only fail to reduce rage because these methods focus on rage itself rather than shame, rage's cause. Perhaps forgiveness rather than punishment, and understanding rather than humiliation, need to shape our view of correction. Obviously, more humiliation and punishment will not stop the shame-rage spiral.

My interpretation of the conversion of prolonged shame into depression and rage reveals the powerful consequences of this emotion. The inability to confront repeated shaming experiences and the inability to withdraw from the shaming world combine to force the person to adapt other strategies for survival. In extreme forms, the suffering individual manifests rage or depression, and in the most extreme forms, the individual experiences deterioration of the self to the point of psychosis.

9

Pathologies of Self

Narcissism and Multiple Personalities

Disorders arising from disturbance in the self system have become more prominent. The idea that disorders change over time is a rather puzzling one, especially when the disorders are psychological. We know that physical disorders and diseases change. Some changes are the result of new information; the discovery of inoculation has eliminated smallpox and greatly reduced the occurrence of many other diseases. Other physical disorders have become rarer because of our greater control over the environment; the draining of swampland has caused a drop in malaria cases, for example. Antibiotics have eliminated a variety of adult and childhood diseases. But as we gain more control over some forms of disease, new ones appear; AIDS is a dramatic example, but herpes simplex infection and Legionnaires' disease also come to mind.

But what about psychological illness? Here, too, changes in the environment probably bring about new and eliminate old disorders. However, we do not as yet have good theories to account for these changes. The appearance of some disorders might be explained by better record keeping or by a greater willingness to report them. Sexual abuse appears to be such a problem. Although sexual abuse seems to have increased, in truth it was always present, but hidden. What has changed is our recognition of the problem, not the problem itself. The same is true of child abuse and neglect. Some disorders appear to have decreased. Hysterical patients, so common in Freud's day, are rare today, and obsessive compulsive disorders seem to be declining.

Two disorders for which I have a special interest have been reported to be increasing: narcissistic illnesses and multiple personality disorders.

Both are related to self systems and to shame. Because of their relevance for a theory of shame, I now wish to focus attention on these two illnesses. Their increase, if true, enables us to explore changes in the self system and shame in Western culture historically, because it is in the United States and Europe that increases in these disorders now are being observed.

Narcissism

Narcissism and Unacknowledged Shame

I must first try to distinguish between narcissism as a description of people's action in the world and narcissism as a disorder.[1] Unfortunately, the use of the term for both normal processes and psychopathology continues to cause difficulty. For example, Freud distinguished two forms of narcissism: primary narcissism involved the initial libidinal investment of energy to the as yet undifferentiated ego, while secondary narcissism made reference to a withdrawal of psychic energy from objects back to the ego.[2] Freud saw self-regard or self-esteem as being related to primary narcissism; however, he never revised this idea in terms of his structured theory of personality. In some sense, then, Freud viewed primary narcissism as a normal phase, a position developed by Kohut.[3] Kohut, unlike many of the ego psychologists before him, argued that narcissism is not necessarily pathological but, instead, leads to object love (love for another) at the beginning of life. In its more mature form, narcissism leads to other skills, for example, to creativity, empathy (putting the self in the place of the other), and humor. From another perspective, we can think of narcissism, at least nonpathological narcissism, as a will to power, assertiveness, or even anger and intention.[4]

The difficulty in the use of this term for both normal and abnormal processes becomes compounded when we deal with self psychologies. I think that the term narcissism should be reserved for the psychopathological, a belief that dictates my use of terms here. My work with newborns, infants, and children informs me that, from the moment of birth (and perhaps even before), the infant is an active organism in pursuit of biologically adaptive goals, which I term *competence* or *efficacy*. One of the great discoveries of the research effort with infants over the last 30 years has been our recognition of the degree and speed with which infants show competence. For example, the infant, by a few weeks of age, can learn to pull a string to produce a desired outcome and, when that outcome ceases, becomes angry and tries harder to produce the effect. This will or efficacy exists on a variety of levels. He does not become self-reflective, however, until objective self-awareness emerges in the second half of the second year of life. Nevertheless, the competency can be observed early. Desire, in the form of goal-directed behavior, exists from the beginning of life.

Narcissism as pathology has been interpreted in the *Diagnostic and Statistical Manual of Mental Disorders* (DSM-IIIR)[5] as a pretentious show of self-importance, such as an obsession with illusions of endless success, power, radiance, beauty, or ideal love; exhibitionism; a cool indifference or rage, subservience, shame, and emptiness; a conviction of entitlement, manipulation, overidealization, or deflation; and lack of compassion. This definition appears to be a distillation of a variety of thoughts ranging from Freud's original statements to Kohut's and Mahler's more recent views. Throughout this volume, I have suggested that a structural approach to the self-conscious emotions might be helpful in defining narcissism. This I will do now, arguing that an inability to cope with shame and humiliation underlies this pathological disturbance. I will then employ the mechanisms used to cope with shame to describe narcissists in their daily interactions.

The focus of this analysis of narcissism is shame-based.[6] For reasons yet to be considered, narcissists are readily shame-prone and, because of this tendency, act to avoid experiencing shame. They try to avoid shame either by utilizing a set of ideations designed to avoid shame, or, when this process does not work, by engaging in emotional behavior that masks their underlying shame. Let us return to my model.

I start with the most critical feature, namely, that some people are disposed to making global evaluations of themselves, especially around negative events. The underlying cause of narcissism is this propensity to focus on the whole self when evaluating failure. Because of this focus, failure is likely to result in shame, and success is likely to result in hubris. Narcissists are prideful people. Their tendency to make a global evaluation affects both their standards and the evaluative process of failure in regard to these standards. An individual can avoid shame by never experiencing failure; the individual can avoid failure by setting her standards low, so as to never risk her inability to meet them. But low standards, because they are easily met, create the feeling of hubris. People prone to making global attributions of negative events are likely to set standards that are too low. In a sense, their behavior is sociopathic because their values and goal structures reflect a lower level than those commonly set by people around them. We have the feeling with such personalities that they are willing to try to get away with more.

But global attribution–prone individuals also set unrealistically high standards, which has the effect of increasing shame. Why, then, should such unrealistic demands be made? Perhaps their expectation of shame leads them to create this raised standard. Alternatively, past successes probably led to hubris, a feeling that they want to reinstate. Finally, and perhaps most likely, they have just not learned to set appropriate standards. If they are readily shamed, they may not have learned how to set realistic goals and therefore set goals that are either too low or too high.

However, other ideational defenses related to evaluation are also possible. All people evaluate their behavior relative to a standard in terms of success or failure. But some people are likely to claim success unrealistically, that is, most other people with the same standards who enacted the same behaviors would be likely to evaluate their behavior as failure. An unrealistic evaluation of success is characteristic of grandiosity. Such unrealistic evaluation is designed to increase hubris and to avoid shame. A narcissist evaluates an action that most other people would interpret as a failure as a success. Such unrealistic evaluation marks the self-aggrandizing way in which a narcissist behaves.

If a narcissist can not judge a particular behavior successful relative to her standard, she enlists other techniques of evaluation in order to avoid shame. For example, the narcissist can recognize failure but still avoid shame by deciding that the failure is not her own fault. This form of ideation allows global attribution–prone individuals to defend against failure by the expedient device of claiming that it was not their fault but instead the fault of someone else, or of chance. Narcissistic personalities exert large amounts of interpersonal control in an attempt to ensure that failure does not occur. The habit of blaming others rather than the self obviously makes for difficult interpersonal relationships.

> *I had a patient, a woman, who was so shame-prone that she could not admit to any fault. To admit fault resulted in such intense shame feelings that she could not function. Her device, then, was to blame all those around her so that she could avoid feeling badly. Her marriage was falling apart because her husband could not understand why she was not able to assume some of the blame for their problems. Marital therapy was unsuccessful, since she was unable to arrive at an equal distribution of fault because of her shame problem.*

The attributions necessary to avoid shame involve unrealistic standards, blaming others for failure, and claims of success that are out of keeping with group norms. One final set of behaviors, having to do with control, is also involved in warding off shame. Shame-prone individuals need to control events around them in order to be able to effect the proper attributional stance. They need to pick which standards to accept, which to discard, what behaviors in their service need to be initiated, and who evaluates the outcome. Since they have little control over the global attributional aspect of the process, they attempt to exert control over all other aspects. These features match the characteristics associated with a narcissistic personality. They are related to a global or self-focus evaluation rather than an action focus.

Before leaving this analysis, I must mention one last set of behaviors associated with narcissism. Given the need to avoid shame and given the likelihood that shame cannot always be avoided, the narcissistic personality is likely to employ the more extreme forms of response to experienced shame. When shamed, the narcissist is likely to employ the emotional substitutions of depression or rage. Given our cultural constraints, in general female narcissists are likely to employ depression, males, rage.

Socialization of Narcissism

Narcissistic disorders refer to a class of difficulties that have as their core the likelihood of making global attributions about self failure. Notice that the diagnostic criteria I referred to earlier contain a broad and contradictory set of descriptions, including a sense of self-importance and feelings of inferiority. The best way to understand this divergent set of behaviors and feelings is to make reference to its relationship to shame avoidance. Narcissistic disorders can be found in both men and women, and are associated with individuals who are likely to make a global evaluation of their own failure. It is likely that the form of the disorder will be different for men and women. This difference can be traced to the different roles men and women have in our society and also to the different types of socialization they experience. Men, as we have seen, are likely to show those behaviors related to action: power, exhibitionism, rage, exploitation, etc. Women are likely to show overidealization, devaluation, ideal love, etc.

I have already considered the critical factors in socialization, and so I will not dwell on them again. Summary however, might be useful. Many parental factors lead the child toward a focus on the self rather than on the action. These include the use of global self rather than specific action attributions, for example, saying "You are bad" instead of "What you did and the way you did it is wrong." In addition to these attributions, the parent's tone of socialization and use of shame and humiliation as socialization devices may lead to the global focus. Moreover, withdrawal of love and traumatic events such as the death or even the serious illness of the parent may lead to this type of attribution.

One other parental practice also may lead to the global, self-focus style. This practice is not considered negative; indeed, it is a recommended parent behavior. This behavior is praising our children. There has been an increase in this type of parental behavior, and it may have more serious implications than anyone realized. Extreme praise and overindulgence may increase global self-focus. Praise of the what-a-wonderful-person-you-are kind focuses the child toward the global self. Such parental praise, although not negative in nature, may focus the child on global features rather than on action. The Japanese avoid praise because they believe that such praise leads to individuation and self-focus rather than to the self-in-group focus that the Japanese culture wishes to promote.[7] We need to keep in mind that global attributions can be caused by too much of a good thing as well as by too much of a bad thing, such as trauma and pain. The modern view of parenting orients adults toward overpraising their children, and may be associated with more narcissistic disorders. Early experiences are most likely to promote global self-focus. Once established, the mechanisms of attribution that I have discussed are likely to generate "narcissistic-like" behavior. Different behaviors or expressions of this type are the consequences of socializing experiences having to do with such factors as emotional expressiveness and the societal acceptance of aggressive behaviors.

Multiple Personality Disorders (MPD)

The phenomenon and study of multiple personality disorders (hereafter called MPD) are valuable since they inform us both about the nature of the self and the role of shame in self development. Some people are inclined to consider MPD a fraud, the device of individuals wishing to fake mental illness, perhaps to avoid the blame for some crime or other serious transgression. Certainly, it is useful to say, in effect, "It wasn't me, it was someone else who did it." Many people have expressed serious doubt about the phenomenon's authenticity. Alternatively, MPD may be part of the psychotic ideation of a borderline personality.[8] It may be just one aspect of a general delusional pattern of thought and feeling. Indeed, some have argued that MPD is caused by patients' susceptibility to the clinician's or hypnotist's suggestions. None or all of these ideas may be true. The phenomenon, however, is fascinating, and until recently there has been little information concerning it.[9]

My fascination with the topic reflects the hidden belief we all have about the nature of our selves. The idea that multiple forces exist and vie for our attention and control is, in fact, quite popular. The notion of devil and angel, one on each shoulder, reflects this divided self. The belief that there is "more than one of us in here influencing our behavior" is based on our observation that we often do things we neither want to do nor think of doing. For example, I often promise myself that I will not snack when I am working but then find myself doing so anyway. The idea of multiple selves, with good and evil battling for our souls, is a Western belief thousands of years old. This belief was given a new form by Freud's structural analysis of the personality. The id, ego, and superego battling each other for the control of impulses represents a modern, scientific version of the older Christian view of the struggle in the soul between good and evil. The multiple aspects of our personality are well recognized, although always within the idea of the unity of the self.

We act in ways that naturally lead us to the idea that there are different selves within us. Some of these processes we are aware of (they are called conscious), and some we are not aware of (unconscious). Interestingly, until recently, personality theorists as well as psychiatrists considered these different processes as part of a whole, the whole being one personality. Cognitive theories attempt to deal with this same problem by talking about levels of knowledge and the organization of these levels.[10] I have already discussed these levels or modes in terms of intentionality, suggesting that a levels approach allows us to explain such problems as intentions of which we are objectively aware and intentions of which we are not objectively aware.[11] As I tried to show when discussing the self, it is possible to have a knowledge of a thing but not to have knowledge of the knowledge of a thing. These different levels of self all exist within ourselves. The concept of a unity of self is our construction to explain these diverse and, at times, contradictory actions.[12]

Disassociation in its extreme form characterizes MPD. However, disassociation can also occur at less pathological levels. In the simplest case of disassociation, we do not focus on certain aspects of ourselves objectively, and therefore we do not know of certain actions. For example, while driving to work we suddenly arrive at a particular street and do not remember getting there or making the turns necessary to get there. Of course, throughout the period of driving we had some level of awareness since the route involved elaborate memory about turns and distance and physical actions such as braking, shifting, and signaling our intention to turn. This kind of disassociation is an example of removing objective attention from ourselves.

In more severe cases of disassociation entire aspects of ourselves are objectively unavailable to us. As Ross has pointed out, in disassociation, especially in MPD, there is a breakdown of the unity of self.[13] Modern neurophysiology also supports this view of multiple selves. Split brain research and studies showing hemispheric differences in function, both cognitive and affective, have led to the view that there are at least two selves, each corresponding to a different brain hemisphere.

The most recent work on neurophysiology supports the notion of multiple sites of higher mental processing. For example, Joseph LeDoux associates the amygdala in animals with emotional encoding.[14] Similar findings have been reported in humans.[15] These new findings in neurophysiology support the general proposition that multiple areas of the brain are capable of processing information. Moreover, these different areas may not be in direct communication with one another. If this were true, then we would have solid evidence to support the idea that humans process information, especially affective information, in a variety of locations in the brain. This idea gives physiological support to our notions of multiple selves and disassociational processes. MPD, then, fits into a new frame of viewing the self.

The *Diagnostic and Statistical Manual of Mental Disorders* (DSM-IIIR) describes MPD as consisting of two features: that there is within the person two or more distinct personalities or personality states, each having its own relatively lasting pattern of perception, thought, and relation to the environment and self; and that at least two of these personalities or personality states periodically take over control of the person's behavior.

The reported increase in the diagnosis of this disorder is amazing. Several investigators report an incredible rate of increase in the Western world—for example, 33 cases from the period 1901–1944, 14 from the period 1944–1969, 500 by 1980, and 6000 by the middle of the 1980s.[16] This increase may be due to two different factors. First, the disorder may be totally new. For whatever cultural reasons, modern times may have produced multiple personalities. Second, the disorder may always have been present, but was not attended to or, if attended to, was seen as a part of another disorder. The last seems the more likely case. MPD may well have been classified under schizophrenia in the recent past. Remember that schizophrenia comes from the Greek meaning "split mind." Indeed, schizophrenia was used originally to describe this disorder. Before schizophrenia was introduced as a diagnostic category, there were many reports of MPD. However, when the schizophrenia classification caught on, in the 1920s and early 1930s, there was a sharp drop in the use of the term MPD. Thus, it seems that the multiple personality phenomenon has been around for some time, though previously it was often called something else. The increase in identified cases of MPD most likely reflects a renewed focus on these patients.

The idea that MPD existed prior to its dramatic increase in the 1980s is supported from a number of sources. Demonic possession, an accusation leading to death at the stake in the Middle Ages and Renaissance, may have been an earlier example of MPD.[17] The classification of MPD is very close to a description of those supposedly possessed by a demonic force. Even the early psychological literature makes reference to multiple personality. Although William James, at the turn of the century, discussed the various selves that made up the normal self, it is unclear whether he had MPD in mind. Nevertheless, another early psychologist, Morton Prince, first editor of the *Journal of Abnormal Psychology*, wrote about MPD and described a case fitting the description of a multiple personality.[18] Ernest Hilgard has reported much of this research under the general theme of dissociation.[19] It appears certain, then, that this disorder is not new, but for some reason it has not received the attention it deserves.

The etiology of MPD has been explored from a clinical perspective. In general, the female to male ratio is on the order of 10:1; some believe, however, that more men could be identified. The causes of MPD appear to be early childhood trauma, almost always in the form of sexual abuse. The sexual-abuse origin of the disorder may be the main reason for the female to male ratio, for females are thought to be the more likely targets of such abuse. But recent evidence suggests that boys are sexually abused more often than we have thought.[20] Early childhood sexual trauma may lead to dissociation, with the child in effect saying, "This isn't happening to me, it's happening to her!" It may be important to note that Freud and Breuer originally thought that their female patients had been sexually abused and that this abuse was the cause of their hysteria symptoms. But these symptoms might also have been a sign of MPD. "Anna O." was an important patient for their studies on hysteria. Ernest Jones, in his biography of Freud, writing about her, noted: "More interesting, however, was the presence of two distinct states of consciousness: one a fairly normal one, the other that of a naughty and troublesome child, *rather like Morton Prince's famous case of Sally Beauchamp. It was thus a case of double personality.*"[21] Breuer, too, noticed this double personality: "Two entirely distinct states of consciousness were present which alternated very frequently."[22] These studies, as well as the case histories now collected, reveal that sexual abuse can lead to a wide variety of disorders, including such severe dissociative disorders as multiple personality.

Let us, for a moment, accept the idea that dissociation occurs as a consequence of early and severe childhood trauma, usually of a sexual nature. If such events occur and lead to dissociation, we need a mechanism to account for this process. Clearly, a powerful emotion needs to be at work. From the analysis up to this point, it appears reasonable to conclude that abuse, sexual or otherwise, leads to shame. The shame produced is too powerful and painful and needs to be transformed. During the shame-avoidance process the dissociation occurs. Recall that I have argued that, when shamed, the self attempts to remove itself from the shamed self. One can remove oneself in a variety of ways, many of which I have already discussed. The easiest ways include forgetting and laughter; more intense ways include emotional substitution; the most intense way may be the splitting of the self. The etiology of MPD may tell us that *traumatic and prolonged* shame experiences are likely to lead to this extreme form of dissociation, this fragmentation of the self.

I believe that shame and dissociative processes have some systematic relation. Under simple and short-lived instances of shame, the dissociative process may be as mild as laughing with the other selves at one's own failure. With more intense shame experiences, the dissociation process becomes more complex: emotional substitution with depression and rage are the likely consequences. Under the most severe and prolonged shame, the most intense dissociation occurs: MPD. I suspect that this extreme form of dissociation is not available to every person. It is likely that some disposition requirement is necessary for this disorder to appear, the nature of which remains unknown but of interest for further study. Not everyone who suffers extreme and prolonged early childhood trauma develops MPD. Other escapes from prolonged and intense shame are possible, including other psychoses and suicide.

Many theorists think of MPD in terms of unconscious versus conscious processes, but it may actually be an extreme phenomena of different levels of focal attention. Ross has said, "There is no need for repression or for a concept of an unconscious. . . . the discarded products of mental con-sciousness in *dissociated form* are what is being observed."[23] Or, again, when talking about phenomena usually considered as unconsciousness: "For me, multiple personality disorder demonstrates that the so-called unconscious is not unconscious at all—it is wide-awake and cognitive in nature, but dissociated."[24] Ross goes on to say that a patient who misses a session is not unconsciously repressing the memory, but, rather, it is the work of an "alter," a dissociated other who is part of the self of this patient. This "alter," when contacted, is conscious and will "readily explain her motivation for taking executive control prior to the session and ensuring that she (the patient) missed it."[25] The usefulness of a cognitive levels approach or a dissociated approach rests on our willingness to suspend the idea that the unity of self exists. The unity of the self exists but not at the level of the actions of our bodies, including thinking, feeling, and behaving. It exists at the level of our objective self-awareness.

MPD has important implications for our study of self and self processes. We have seen that prolonged and severe early childhood trauma can lead to the creation of multiple selves. Two alternative views present themselves in relation to the organization of the self system. The first possibility grows out of the belief in the unity of the self. This is the idea of a single self as the natural, mature, and final state of human life. This state is disturbed by trauma. The trauma has the effect of splitting this unity. But we do not have to hold to the unity of the self as the final process. Here, the effect of the early trauma is to further split those selves who, under normal conditions, remain more integrated and in contact with one another, although not constituting a unity. That is, early childhood traumas can serve to accent the process that already exists. The answer to these two possibilities can only be found in our own view of the nature of the self. As we will see, different cultures, even technologically advanced cultures such as the Japanese, have very different views of the unity of the self and its relationship to other selves. MPD may be only an extreme form of these cultural artifacts.

10

Individual Differences and Shame Fights Between Couples

Some people appear to be more shame-prone than others. But individual differences should be expected because people differ in both their interpretation of failure and their willingness to acknowledge responsibility for it. Because of a paucity of data concerning individual differences, we will have to go far afield in our search for their origins. Most of the research literature focuses on guilt rather than shame and on achievement as the eliciting situation.

Individual differences are best studied by clinicians and by researchers analyzing groups. There has been little clinical study, so I will draw more on research, especially on those studies that examine sex differences in achievement.

Shame is a naturally occurring event. Like all emotions of which human beings are capable, shame has adaptive significance. As individuals, we have no desire to experience shame, but as a group few of us would care to live in a world in which shame was absent. Moreover, because shame helps us fixate on our behavior and focus on ourselves as well as our actions, it serves to define who we are and who we wish to be. For example, when patients finally recognize and admit that they are ashamed of a certain action, they have a very powerful motive for affecting their behavior and altering it. Thus, when I talk about shame and individual differences, I do not necessarily mean to imply that such differences are maladaptive. Clearly, in the extreme, they are; the psychopath who feels no shame and the shame-ridden or narcissistic individual both suffer from disorders and need treatment. But my focus will be on the normal range of individual differences in shame.

Shame in Individuals

Individual differences in shame are apparent once we care to observe them. A therapist, if prepared to look for shame, will notice that many patients initiate therapy because of their shame. Of course, not all problems derive from shame; various forms of psychosis are not necessarily shame-driven. But many character disorders in interpersonal relationships are associated with shame. Anyone who carefully observes people's emotional behavior will see that the incidence of shame is quite common, and that individuals have a wide variety of shame problems.

> *I recently overheard two women graduate students talking. One said to the other that she was ashamed of the presentation that she had just given in their seminar. Her friend replied that she was surprised to hear this admission because she thought the other student's performance had been excellent.*
>
> *A young patient of mine reported that she was ashamed of her body shape because she had "very small breasts while Jane [her best friend] had large breasts." When I asked her what Jane thought about her figure, she reported that her friend found her smaller figure quite attractive and often wished she was smaller so that she might fit into designer clothes.*

Such differences in shame experience may be useful in informing us about eating disorders, especially among females who are likely to be shamed over their physical appearance. Individual females differ in their responses to their perceived physical appearances. Some are unhappy about the way they look, but are not overly shamed by their appearance. Others are shamed but are able to cope with that shame and live relatively normal lives. But some women find their bodies so shameful that they go to such extremes as anorexia or bulimia in order to change what they perceive as a shameful appearance.[2]

Individual differences in shame are apparent early in life, as soon as objective self-awareness becomes possible. In a number of studies looking at children's performance ability in laboratory settings, people have observed marked differences in individuals' responses to failure. In a study discussed earlier, parents were asked to give their 3-year-old children a set of increasingly difficult tasks to solve. Only one-quarter of the children showed shame when they failed to solve an easy task. Only 1 out of 10 children showed shame when they failed to solve a difficult task. Such individual differences at the beginning of life reflect the processes likely to produce the differences we see in adults. The three children who demonstrated shame as a result of failing the hard tasks may already have had an overdeveloped notion of what constitutes success or failure; using a more familiar term, they may have had too strong a superego. During this study, I interviewed the parents and their children and discovered six pairs of parents who made strong demands on their children concerning performances. Three of these pairs had children who responded with shame response when failing a difficult task. All six parent pairs had children who showed shame responses at some time during the experiment, and three of the six were the parents of the children who responded with shame to failure on the difficult task.

In another study with 2 to 3 year olds, we observed children's responses after they transgressed a rule, in this case, peeking when we told them not to peek. About two-thirds of the children who peeked did not admit to the transgression—one-third lied, and one-third refused to answer the question "Did you peek?" Observation of the facial and bodily expressions of the children who refused to answer the question revealed behavior indicative of shame. Failure to answer was often accompanied by confusion and loss of speech, two other signs associated with shame. But the children who lied did not show any shame response. Again, individual differences in shame to a transgression were apparent.[3]

These data are consistent with observations of others. Barrett and Zahn-Waxler, for example, also found individual differences in the shame response.[4] In sum, these data, both the observation of adult differences in reported shame and the individual differences seen in the opening three years of life in the experience of shame, point to wide differences in degree of shame response.

I have already pointed to some of the reported sex differences between girls and boys and women and men concerning the likelihood of having shame. Sexism complicates our understanding of these differences. Until recent times psychology was a male-dominated field, and therefore reflected male bias. Men are more likely to experience guilt than shame, and when they do experience shame, are more likely to transform shame to anger, while women are more likely to experience shame than guilt, and tend to transform shame into depression. Men, probably because they are more guilt- than shame-prone, have, throughout history, focused far more on guilt (and morality) than on shame. Recently, Masson raised this issue in relation to Freud's theory of impulse control and guilt.[5]

Recall Freud's earliest cases, those that he and Breuer used to evolve the original theory on hysteria. Freud first argued that neurotic symptoms were caused by sexual abuse in childhood.[6] He reported that his first 16 patients, all women, had been sexually abused in one way or another. Thus, Freud's original formulation related sexual abuse to later psychopathology. Recall my earlier discussion of the relationship between sexual abuse and shame. It would be only a small step to go from being ashamed about being abused to developing neurotic symptoms. In other words, sexual abuse leads to shame, which leads to neurotic symptoms. But Freud altered his thinking so that neither sexual abuse nor shame caused the neurotic symptoms. In his revised theory, fantasy and impulse control, or its lack, were postulated as the cause of the neurotic symptoms, an explanation based upon anxiety and guilt. In other words, a male tendency to focus more on guilt than shame may have led Freud to substitute a guilt origin for a shame origin of neurotic symptoms.

H. B. Lewis believed that Freud's lack of attention to the topic of shame and his focus on guilt were related to his turning away from the seduction theory. Freud discussed shame in terms of the psychology of women, but only around his fantasy theory: "Shame, which is considered to be a feminine characteristic par excellence, has as its purpose, we believe, concealment of genital deficiency."[7] Freud's male bias and his failure to understand the psychology of women led him away from the study of shame. Discussing Freud's concern with guilt rather than shame, Lewis remarks, "Freud thus describes the superego of men in terms of the Kantean categorical imperative of guilt—as an internal Prussian gendarme (policeman), as what Marx once put it—while the superego of women took the inferior form of shame."[8]

Freud based his sex difference theory first on the Oedipus complex and on the compromised superego, which was not "independent of its emotional origins as we require it to be of men." This view of sex difference in moral development was also voiced by Lawrence Kohlberg. As Lewis says:

> In the literature, guilt more often signified an unconscious force that motivated behavior rather than the experiential state. Even more troublesome was how the literature treated the term "superego." The superego, although formally acknowledged to be a theoretical construct, was nevertheless treated as an established fact or an explanatory system. The superego was heir to the Oedipus complex. Both the superego and the Oedipus complex were regarded as established facts instead of as theoretical constructs. If women could

not live through the Oedipal complex because they were castrated, then their superegos were necessarily relatively underdeveloped.[9]

I will not linger on Freud's ideas concerning women's less developed moral sense since Carol Gilligan, in her book *In a Different Voice,* has made it quite clear that the male perspective on what constitutes moral behavior may have limited our understanding of our moral emotions and imposed a burden on gender differences, namely, that women have less moral sense than men.[10] Men may be more guilt-oriented than women. However, this orientation does not necessarily reflect sex differences in moral behavior; rather, it may well reflect sex differences in response to shame and guilt, or sex differences in the situations likely to elicit shame.

I questioned more than 200 students about situations likely to elicit shame and found some interesting sex differences. For men, there were two categories of situations most likely to elicit shame. The first is failure over a task deemed important. Such tasks are related to what I have called the core capacities, that is, those capacities deemed important for the definition of the self.[11] Such situations, of course, are individually defined, but they include performance in school and sports, and activities such as earning money. The second class of situations likely to elicit male shame is sexual potency. This, too, is individually defined, but it includes premature ejaculation, failure to have an erection, and a girl's refusal to go out on a date with them.

There also were two classes of situations that were most likely to elicit shame in women. The first is physical attractiveness, which has been found by many investigators to be an important characteristic for women.[12] Physical attractiveness has to do with appearance or with exposure. In this regard, it should be noted that in the study about embarrassment described earlier, we found that girl children showed significantly more embarrassment than boy children, and this difference was already apparent by the end of the second year of life! During the study the experimenter praised the children's appearance. Girls showed greater amounts of embarrassment than boys when praised. This finding at 22 months of age may well mark the onset of female attention directed to their physical selves.

The second class of events likely to elicit shame in women is failure in interpersonal relationships, which includes failure in regard to peers, boyfriends or husbands, parents, and children. Obviously, this second class is a rather broad category. It reflects the female interest in and concern for relationships. In this regard, it is important to note that females' moral sense, as Gilligan describes it, is influenced more by their relationship to others and how others might feel and react than it is to internal standards and rules. Thus, women's moral standards are consistent with the types of situations which, for them, are likely to elicit more shame. Interestingly, the failure of interpersonal relationships, although often mentioned by men as a situation that causes shame, did not receive a high overall rating; failure in interpersonal relationships was not in the top four male responses.

While I believe that the differences between the sexes in prototypical situations likely to lead to shame reflect socialization differences, we cannot ignore the possibility that sociobiological forces may also be involved. For example, the physical attractiveness of women and the sexual potency of men, both of which are elicitors of shame, can be related to reproductive success.

Until further sociobiological evidence is produced, however, socialization issues related to sex differences remain the most likely explanation for male and female shame differences.[13] It seems clear that women are the kin keepers and grow up more oriented to connectiveness and loving others as a central value in their lives, while men value more aggressive behavior in order to compete in economic systems. Other socialization factors also have been raised.

The sex differences that we observe in adults make their appearances in childhood. As I already have shown, most children respond with embarrassment when praised, but girls show significantly more embarrassment over exposure than boys. Moreover, in response to performance on a task, girls are three times more likely than boys to show shame when an easy task is failed. Finally, in our study of deception, we found females more likely than males to lie about whether they had peeked. Explanations for the sex differences in deception vary and could include sex differences concerning fear of the experimenter's reprisal. However, observation of facial expression indicates that the boy children who transgressed and did not respond to the experimenter's question showed less shame than the girl children who did not respond.

Perhaps the most significant work on early sex differences is being done by Carolyn Zahn-Waxler and her colleagues who have been observing children from 1 to 3 years of age.[14] Their findings on sex differences tend to support the difference that we see among men and women in terms of sensitivity toward others. Women, more than men, are interpersonally sensitive and place importance on relationships in situations of interpersonal conflict and distress. They are better able to interpret other people's emotions and psychological defenses, and they are more empathic. Finally, they appear to feel more guilt concerning their aggressions toward others.[15]

Most of the research on children's empathic response to others' distress indicates sex differences in this behavior as well.[16]

Another interesting sex difference, revealed through study of older children, concerns helplessness versus mastery orientation on school tasks. The helpless child is one who is concerned about performance goals and therefore is globally self-focused, whereas the mastery-oriented child is interested in learning and therefore is specifically focused. Girls tend to be global-, and boys specific-focused. These sex differences in orientation may account for differences in school performance.[17] These data appear to indicate that, on the one hand, women are globally oriented, but, on the other hand, they are more other-oriented and empathic, a specific attribution orientation. This suggests that women may be more prone than men to both shame and guilt. Unfortunately, most of the early sex difference literature fails to distinguish between shame and guilt. It might be the case that, because women are more empathic than men and because they focus on others, failure in interpersonal relationships with others will lead them to feel badly about themselves. In this case, feeling badly about one's self should lead to more shame. If this were true, then it is likely that the sex differences that have been suggested are true.

That individual differences exist in the likelihood of being shamed leads to a rather interesting possibility: people live in different emotional worlds and these differences cause interpersonal conflict. This is particularly true for heterosexual couples, since with couples both individual and sex differences can combine to promote interpersonal conflict.

Couples and the Two Worlds Hypothesis

Individual differences in behavior, within a dyadic relationship, can cause difficulty, not because of the fault of either person, but rather because of misunderstanding and misinterpretation of the behavior taking place. The example that follows helps to illustrate what I call the Two Worlds hypothesis. In this example and throughout subsequent discussion, I deliberately stereotype male and female behavior. The stereotypes are meant only to facilitate discussion. While it is often the case that arguments take a particular male-female form, there is no reason to assume either that this *must* be the case or that it *always* is the case.

A couple who had been fighting came to my office. The husband, Charlie, related the following story as an example of their difficulties. They had had a dinner party the previous weekend. His wife, Rita, had set the table and had prepared a lovely meal. After the guests had left, he complimented her on the lovely dinner, but then he said to her, "Dear, don't use that tablecloth again. It's old and stained." He reported that she became quite angry with him. He could not understand why she was so angry because all he had said was that he didn't like the tablecloth. Unbeknownst to him, his statement had shamed his wife. She made a global attribution around her failure which resulted in shame. Her shame made her feel angry with her husband. Moreover, she did not understand that he was unaware that he was shaming her. She believed that he had deliberately shamed her. He recognized that he had criticized his wife, but not that he had shamed her. For him, personally, criticism did not result in shame.

The wife later related a story about her husband's behavior. On another occasion, also related to having guests at their house, the husband bought some flowers and put them in a vase on the coffee table. After the guests left, the wife commented, "Don't use that vase again, it's really ugly." His response to her comment was quite different than hers had been during the tablecloth incident. Rather than becoming angry, he said, "Gee, you're right; next time I'll use the blue one."

We see that the husband in this case does not show shame. His emotional response over his failure is one of regret, or possibly even guilt. He realized that he had done something wrong and thought to correct the wrong. His wife's response to his statement of reparation confused him. She said, "Charlie, why don't you ever listen to me?" This was surprising to Charlie, since he believed that he did listen to her. His response was, "Rita, what do you mean listen to you? I can repeat every word you said."

In our discussion, I came to understand that the phrase *"You are not listening to me"* did not in fact refer to whether he heard her message. Rather, it was related to his emotional response to receiving her message. Unlike Rita, who registered shame when criticized for a recognized failure, Charlie offered reparation. Reparation is a clear marker of regret or guilt. It is not a marker of shame. Rita's comment, "You are not listening to me," was her method of indicating that she did not think he was having the correct emotional response, that is, that he is not feeling the same emotion she feels when the situation is reversed. That Charlie experienced regret or guilt rather than shame went unrecognized by Rita because she did not see regret or guilt as a legitimate and meaningful emotion. Parenthetically, it is interesting to note that men widely report that their wives use the expression "You are not listening to me." I am sure that this statement reflects a failure in empathic emotional understanding.

The problem for this couple was not undue shaming and pathology.

Their interpersonal problems arose from individual differences in emotions: under similar circumstances, Charlie and Rita will likely experience a different emotion. For Rita, the emotion she is most likely to experience when faulted is shame, whereas for Charlie, the emotion he is most likely to experience when faulted is regret or guilt. They were both unaware that their emotional lives differed to this degree. Because of lack of awareness, they were unable to negotiate this difference. Misperceptions concerning emotional states, misperceptions arising from individual emotional differences and the very human tendency to assume that the other feels what I would feel if I were in the other's place, lie at the root of many troubled interpersonal relationships.

Why do individuals, even those bound by the special ties of intimacy, fail to understand and properly interpret each other's emotional states? We could argue that such failure is due to some underlying pathology in each of them. Alternatively we could argue that an empathic stance is missing so that they cannot comprehend the feelings of the other. But this is not likely. I would argue instead that not lack of empathy, but the empathic process itself leads to misinterpretation. For example, Rita experiences shame, and she mistakenly assumes that Charlie knows she is ashamed. Because of this first assumption, she also assumes that he is *intentionally* shaming her, and she becomes angry as a response to his aggressive behavior. Charlie, in contrast, through his empathic processes, assumes that Rita feels regret or guilt when he criticizes her, and expects to see reparation around specific action. He is unaware that he is shaming her, and he does not understand either her anger with him for making a simple suggestion or her complaint about not listening. Thus, their empathic stance is likely to increase interpersonal struggle rather than alleviate it.

Therapy involved pointing out to Charlie that his comments were shaming Rita. Likewise, Rita needed to understand that Charlie did not intend to shame her. She also needed to learn that his response of regret or guilt was a genuine response to her criticism. He *was* listening, but reacting in the manner natural to him, not in the way she would react. Finally, Charlie came to understand that Rita's anger was caused by her feeling shame and believing that he was intentionally shaming her. The success of the therapy rested on their becoming aware of the differences in their emotional response to similar situations.

It seems reasonable to assume that the experience of Rita and Charlie has a much wider occurrence. In the majority of couples, it is the woman who is likely to make attributions that lead to shame, and the man attributions that lead to regret and guilt. Nevertheless, there are couples in which the reverse is true. What is important for the analysis is that many couples' failures can be traced to misunderstandings about the different emotional experiences each member of the couple is having. It makes little difference in the analysis that I use particular man/woman beliefs. Indeed, even in same-sex couples or among peers, the same dynamics are likely to be at work. The proposition is quite broad: dyadic relationships often fail, not due to specific pathologies related to the individual members, but rather due to the failure of the members in the relationship to negotiate the Two Worlds hypothesis. Given that discussion of shame is so difficult for individuals (keep in mind my earlier belief that talking about shame leads to shame), it is likely that misunderstanding in the realm of shame is not readily repaired. What is needed is the type of analysis and explanation given here, because what is remarkable in this case and in others involving personal friends and couples is the ease with which such misunderstandings can be corrected once understood.

This Two Worlds analysis allows for a consideration of a broad set of problems. For example, I have talked about women students who are unable to take criticism around specific failures in a course. What goes on in such situations, often between a male teacher and a female student, is the negotiation between individuals, one who is likely to see the error in terms of shame and the other who is likely to see the error in terms of a mistake unrelated to the self. The shame felt by the student is not intended by the teacher, who wishes simply to point out that the student did a particular thing wrong that needs correction. The failure of the professor to understand the attributional process is likely to result in his inability to empathize with the student's serious distress or to empathize with the student's withdrawal or failure to complete the task. If the professor understood that he is unintentionally creating shame in the student, he could change his behavior so as to help the student learn by means of the criticism process instead of not learn because of the shame experience.

Examples of this Two Worlds hypothesis are almost endless. I will mention one briefly before applying this concept to more general relationships between men and women.

A husband and wife are enjoying an intense discussion over some intellectual idea. They are arguing vigorously, with loud voices. Deeply involved in their discussion, each is defending a particular position. In the course of the discussion, the woman suddenly says, "Why are you talking to me that way?"

Change of focus from the topic under discussion to the interpersonal relationship usually is indicative of a shame experience. I call this movement *personalizing the interaction*. One member of the dyad stops focusing on the discussion itself and, instead, focuses on the disagreement. Focus on the disagreement, in turn, becomes the basis of a self-evaluative process. In the example above, perhaps the man's argument became too intense or too loud. The woman stopped focusing on the content of her husband's remarks, and started registering the tone of his remarks. Next, she decided that the tone indicated disparagement of her (even though it was not meant to), and then she felt shame. Meanwhile, her husband remained totally unaware of this internal progression, and therefore is totally unprepared for his wife's accusation, which to him seems to come from nowhere. Although based on the husband's intense argument and the wife's personalization, the ensuing disagreement is due to their ignorance in regard to each other's emotional life.

The Psychic War Between the Sexes

This sex difference that I have noticed in couples appears to be a more general difference. Men think that women are too sensitive, and women think that men are too aggressive. These different views are based upon differences in response to shame. Consider men's interaction without women. A common feature of men in groups is the high level of reported aggressive behavior that takes place between them. In young men, this aggressive behavior used to be called "ranking." Ranking consists of saying rude things to, or making fun of, another. When I was growing up in New York City, young men learned how to rank and how to receive ranking as part of their peer group interaction. I can recall few instances where ranking behavior caused aggression among my male peers. Although there is no evidence to confirm such a view, I suspect that ranking was not shame inducing, either because of the nature of the ranking itself or because of male training not to make global attributions of failure. Some men do not find this kind of behavior aversive; indeed, many men rather enjoy it. Ranking does not occur among adolescent females, nor among adult females. If such ranking were to take place, it would be viewed as offensive and hurtful. Women would consider ranking bad manners because it might induce bad feelings, including those of shame and humiliation.

Ranking behavior provides us with a simple example of the difficulty men and women have when they come together. Men do not find ranking negative and it does not elicit overt shame. But this is not so for women. If men engage in ranking behavior with women, the women are likely to interpret this behavior as aggressive and to believe that the men intend to humiliate and mortify them. Men, being used to this behavior, are unaware that this behavior causes pain and shame. They are surprised by the women's reaction. Stereotypic male/female descriptions are thus likely to be generated by both parties in the interaction. Males are considered aggressive and brutish; females are considered oversensitive and childlike. In fact, neither stereotype is true.

A Two Worlds view is useful in considering group interactions. One, in particular, has been brought to my attention, the interrupt patterns in conversations and in holding the floor at meetings. Men are more likely to talk at meetings and at other public gatherings. This finding is surprising in view of the common belief that women are more talkative, gregarious, and social than men. The explanation for male talk dominance in group situations, accepted by both men and women, is that men are more aggressive than women. Men are less willing than women to give up the floor and are more likely to interrupt other speakers. But our analysis of interrupt patterns reveals that men interrupt other men as well as women. Moreover, men do give up the floor. One possible explanation for this behavior is that men are more collegial to other men than to women and allow other men the floor. This idea supports the stereotyped differences between the sexes. While such a hypothesis is worth considering, alternative ones exist. In particular, I suggest that men speak more than women, not because they are aggressive, but because they are less concerned with the global self-evaluation related to failure in performance. If this analysis of sex differences in self exposure and attribution is correct, failure for men has less serious consequence than for women.

While men are more likely than women to speak at public meetings, it may not be because men are more aggressive, or because they are more likely to interrupt, or because they join together to prevent women from talking. One could hypothesize that women's attributional style and concerns about self exposure are the true cause for women's talking less. Women might restrict themselves through their own attributional processes. Such attributional processes are facilitated by men's behavior. As I suggested above, men are more likely to disagree with the statements of others, both men and women. Men are thus likely to disagree with what women say. Because women are likely to make global attributions over their failure, the threat of such failure serves to inhibit certain behaviors, in this case, public speaking.

Clearly more evidence is necessary to support this radical hypothesis. As I have suggested, it may be that both men and women have the same shame response. When shamed, women are more likely to become depressed, men, angry. Depression typically results in cessation of speech, but anger may promote more talking. It is much easier to continue our stereotypes and believe that men are more aggressive than women, and thus the cause of women's inhibition. However, it is clear that women's inhibition must have some dynamic process in its own right and, in part, must be independent of men. Although the process of self evaluation and attribution involves others, the attributional process itself resides in the individual rather than in the interpersonal relationship. One person in a couple feels shame over drunken behavior while out for the evening with another couple and never wants to see the other couple again, while another person in the same situation feels regret and wants to repair the relationship. In the same way, it may be the case that women, using their unique attributional style, are likely to inhibit themselves. That men are more aggressive both to other men and to women cannot be denied. Their aggression notwithstanding, it is unlikely that this is the only cause of women's behavior. The historical difference in status between men and women may, in substantial part, be based upon differences in shame evocation. Men may be more able to evoke shame in women than women are able to evoke shame in men. If this were the case, then men would be dominant not because they are aggressive (they are), but because they can evoke shame in the other without being easily shamed themselves. The fact that men are considered to be aggressive and women nonaggressive may be best understood in the context of shame differences. Once again, an understanding of the Two Worlds hypothesis provides us with an opportunity to understand the dynamics of individuals in social networks.

Pathological Shame and Couples

I have focused on adult relationships that fail at times, not because of undue individual shame-proneness or individual differences in aggression, but rather because of individual differences that lead to a failure to appreciate what is happening in the psyche of the other. But there are some interpersonal dynamics which are more pathological in nature. One or even both of the individuals in a dyad can have a serious problem with too much shame.

Fighting over Not Doing Enough

A recent case of a shame/anger situation indicates how a pathological shame-proneness in one partner elicited a fight.

David had to go on an extended business trip, and regretted leaving his wife, Carol. After three weeks of separation, David called Carol. During the conversation, he said, "The next trip I go on, I don't want to go by myself. I want you to come with me. I miss you and I don't like not being with you." From David's point of view, his statement was a sign of his love for Carol. But Carol, who was shame-prone, heard his words not as a statement of love, but as a statement of demand. Her response was, "I can't go with you on the next trip. I have a life of my own, and I need to do what I need to do." She said those words in an angry tone. David, in turn, became angry, since he was hurt because his statement of devotion had been rebuffed. The conversation quickly ended with both husband and wife feeling badly.

An analysis of this situation reveals several interesting features. Carol heard David's statement as a demand; thus, according to her perspective, her angry response was justified. Therapy enabled Carol to realize that her angry response to David's positive declaration indicated shame. Because she is easily shamed, his desire, which she could not satisfy, shamed her. She pointed out, correctly, that she often became angry when she felt that she had failed in her interpersonal obligations. Carol substituted anger for her unacknowledged shame.

David's reaction to Carol also throws light on the shame/rage spiral. Having declared his love and his need for Carol, he was surprised and angry at her response. In therapy, he came to appreciate the fact that his anger also was preceded by shame. In his case, the shame was produced by her rebuttal of his love statement: anger was his way of dealing with his unacknowledged shame. The spiral here was initiated by Carol's shame-proneness, but David also contributed to it. It became the material around which much of their interpersonal difficulties, due only in part to her shame-proneness, were based.

Shame and Silence

Interpersonal difficulties around shame can be seen in situations other than a shame/rage or shame/depression axis. In the next example, we see a shame/shame interaction. Recall my earlier discussion of how shame is capable of eliciting shame in others. The shame arising from public error not only shames the performer, it also shames the audience. The case of Paul and his father presented in chapter 1 offers a perfect example of contagious shame. In the case I wish to present here, this contagion is manifested by a couple with a sexual problem.

> *A sex therapist met separately with a husband and wife referred to him because of sexual dysfunction. Upon inquiry, he found that the husband was suffering from premature ejaculation. The wife, who was quite inexperienced when they married, was under the impression that her husband's problem was caused by her inexperience. Because both members of the couple were shamed by their behavior, they sought to avoid all sexual contact. For the last nine months they had avoided all sexual activity. They were quite happy together as long as this lack of sex was not raised as an issue. Difficulties arose—and they sought therapy—after the woman announced that she wanted to have a child.*
>
> *The therapist attempted to get the husband and wife to discuss sex. However, neither was able to approach the subject. No amount of coaxing would elicit from either anything more than the most minimum statements concerning their sex life. After two months of unsuccessful therapy, the therapist suggested that, since they could not discuss the problem, therapy be discontinued. Because the woman desired a child, this threat seemed to energize her into finally discussing her feelings. In one important session, she revealed how ashamed she was at her husband's lack of control. Her discussion of her shame helped her husband to discuss his shame concerning his premature ejaculation. The discussion of shame and the breaking of the silence associated with this shameful experience allowed the couple to deal with the immediate problem of their sexual dysfunction. Once shame was brought into the open, it was possible to discuss various sexual techniques. Sex therapy was ultimately successful. Once a discussion of mutual shame took place, the sexual problem itself could be dealt with.*

This case reveals one of the most insidious features of shame, namely, the repression and the denial associated with the feeling. Until the therapist could induce the couple to discuss the feelings associated with their dysfunctional interaction, he could not move the couple forward to solve their dysfunction. The silence associated with two people's shame is unbearable. It presents a barrier or a wall to interpersonal freedom and expression. Suzanne Retzinger, in a paper on marital conflict, has written, "Isolation and shame are inseparable. When shame is not acknowledged, it is almost impossible to mend the bond. In itself, unacknowledged shame creates a form of self-perpetuating entrapment in one's own isolation. If one hides this sense from the other due to shame, it creates further shame, which creates a further sense of isolation."[18]

Intergenerational and Sex Differences in Shame: The Oedipus Myth Revisited

Shame can be useful in understanding intergenerational struggles. If men are socialized differently than women in regard to shame, it may be the case that mother-son, father-son, father-daughter, and mother-daughter relationships are influenced by this factor. Recall that women typically both acknowledge their shame more than men and handle their unacknowledged shame more often with depression (sadness) than rage (anger). As we have seen, this Two Worlds view affects adult relationships between the sexes. There is every reason to believe that the Two Worlds view may also be at work between parent and child.

Sons and Mothers

Let us first consider the mother-son relationship. I believe that the socialization practices of the mother toward her son are designed to promote overt feelings of shame and, when shame is unacknowledged, to express more sadness than anger. Given that the boy child is simultaneously being socialized for his male role, there should be a competing disagreement and struggle between them: without knowing it, the mother wants her son to express more shame, while her son wants to feel and express less shame. The struggle takes many forms, but its net result is to push the son away from his mother; his expressions concerning her wanting to "baby him" and to keep him dependent may indicate this struggle. In our longitudinal study, we have been interviewing adolescents about their relationships with their parents. A consistent theme that emerges from the boys is that "their mothers want them to behave better." Inquiry into what this complaint means, especially in regard to interpersonal relationships, points to mothers who want their sons to be more open with them and to own up to their inappropriate behavior. Although I cannot be sure, this "owning up to inappropriate behavior" appears to be related to how boys say they are sorry when they violate some rule. One mother told me that she thought her son "is psychopathic because he never feels sorry for what he's done." If our data on adult couples can be applied to mothers and sons, and I think it can, mothers and sons are caught in a misunderstanding trap based on sexual identities and differences in emotions. Boys who violate some parental standard probably express regret or guilt and a desire for reparation. But their mothers, being women, and viewing the violation from a woman's perspective, expect the boys to express shame. When a shame response is not forthcoming, they read its nonappearance as a sign that their sons are not truly sorry for their transgressions. In other words, the mother unknowingly tries to make her son feel the way a woman (herself) would feel, but the growing boy finds the desired shame feeling uncomfortable and incompatible with the male role he is struggling to acquire.

This intergenerational struggle over shame should appear as soon as shame and its socialization appears. Since we have marked this around age 3, I have reason to believe that the mother's attempt to impose a female emotional state on a male child bears some relation to what was seen as the Oedipal struggle, which begins to take place at this same point. The male child struggles to achieve autonomy and to reduce shame (Erikson's third stage), while his mother attempts to socialize him so that interpersonal relations, rather than achievement, and shame, rather than guilt, dominate his social life. The son, who still needs his mother, her care and her affection, is both pulled toward her and repelled by his male role needs. These goals are incompatible and lead to the intense psychic struggle taking place. The form this struggle takes can be seen in this example.

An 8-year-old boy wants to go out and play with his friend. His mother says, "I want you to stay in. Play with Tommy [his 5-year-old brother], he's sick." The boy answers, "No, I want to go out." She says, "Tommy will be sad, he's alone." The boy becomes angry. The anger reflects not only his frustration over play but, I suspect, his upset over being made to feel shame.

Daughters and Mothers

The struggle around shame and its expression between daughters and mothers should be less intense than that between mothers and sons. There are two reasons for this lesser intensity, the most obvious being that mother and daughter have no sex role difference to complicate their interaction. In general, daughters, like their mothers, are expected to feel more shame and to express it in a way consistent with the feminine role. The typical daughter has no struggle with her mother in regard to shame and its socialization. If she does, then her anger at being shamed also has to be negotiated. In fact, the anger around shame may be the most difficult for a daughter to deal with since the anger itself may be shameful. This bind, if anger does arise, has been the focus of recent discussions in feminist literature.[19]

Because we are in the midst of important role changes for women, the negotiating of shame and its manifestations should become more difficult for girls. The attributions associated with shame and the socialization processes do not necessitate the typical female and male behavior. There is no reason to think of these differences as genetically driven. They are role-driven and, as such, are open to modification as roles change. Given the role changes for women emerging in the last 25 years, I would expect to see some of the same mother-daughter intergenerational struggles over these issues that we have seen for mothers and sons. One female adolescent in our study, very much achievement-oriented and not yet interested in boys, expressed views similar to boys in regard to her mother's behavior. She found that it was very difficult to make up after a fight with her mother because she felt her mother did not think her apology was sincere. I suspect the adolescent was expressing regret, not shame, to her mother.

In general, though, role changes are not as marked as we might assume. Because of this, role similarity makes the struggle over shame issues less relevant. Besides the similarity of roles, daughter-mother relationships may remain more intimate because both parties in this relationship share a similar ability to feel shame and follow the same emotional substitution rules. Consider that, when sons and mothers struggle over shame, the boys typically respond with anger to their shame, while their mothers typically respond with sadness. Thus, anger expression versus sadness expression is apt to drive them apart. In the case of girls and their mothers, a similar sadness expression is likely to bring them closer together. Even if the daughter feels anger, her anger is likely to lead to shame, and this combination binds them rather than separates them.

———— • ————

Shame operates differently between a mother and her children, depending upon whether they are sons or daughters. For sons, the shame struggle separates child and mother, while for daughters, there is no struggle, so that the shame negotiation actually helps to bind child and mother. This struggle has been seen around the sexuality of parent and child. I prefer to view this struggle around the issues of self, self blame, and the emotions that accompany them.

Fathers and Their Children: Bambi *Revisited*

As usual, the analysis of development leaves fathers playing a minimal role. While men are not usually the prime caregivers, their role in childrearing should not be minimized. Fathers have both direct and indirect roles, and they exert important influence both through their interactions with their children and through their interactions with their wives/mothers of their children. The father's role is significant and less passive than our stereotypes suggest. Recent work by a variety of authors shows fathers' impact in infancy, and we also possess considerable information regarding their importance in adolescence.[20] In fact, the role of fathers in their children's lives increases over time. Fathers are particularly important in the intergenerational struggle over shame.

Many of us remember the Walt Disney movie *Bambi.* You may recall that when Bambi is an adolescent, his mother, who has raised him, is killed by hunters who also set the woods afire. The animals flee and Bambi, who appears trapped and fated for death, is saved by the timely appearance of his father, who leads him from the fire to safety. Children love this story, even though it is sad. The arrival of Bambi's father and his rescue of his son characterizes, in part, the human father's role for his son in the struggle over autonomy and shame. Fathers, through their behavior and action, provide both a model and an ally for their sons. The father's role is to lead his son from the shame struggle with the mother, and, at the same time, to negotiate male-male aggression. Unfortunately, while most fathers are successful in the first task, they are less successful in the second. Fathers and sons have their own negotiation around shame. Since their axis is shame-anger, their interactions are more likely to be around anger, and it is the shame-anger problem that needs to be solved. When they are successful in negotiating the shame-anger-shame axis, their relationship across the life span is ensured. When they are not successful, the son must separate himself from both parents, but for different reasons.

The father-daughter relationship is the most difficult to describe, since the father does not need to serve as a model to lead his daughter from the shame struggle with her mother. Nevertheless, he may play some role even here.[21] Moreover, as the Two Worlds view suggests, father and daughter differ in their shame feelings and are therefore unlikely to be able to negotiate their shame once it appears. The father's primary role may be to serve as a model for the other men his daughter is likely to come in contact with. Unfortunately, because they cannot negotiate the shame struggle, his does not provide a sufficient model to help her in her subsequent male relationships. This, of course, applies when daughters maintain the traditional female role. If they assume the new liberated role, the father has a similar function to that which he serves with his son. It has been noticed, especially with firstborn female children, that daughters form a stronger attachment with, and therefore identify more with, their fathers than with their mothers. When this happens, the father's role becomes similar to that discussed for their sons in the struggle between daughter and mother.

11

Stigma

Erving Goffman, in an acclaimed monograph entitled *Stigma,* talks about the nature of self-presentation and the role of stigma in interpersonal relations. He states that people with stigmas are thought to be not quite human: "[T]he standards he [the person with a stigma] has incorporated from the wider society equipped him to be intimately alive to what others see as his failing, inevitably causing him . . . to agree that he does indeed fall short of what he really ought to be. Shame becomes a central possibility."[1] For Goffman, stigma represents a spoiled identity, the idea that somehow one is imperfect in regard to the standards of the society in which one lives. While the concept of stigma is not easily defined, we can say that it is a mark or characteristic that distinguishes a person as being deviant, flawed, limited, spoiled, or generally undesirable. The deviating characteristics of the person are sufficient reason for the occurrence of the stigma. Stigma relates the self to others' view and, although the feelings of being stigmatized may occur in the absence of other people, the feelings associated with it come about through the stigmatized person's interactions with other people, or through her anticipation of interactions with other people. For example, a woman with one leg shorter than the other, who limps when she walks, frequently notices other people looking at her. Thus, at home, she anticipates walking in public and being observed by others. Stigmatization is a public, interpersonal event; it is a mark much like the mark that God imposed on Cain to punish him for killing his brother, Abel. It is apparent and visible.

We might begin by asking, What are these marks and how can we determine who is stigmatized and who is not? I remember many years ago, my grandmother, while talking to me about a favorite uncle, suddenly lowered her voice and said in a whisper, "Poor Uncle Joel, he has cancer." She said the word "cancer" in such a soft voice that it was almost impossible to hear. For my grandmother, Uncle Joel's cancer marked him and was a stigma, not only to him, but to the family as well.

Stigmas are varied because they are a public violation of what is considered normal. Since standards and rules of normalcy vary, what is considered a stigma in one case might not be a stigma in another.

A List of Stigmas

The list that we could come up with in regard to stigmas in our society would be long and varied. Thus I cannot do justice to all of the things that could be considered as stigmas in U.S. society. But let us look at a few of them. We will have to include sickness, cancer being the current best example. Betty Ford's announcement that she had breast cancer was considered a brave act because she had dared to reveal her stigma. Leprosy and epilepsy have long been considered stigmas. Of course, not all illnesses are stigmas; for example, coronary disease does not constitute a stigma. Physical appearance can be the source of a stigma and a very important one, both for females and for males. For females, the stigma of being overweight is a very powerful social marker. Anorexia and the other eating disorders so prevalent in U.S. females may be due to this powerful sense of being marked and stigmatized.[2]

> *I had a young female patient, who was extraordinarily attractive and quite thin, yet who saw in herself marks that stigmatized her. She thought that her breasts were too small. In spite of the fact that she was considered attractive by her peers of both sexes, her own sense of stigmatization was so powerful, her shame over her appearance so devastating, that she found it difficult to enter into any interpersonal relationship that might lead to intimacy, and thus to the uncovering and exposure of her body.*

For males, the same sort of stigmatization occurs, although for somewhat different reasons. As a child I remember comic-book ads about Charles Atlas's weight-lifting, body-building course intended to relieve the stigma of being puny and nonmuscular. In those days, being a "97-pound weakling" was a form of stigmatization that every young man sought to avoid.

One of the most prevalent stigmas for men involves height. If a man is shorter than average, and particularly if his shortness makes him shorter than most women, he will be subject to stigmatization. The well-known "Napoleon complex" of short men speaks to their attempt to compensate for what is a very clear stigma. A male's shortness constitutes an important physical marker and qualifies as a stigma. Americans tend to vote for the taller of two presidential candidates. Michael Dukakis's presidential race against George Bush is a clear example of the stigmatization of a short presidential candidate. Although short males do win public office, their below-average size is often made fun of or ridiculed by their political opponents, political cartoonists, and the like. Abraham Beame, former mayor of New York, and Robert Reich, the current United States Secretary of Labor, are examples of this stigmatization. Physical appearance is public, and so our appearance constitutes a potential stigma. Being physically ugly, for both men and women, can constitute a stigma. The stigma of ugliness impacts on our sense of identity, and marks us throughout our lives. While our sense of the attractive, and thus of the ugly, is culturally defined, there is evidence that across cultures there are particular aspects of appearance that are universally considered ugly.[3] Ugliness, even without any accompanying physical deformity, constitutes a stigma.

If physical unattractiveness constitutes a stigma, how much more stigmitizing is a physical disability? Think about people who have a hunchback, a limb missing, a limp, or who have facial paralysis. Physical disabilities, because they serve as public markers, cannot help but produce embarrassment and shame in those individuals possessing them. As we will see, many attempts to cope with these stigmas are made. Corrective surgery has been recommended, not so much to affect ability, as to offset the public appearances associated with the disability, for example, plastic surgery on children with Down's syndrome.[4] To our list of stigmas, then, we must add all the obvious forms of disabilities.

Perhaps the most extensive literature on stigmas speaks to the effects of mental retardation. The mentally retarded feel the stigma of their mark. Older children and adults who suffer from mild mental retardation experience their stigma and are shamed by it. Some of us are familiar with the now cancelled TV program "L.A. Law," in which Benny, a mildly retarded character, had an ongoing role. Often Benny's part in the series dealt with his shame, embarrassment, and even anger when he perceives that others are responding to his stigma. It is no television play, but real life that Benny speaks to. Consider a United Press International report that I read in the *Hartford Courant* in November 1981. The headline of the article reads, "Teenager Describes How It Feels to Be Retarded."

*"Sometimes it makes me want to cry inside because I am retarded. I am re-
tarded, but sometimes, other people may forget about me being retarded. I
can't stand it if someone teases me, it makes me feel weird inside. I can't
stand it! Nobody likes that, but when they realize that they are hurting my
feelings, sometimes they come over and apologize to me."*

The stigma associated with mental retardation has a powerful effect: it
not only impacts on the person's sense of his spoiled identity and
prompts feelings of shame and embarrassment, but also impacts on
how he goes about trying to cope with his everyday life. Such an intense
feeling as a spoiled identity, as a self that is no good, as an unworthy
person, must be a public mark almost too hard to bear.

Our list of potential stigmas, since it reflects standards and rules, is
open to change as a function of historical time and culture. For example, in our culture today, being old is a stigma and reflects a spoiled
self. We try to hide this stigma: we dye our hair to hide the grey, use
plastic surgery to remove the wrinkles on our faces, and buy expensive
cosmetics in hopes of masking the effects of the aging process. The
stigma of age affects men as well as women. A friend of mine reported
to me that he had met "a very attractive 30-year-old." Although he was
59, when she asked him his age, he lied and said he was in his early 50s.
While men suffer from the age stigma, women suffer even more because in our society a woman who ages is "ugly."

It should be clear that stigmas, and the age stigma in particular, are
in large part culturally determined. Although youth is valued in all societies, if for no other reason than old age reflects the end of one's life,
there are strong cultural differences between societies. A Japanese colleague told me of an interesting distinction in insurance payments in
the case of an accident. If an elderly person were to die in an airplane
accident in the United States, compensation to his family would be
based on the loss of income his family suffered. Since old men, statisti-
cally, are out of the work force and unlikely to be generating much
income, their families receive little compensation. Conversely, the families of young men who die in airplane crashes receive generous compensation because it is assumed that a young man's family has lost
decades' worth of his earning potential. The case is just the opposite in
Japan, where age is associated with wisdom. An older person, who presumably has acquired more wisdom with his years, is more valuable
than a young person who has yet not accrued such wisdom through
age. Compensation, then, is greater for the old man than for the young
one. Such views of value and worth as a function of different societies

suggest that the idea of stigma not only resides in the marked individual, but in the societal value system, as reflected in its standards, rules, and goals. This conforms to my view that shame is the consequence of the failure around a specific set of standards, rules, and goals.

The Public Cry

The effects of stigmatization have been known for some time. Edward Jones and his colleagues, in their *Social Stigma*,[5] point out the connection between stigmatization and dysfunction. However, the relation between stigma and shame has been less articulated. Nevertheless, stigmatized individuals have been characterized as having disrupted emotional, cognitive, and behavioral response systems, likely to be caused in part by their dysfunction and in part by their feelings of shame. Imagine, for yourself, the effect of stigmatization. Here, we rely on some of the examples taken from the newspapers only a decade ago that Jones and his colleagues brought to our attention.[6]

> *September, 1982. UPI reports that majorette Peggy Ward will be barred from Friday's football game. The reason Miss Ward is one and a half pounds overweight. She is 5'4" and 127 pounds. This weight exceeds the guidelines established by the band director. The school superintendent supports the band director, but Miss Ward is fighting back by fasting to make the limit in time for the game. But the event has been psychologically costly for the majorette. "The pressure and intense publicity surrounding the controversy apparently became too much for Miss Ward, who telephoned her mother in tears . . . and asked to be taken home from school."*

> *An article in the* Chicago Tribune *about Susan Nussbaum, a paraplegic who became an activist for the rights of paraplegic people. Miss Nussbaum reflects on her thoughts after her freak auto accident that left her spinal cord irreparably damaged. "Suddenly, I was one of those people my mother used to tell me not to stare at on the street. I thought if I didn't die in the hospital, I would kill myself when I got out."*

Such examples suggest that the phenomena of social stigmas are all around us.

Listen to some other cases as presented by Steven Reiss and Betsy Benson[7] on people with mental retardation who are aware of their condition.

This is the description of a woman who was moderately mentally retarded. "In therapy interviews, Ms. A complained that her family 'treats me like a baby.' The specific complaints included parental checks on whether or not she had taken her seizure control medication and their mistrusting her with more than a few days supply of medication. She also complained about becoming angry when criticized and when 'people don't do me right.' She reported with sadness instances in which she had been called 'a retard.' She expressed frustration at not being able to read or handle money, explaining that she never learned much at school."

Or the case of Mr. C with dysthymic disorder, a 27-year-old mildly retarded man who had been referred to the outpatient clinic by his adoptive parents because of his sadness. Although he had a part-time job at a grocery store, he was dissatisfied at not being able to find a full-time job that paid more money. His other goals included obtaining a driver's license and living in his own apartment. Most of all, he wanted to meet a "good Christian minded girl" who he would eventually marry. . . . In psychotherapy interviews, Mr. C. cried when he related a series of rejections. He traced these back to his natural parents who had neglected him and had given him up for adoption. Public school students had ridiculed him for attending special classes and for riding the bus for handicapped students. Since leaving school, he had become more socially isolated and spent much of his free time watching television.

Mr. C. saw little hope for any future improvement in his life. "I am so lonely," he said. "I can see myself as an old man with gray hair—no friends, no family, all by myself."

These examples should make clear to us that the stigma felt by the individual is profound, resulting in emotions as diverse as anger, sadness, humiliation, shame, and embarrassment. Examples in regard to the feeling of the stigmatized person are endless, especially for those with mental retardation.

In the last decade extraordinary efforts have been made to reduce the stigmatization of people. This can be seen in our society's commitment to changing the use of language. In the past, for example, people were described as "a handicapped person," "a disabled person," "a mentally retarded person," or "a Down's syndrome child," as if the mark itself described the whole person. Now, working to reduce stigmatization, we have agreed to change our description. Instead of speaking about "a retarded person," we now say "a person with retardation"; the change in wording is meant to indicate that this person has many features, and that retardation is only one of them. Retardation is not the marker by which this individual is to be defined. Such a realization, as reflected in our language, represents a generous social commitment to alter the effects of stigmatization. However, one must wonder whether such language change can be effective in reducing the negative effects of stigma. For example, cosmetically altering the facial appearance of children with Down's syndrome, while improving the way they look, does not alter the way they behave. Because of this reality, their mental retardation is still apparent to the nonretarded, and may still be the source of stigmatization. For this reason, the use of cosmetic surgery has for the most part been discontinued.[8]

When I was a youngster attending the public school system in New York City, there were five or six different classrooms for each grade. The classrooms were given individual letters, representing in descending alphabetical order the smartest or college-bound class down to the vocational class; thus, 8A signified the students in the academic program in the 8th grade. But 8B, instead of being second highest class in regard to academic achievement, was actually the classroom for children who had mental retardation. In this way an attempt was made to fool people into thinking that this was not a class for children with retardation. In fact, the ploy was well known and did nothing to alleviate the stigma of being in a classroom of children with mental retardation.

While such attempts to reduce stigmatization may not be as affective as we hope, the passage of the federal Public Law PL 94-142 was a worthwhile effort. The law attempts to reduce the barriers experienced by stigmatized individuals by increasing their access to public buildings, services, and education. Although parts of the law are resisted and appear foolish and costly, it has forced our society into recognizing the adverse affects of stigmatization. Even so, the impact may not be as great as we had hoped given the psychological and sociological conditions related to stigma and to how people respond, both those who have the stigmas and those responding to others with them.

Stigma Contagion

The impact of stigma is wide: it not only affects those who are stigmatized, but those who are associated with the person so marked. Goffman called this phenomenon "courtesy stigma." Stigmas are contagious: they impact on members of the family and even the friends of the stigmatized person. Like an infectious disease, the stigma not only affects the victim of the stigma but all those who are associated with him or her.

Parents of Stigmatized Children

The parents of children with a stigma are themselves stigmatized and suffer the same fate as their stigmatized child.[9] There is no question that the parents of a child who has mental retardation themselves become objects of stigma. We see the impact of stigmatization in the description of what happens to parents when they are informed that their child has retardation: First they express shock and disbelief that their child is in imperfect health. Second, they experience anger and rage. Third, sadness replaces the anger. Finally the parents enter the coping stage. Whatever stage the parents of a child with a stigma are in, they must learn to cope with their shame and embarrassment over having such a child. The shame at having such a child can last a lifetime and can lead to many family difficulties, including a high rate of marital discord and divorce as each parent seeks to blame the other for the stigmatized child.[10] Given the differences between men and women in their willingness to accept blame, it is not surprising that husbands have a greater tendency to blame their wives for the stigmatized child and that mothers tend to accept such blame much more than fathers do. This coping system enables fathers to blame the mothers of their children, and thus to separate themselves from the shame of the stigmatized child.[11]

The shame of the parents has been revealed in the intervention studies designed to reduce the parental stress of parents who have children with difficulties. The most successful research projects are those that focus on parents' feelings of shame in combination with therapy for dealing with their shattered expectations. Karen Frey, Mark Greenberg, and Rebecca Fewell[12] intervened in order to alter the appraisal pattern of parents, which they claim leads to shame and embarrassment. Without dealing with this problem, they could not get the parents to function appropriately.

Programs treating families suffering from the stress of a stigmatized child reveal that the focus on the parents' attributions, and therefore on their shame, have the best chance of altering the family dynamics and helping the child. Charles Nixon and George Singer describe an intervention program to help mothers with children with mental retardation. The program consisted of 10 hours of discussion concerning how they were thinking about their children. The treatment condition focused on the cognitive distortions that contributed to self-blame and guilt and the best techniques to deal with these cognitive distortions. Using the attribution model, the therapists change the cognitive distortions and the automatic thoughts of parents. The results, although modest, demonstrated that the therapy could alter the emotions of shame, guilt, and depression through altering the cognitive attributional style of parents. The authors, in discussing their findings, conclude that the treatment was effective "in reducing self-blame and guilt in parents of children with severe disabilities, because there were significant reductions in automatic thoughts, internal negative attributions, and depression. There is evidence that cognitive distortions were effectively restructured. Therefore, there is evidence that cognitive restruction was an important contributor to the reduction and parental self-blame and guilt."[13] The authors discuss guilt and make no distinction between guilt and shame. However, a careful reading of this research project as well as many others that use the term "guilt" leaves little doubt that the authors are speaking of shame. Indeed, the very term "spoiled identity" speaks to the all-encompassing total-self feature of stigma.

In a recent study by Robert Marvin,[14] the mechanisms that related parental attribution and child outcomes were observed. Mothers of children with handicaps who were able to cope with their shame were those mothers who were best able to form a secure attachment with their infants. Moreover, it was the securely attached infants who showed the most improvement.[15]

A disability not only directly affects children's functioning, but also indirectly affects children through the children's shame and the shame of their parents. The impact of disabilities on children's development can only be weighed by taking into consideration both the direct and the indirect effects of stigma. The impact of disabilities on the children's development cannot properly be assessed without taking the impact of stigmatization into account. When children with Down's syndrome were placed in institutions, their intellectual capacity seemed to be quite low. It was assumed that their intellectual capacity was caused by their chromosomal deficiency. When children with Down's syndrome were not placed in institutions, but given a normal socializing experience at home, their intellectual capacity seemed to improve. The biological factor, while important, was not the only determinant of their intellectual capacity. In like fashion, the ability to normalize the stigma associated with disability may result in more satisfactory development and outcomes. It is certainly important for the mental health and well-being of all the family members.

Brothers, Sisters, and the Environment of Shame

Although most attention has been paid to the parents of children with stigma, we should not neglect the impact of stigma on the other children in the family.

Years ago, I had a patient who was the younger sister of a child with severe retardation. Sarah's sense of her responsibility for her sister and her feelings of shame connected with growing up in such a household were related to her feelings of depression and disassociation. "I always had to be the good child. My parents used to say to me that I had to represent the family because my sister couldn't. It was always up to me to put on a good face. When the family would go outside, on an outing, although these were not very often, I was always ashamed of my sister and never wanted to be associated with her." What stood out in Sarah's mind was the request of her parents to be the "good child." She could not act childlike, but had to be responsible. She was held to higher standards. Even when her sister was aggressive with her, she could not retaliate: she had to be the good child, the appropriate child. She had to be the child who understood the terrible stress and pain that the family endured. She, of course, carried these high standards with her and it was one of the primary causes of her own feelings of depression and lack of self-worth.

The problems for the siblings of children who are stigmatized impact in many different ways. Ann Gath,[16] in talking about the brothers and sisters of mentally retarded children, points to this difficulty. Clearly, a child with disabilities is a source of shame to his brothers and sisters. According to Gath, siblings of children with a stigma must bear the emotional distress and disappointment of their parents. Their parents' grieving and stress impacts on them. Moreover, the parents' energy must be directed toward the stigmatized child, thus leaving less time and energy for the "normal" siblings. In addition, the siblings without stigma are required to share more of the load of family life than they might normally bear. They have to take care of the sibling when the parents are not available. The issues of fairness and the issue of sibling rivalry also are problems for the siblings. The normal competition between siblings is likely to be settled in favor of the stigmatized child. The sibling who is without stigma is likely not only to be neglected, but also to assume greater responsibility. For example, Sarah reported that even when her sister did something wrong, her parents insisted that she, "the normal sister," understand and make allowances for her sister's behavior.

Although no accurate data exists on the effect of stigma on other members of the family, there can be no question that the stigma associated with having a sibling with difficulties is a burden for the nonaffected siblings, a burden which, given their young age and their lack of coping behavior, may create a serious stress for which they are ill-equipped. Moreover, the support that they might receive from other adults around them is likely to be limited given the need of the parents to support themselves and the stigmatized child. Thus, the prognosis for the siblings appears to be risky. The little clinical literature on the topic suggests that siblings of children with disability are a group particularly at risk for problems related to high standards, self-blame, and the accompanying emotions of shame, embarrassment, and guilt.

Parents as Stigma

We have been focusing on the stigma associated with families where one of the children has difficulties. Now we need to consider the issue of a parent who has the stigma. A child who has a parent with a stigma is likely to suffer in the same way as the parent's spouse.

Many years ago, I knew a young woman, who was the daughter of parents who were deaf and unable to speak. The child herself was normal. Her description of her childhood was filled with the same heart-wrenching descriptions that I hear from parents of children with stigma. I recall her telling me of the embarrassment she felt when she had her friends over to her house and how upsetting it was when she had to help mediate conversation between her parents and the school authorities. She described her life "as always being different, as always being marked by the fact that I was the daughter of deaf-and-dumb people." Surprisingly, although she had claimed little sense of self-blame for her parents' stigma, she nevertheless felt as though there was something wrong with her for being the daughter of such parents. She discovered that her best coping strategy was not to think of her parents as "deaf-and-dumb," but to focus on their positive features, of which there were many: they were loving and considerate parents. Nevertheless, when she went off to university she was greatly relieved of her assigned identity as the daughter of stigmatized parents and did not tell her friends and acquaintances about her parents and their condition. She left home to go to university and did not return, marrying in her second year of college. She found a way of escaping her spoiled identity by separating herself from it. She also told me of her parents' sadness, which she learned about later in her life. Because they understood the burden she must have experienced as their daughter they suffered once again from their stigmatization, the first time as victims, and the second as the source of victimization of their daughter.

The stigma of the parent is visited on children in many ways. For some children, the stigmatization carries with it self-blame and is likely to lead to shame. Several examples of this problem come quickly to mind. An alcoholic parent is a stigma even without public notice; however, the child living with an alcoholic who is abrasive or violent becomes much more stigmatized. It is a source of shame even if the child does not feel responsible for her parent's drinking, but is much more so if they see themselves as responsible for it. The same effects can be true for any of the other stigma conditions of the parents, including parents who are depressed, parents who are psychotic and hospitalized, or even parents who have lost their jobs and need to go on welfare. The stigma associated with being the child of such a parent is largely mediated by the degree to which the child accepts responsibility. Even so, such children feel stress, and their feeling of an identity spoiled has to be the consequence of having parents who have problems that are publicly marked. Shame for the child will occur for any of the conditions that may constitute a stigma for the target person.

Stigma, Attribution, and Shame

Throughout much of this book, I have attempted to show how shame, a much misunderstood emotion, impacts on human life. The relation of stigma to shame has been noticed by others, yet the analysis of stigma, at least from Goffman on, has been plagued by the problem of what "stigma" might be. Clearly, from Goffman's point of view, it is a public mark, something that can be noticed by others and that involves a "spoiled identity." On the other hand, it has been noticed by social psychologists that the issue of stigma has to be related to social values and social good.[17] These conflicting ideas about stigma are readily satisfied by our analysis of the attributions related to the self-conscious emotions and, in particular, to those of shame. Perhaps the single biggest discrepancy between the theory of shame that I have proposed and stigma is related to the issue of public versus private acts. While the issue of public failure is relevant to the emotion of embarrassment, it is not so for the emotions of shame, guilt, or even pride. For the occurrence of these self-conscious emotions, one can have either a public or a private act. Shame can take place privately as long as the attributions that give rise to it occur. Stigma for the most part constitutes a public violation or action. For the fear of such a violation, it must be transparent, such as in physical appearance or action. As Goffman points out, "The immediate presence of normals is likely to reinforce this split between self-demands and self, but, in fact, self-hate and self-degradation only can occur when he and a mirror are present. The awareness of inferiority is what the stigmatized person is unable to keep out of consciousness, the formulation of some chronic feeling of the worst sort of insecurity, the anxiety of being shamed."[18]

The literature on stigma reflects my concern with shame as a self-destroying emotion. Let me return to my early analysis of shame in order to see how stigmatization produces shame.[19] To begin with, standards, rules, and goals are necessary and need to be incorporated in an individual's cognitive capacities in order to make a judgment about whether his behavior meets or does not meet these standards. From the point of view of standards, it is quite clear that the stigma that an individual possesses represents a deviation from the accepted standards of the society; this deviation may be in appearance, in behavior, or in conduct. Nonetheless, the person is stigmatized by possessing characteristics that do not match the standard. It is, of course, well recognized that these standards may change with time, and change with culture, but such standards exist and individuals whose appearance and behavior deviate from them can be said to suffer from a stigma.

The second critical feature in the elicitation of shame, as well as the other self-conscious emotions, is the issue of responsibility or self-blame. Here again stigma and shame analysis lead to the same conclusion: the degree to which the stigmatized person can blame herself or is blamed by others for her condition reflects her degree of shame.

The idea of responsibility and perceived responsibility is central to stigma and shame. Bernard Weiner has recently discussed this topic of perceived responsibility.[20] For example, overweight people are perceived as responsible for their condition because they presumably have control over their eating; therefore, overweight is a stigma. Weiner describes a study in which he examined the relation between stigma, perceived responsibility, and emotions. Adults rated 10 stigmas in terms of personal responsibility: AIDS, Alzheimer's disease, blindness, cancer, drug addiction, heart disease, obesity, being a paraplegic, being a child abuser, and having Vietnam War syndrome. Adults also were asked to rate their reactions in terms of anger and sympathy to each condition. The results revealed that six of the stigmas—Alzheimer's disease, blindness, cancer, heart disease, paraplegia, and Vietnam War syndrome—were rated low on perceived personal responsibility. But having AIDS, being a child abuser, having a drug addiction, and being obese were rated high on personal responsibility. Conditions where people were not held responsible elicited pity, but not anger. Responsibility and self–blame or the blame of others toward the self are therefore very uch related. Thus, social rules involve not only standards and rules, but also societal issues about controllability.[21]

Responsibility is not only a personal task: it involves the perceived responsibility that others hold. For example, a mother who gives birth to a child with mental retardation can blame herself for the condition, claiming that she did not do the correct thing during pregnancy, for example, not eating well or not taking care of herself, or she can see it as a chance event with no self-blame. However, we need not only to convince *ourselves* that we are not responsible, but we need to convince *others* that it is not our fault. For example, an overweight woman may know full well that her condition is glandular and that there is nothing she can do to control her weight; yet, it still remains a stigma for her because she knows others see her as responsible.

Holding one's self responsible is a critical feature in stigma and in the generation of shame since violation of standards, rules, and goals are insufficient in its elicitation unless responsibility can be placed on the self. Stigma may differ from other elicitors of shame and guilt, in part because it is a social appearance factor. The degree to which the stigma is socially apparent is the degree to which one must negotiate the issue of blame, not only for one's self but between one's self and the other who is witness to the stigma. Stigmatization is a much more powerful elicitor of shame and guilt in that it requires a negotiation not only between one's self and one's attributions, but between one's self and the attributions of others.

The major distinction that I have drawn between shame and guilt or regret rests on the idea that in shame the entire self is no good, as captured in the expression "I am a bad person." Goffman's expression of stigma as a "spoiled identity" makes clear that stigma constitute a global attribution about the self as no good. A spoiled identity reflects a whole self spoiled by some condition or behavior. Much of the pathology associated with stigma follows from the idea that the stigma defines the individual; thus the whole self becomes defined by the stigma. The expressions "the Down's child," or "the mentally retarded person," or "the fat lady" all reflect an unescapable realization that the stigma is the defining feature of the self.[22] That a stigma reflects a spoiled identity shows its similarity to our concept of shame and allows us to appreciate how the very act of stigmatization is shame-inducing. It is not surprising to find in the descriptions of stigma associated feelings of low self-esteem, and, with it, depression and acting-out behaviors.[23] Stigmas speak to the idea of difference and how difference shames us and those we know.

12

Shame Across
Time and Place

There are two views of emotional states. In what I will call the *universal* view, emotional states are assumed to be the same over place and time. Universalists think that the way things are here and now is the way they always were and will be; they may appear to be different, but they are not. The universalist holds that the feelings of shame, for whatever reasons, are the same whether you are a 10-year-old American child or a 40-year-old American adult, or, for that matter, a 40-year-old Indian, Balinese, or Japanese adult. What precipitates the shame, how the shame is expressed, and whether you attend to it or not may differ, but the shame *feeling* (if we could measure it) is always, and in every culture, the same.

In what I will call the *relative* view, emotional states are assumed to vary across time, and from culture to culture. Relativists emphasize differences. They believe that feeling states are related to what causes them. Your age, your manner of expressing them, and whether you experience them or not alters the feelings. Shame over an action that disrupts your social group, shame over aggressive impulses, and shame over your individual failure at a task are different feelings. Shame for a 10 year old is a different feeling than shame for an adult.

This universal-relativistic argument permeates the study of cultures and history, and colors debates about the nature of self and feeling. Irving Hallowell, a universalist, argues that all people have some belief about personal identities that exist over time and whose boundaries separate the individual from others.[1] Clifford Geertz, in contrast, argues from a more relativistic point of view that the Western concept of the person, "however incorrigible it may seem to us, [is] a rather peculiar idea within the context of the world's cultures."[2]

All human beings are similar in some important ways: no matter where or when we exist, we all need to perform certain essential tasks such as eating, regulating our body functions, reproducing, and the like. Moreover, and perhaps even more important, we have the same bodily features. Logically, similar physical structures are likely to give rise to certain universals. For example, facial expressions of the basic emotions share a universal neuromusculature that is organized in the same fashion across cultures and time. People who are joyful show a happy face everywhere and in all times—if they are willing to reveal their joy.

I am a universalist, and I will therefore argue that the state of shame is the same over place and time. I have read about cultural differences, but I have discovered no evidence to challenge the view that shame everywhere is produced by self blame following an important failure of the self. I further hold that, because the state of shame is so intense and aversive, humans everywhere attempt to rid themselves of it, through processes we have already considered, which include laughing, forgetting, confessing, and making elaborate emotional substitutions.

What is not universal is the nature of the internalized standards, rules, and goals whose violation precipitates shame. These do vary over time and place. The likelihood of attributing self blame in response to failure to meet standards also varies, as do the ways in which shame is expressed and the ways by which we attempt to rid ourselves of it. Clearly, culture is an important frame of reference, one that gives meaning to universal experiences.

In a series of studies, Jeannette Haviland and I observed that 3-month-old infants differed in their facial response to the approach of strangers. Boy children tended to lower their eyelids, while girls tended to open their eyes wide. The same sex differences were seen when these children observed pictures of geometric patterns. The behaviors seemed associated with the observation of new things. But what did they mean?

We asked a group of adults what open eyes indicated. Their answers varied, but most suggested interest, friendliness, openness, invitation, and naiveté. In contrast, eye narrowing conveyed to them suspicion, hostility, defensiveness, and thoughtfulness.

If we applied the meaning system of contemporary American society to the behaviors of 3-month-old infants, we would capture, in part, our (admittedly slowly changing) male and female stereotypes. But if we applied the meaning system of an isolated tribal people in the Amazon rain forest, the meaning of these behaviors might well be different. In fact, the eye pattern we observed with American children may have no meaning other than the meaning imparted by the American cultural frame.

The universal view and the relativistic view are not antithetical. Some universals may appear only at the level of behavior; these universals must wait for culture to assign them specific meaning. Other universals may be related more to deep structures that carry with them a specific meaning, but even here different meanings may well be assigned by different cultural frames.

Although the self differs in time and place, a point to which we shall return in a moment, all self systems include knowledge of, and beliefs in, standards, the prerequisite necessary for the elicitation of shame. How could they not? All selves exist in a world with other selves, a community with established standards for actions, thoughts, and feelings. All people evaluate their actions against some set of standards. When human beings fail, they look for a cause. All thinking human beings, no matter what their cultural differences, recognize cause and effect. Experiencing failure, they look for its cause in themselves, in others, in the nature of the world as they understand it, in the work of God or gods, in fate or chance. If they choose to locate the cause of failure in themselves, and this seems likely at least some of the time, then the focus of the fault has to be something that they themselves have done wrong. This reference to the self may confine itself to one aspect of the self, the "specific self," or it may reflect on all of the self, the "global self."

Knowledge or belief about the self system and its meaning plays a critical role in the shame process. How does the idea of a specific self, as opposed to that of a global self, affect our understanding of shame? I have chosen until now to consider the self and shame within the frame of modern Western culture. All humans are located within their own meaning systems: an American has a meaning system that differs in many respects from an Indian's meaning system, just as the meaning system of a Hindu Indian and a Muslim Indian differ. Now it is time to widen our frame and look at self and shame across place and across time. Within a different frame, we may be able to understand, for example, the disappearance of hysterical illness and the rise of new disorders such as narcissism and multiple personality.

Changes Across Place

When we look at cultural differences in the concept of a person or self, we see a wide diversity of forms. The modern Western idea of self is only one of many. Even so, the same situations that elicit shame in the West elicit shame universally. We must rely for the data on the work of cultural anthropologists who give us a view of many cultures; those I will discuss here include the Javanese, Balinese, Moroccan, Ilonget (of the Philippines), Indian, and Japanese cultures. Although we will see differences, I agree with Geertz that "one feels reasonably safe in saying, that the concept of person exists in recognizable form among all social groups."[3]

Geertz's view of the Western concept of person is a useful starting point. For Geertz, the Western tradition conceives of a person as "a bounded, unique, more or less integrated, motivational and cognitive universe, a dynamic center of awareness, emotion, judgment, and action organized into a distinctive whole and set contrastively both against other such wholes and against its social and natural background." As Europeans or Americans, we see ourselves as unique, bounded in space and over time as a unit; this unit can be defined independent of other units. These units live together, but not within each other. Moreover, although each unit is made up of parts, these parts are highly integrated.

The Many Selves

Other views of a person are certainly possible. Outside the Western tradition, the idea of multiple selves is quite common. The Javanese, according to Geertz, for example, conceive of a person made up of two sets of contrasts, an inside ("lair") and an outside ("batin"), that are not related. We might categorize the inside self as the subjective self, and outside self as the behavior of the self. These two aspects are independent. The task associated with achieving a good life is to put each into a proper order. The Javanese have "a bifurcated concept of self, half ungestured feeling and half unfelt gesture."[4]

Geertz contrasts the Javanese with the Balinese. The latter stylize all aspects of individuality so as to mute or flatten their roles as individuals. They define themselves not as unique individuals, but as part of a pattern within the wider culture. The person is conceptualized as a representative of a generic type. These generic types are varied; so, too, then, is the self. What we would recognize as personal expression or idiosyncratic aspects is absent, since the Balinese define and are defined by a nexus of roles. They are assigned forms around a variety of positions in the nexus. A particularly telling feature of Balinese culture is the significance of birth order as a means of categorizing people. There are four birth orders: first, second, third, and fourth. All children are assigned to one of these positions, an assignment that marks identity throughout life. If a child dies, this death has no effect on birth-order designation: the next born keeps the same birth order, even though the earlier position is empty. After four children are born, the system repeats as necessary (a fifth-born child is assigned to the first order, a seventh-born child to the third order). Birth order is a significant component of identity in Balinese society even though it does not reflect anything unique about the individual. Geertz informs us that the Moroccans, on the other hand, are defined chiefly by their relationships to others, and by group membership; however, they segregate their inner selves.[5]

In each of these three cultures, the self is defined differently. The Javanese and Moroccan sense of self appears more fragmented than our own. The Balinese attempt to reduce the uniqueness of the self through a flattening or muting of roles. Nevertheless, despite significant differences, all three cultures have a concept of self and standards in regard to that self. Moreover, in all these cultures violation of these standards leads to self blame and to shame. The Javanese attempt to order themselves both inside and outside to achieve "alus," a refined state, rather than "kasar," a vulgar state. For the inside, religious discipline, and for the outside, etiquette, provide the rules needed to arrive at the perfect order. We can logically surmise that failure in one or both areas represents failure of that self, and so is likely to lead to shame.

Failure also leads to shame for the Balinese. Failure consists of exposure of the individual's self, the lifting of his elaborate mask of role and position: "When this occurs, as it sometimes does, the immediacy of the moment is felt with excruciating intensity and men become suddenly and unwillingly creatural, locked in mutual embarrassment as though they had happened upon each other's nakedness."[6] Notice here Geertz's use of the terms "excruciating intensity," "embarrassment," and "nakedness." Surely these terms indicate a state of shame. The failure of the self is the failure of role and the dissolving of the standardized public identity. The point I wish to stress here is that shame occurs when standards are violated, when fault is attributed to self (that self or part of self that is involved), and when self rather than action (or its part) is focused upon. *The context and nature of the standards and the expressions of shame may differ; however, the mechanism for eliciting shame remains intact.*

We can see that self in these cultures differs from the Western self in at least one important feature. Neither the Javanese nor the Moroccans have the idea of a single unified self. For these cultures, different aspects of the self can exist independently, each having standards and each being capable of fault.

The concept of multiple selves is also found among the Ilongets of the Philippines and the Gahuku-Gawa of New Guinea.[7] The idea of an "I," a consistent self, is absent where selves are defined by the contexts in which the person is engaged. In cultures in which roles and role changes occur according to context, and in which one's nature is defined by specifics rather than abstractions, the qualities of the self remain fluid. For the Ilongets, "their deepest sense of whom they are is located in a set of actions." There is no core self, only a changing entity without a personal history. Nevertheless, Ilongets know shame, even if "only with reference to occasional sorts of contexts and relationships."[8] Because the Ilongets have standards, these standards can be violated, and their violation can lead to shame. "Thus, whereas the affect 'shame' may everywhere concern investments of the individual in a particular image of the self, the ways that this emotion works depends on socially dictated ways of reckoning the claims of selves and the demands of situations."[9]

These cultures provide us with examples of self systems in which the self is embedded in the actions of the person and changing roles, defined not by a core invariance, but by roles that change in the context of specific actions. As Richard Shweder points out, this type of thinking extends beyond the idea of self and characterizes classification processes in general.[10] Luria's studies of classification point out that, for preindustrial people, the ability for abstract classifying is almost absent.[11] Testing peasants in Central Asia prior to industrialization, he found that they could not classify objects as the same, based on some abstract similarity. For example, he showed people four different objects—a blue plate, a blue flower, a blue sky, and a blue cloth—and asked them in what way they were similar. While industrialized people would answer "They are all blue," the peasants ignored the color similarity. In fact, when he pointed out a common blueness, they objected, arguing that they were not the same. The ability to find invariance across change was not meaningful for them. Luria related their way of thinking to the type of lives the peasants lived, and suggested that when they became industrialized, their way of thinking would change.

In the same way, we can argue that the specific structure of the culture determines whether people embedded in this culture will abstract an invariant self from the flow of diverse actions and roles. I believe that some form of invariance exists, at least at the level of memory and action, if not at the level of objective self-awareness, in all cultures. But this remains to be proven.

The idea of multiple selves raises some concerns about my view of shame. Recall that shame is activated when the self, rather than its action, fails in regard to important standards. If the self is fragmented, how can the self fail? Perhaps my use of the term *global* has been misleading. Global can refer to all of the self if there is unity, but also to a self of the moment if there is no unity. In other words, evaluation of the self's action does not have to encompass all possible selves in the case where there is more than one self. The self at the moment fails, and this self is shamed. Other selves may not be simultaneously shamed. If the shame is only attached to one self, that may encourage movement to a self not ashamed.[12]

I-Self and We-Self

The Western view of self encompasses not only a single self, but a self alone. As Geertz has stated, the unit of the self in the modern Western view contrasts with other such units and against the natural and social background. While we in the West recognize that the self grows through interaction with the social nexus, we believe that its mature state is marked by separation from this social nexus. Margaret Mahler argues that the most important phase of self development takes place in the *individuation-separation* period. What, then, could be clearer? For us, now, a whole self is a separated self, unbounded and free. This idea of personal freedom may be the cause of increasing shame.

In the cultures I have mentioned, we see that people and their identities are embedded within a social context and within the context of their actions. I have referred to a we-self as opposed to an I-self in accordance with the usage of others.[13] The embeddedness of individuals within their social and natural context can occur whether the context is a fixed entity or a changing pattern of action. In a changing pattern of action and role, the self assumes many different forms; in a fixed pattern, the self may not. Even so, in both types of context, the self is embedded in other we-selves and is defined by these we-selves.

Embeddedness is especially characteristic of the Indian and Japanese cultures. As we examine them, while noting some differences between the two, especially those related to achievement, I will stress the similarities that unite them. I am particularly indebted to the ideas of Alan Roland, but I have also consulted the ethnographic work of Richard Shweder, the *Oriyas of India,* and Ruth Benedict's classic work on the Japanese.[14] I do not have time or space to consider the fascinating issue of different selves, for example, the spiritual self versus the familial self. Evidence indicates, at least for the Japanese, that the private self is kept very secret. Roland points out that conducting therapy in Japan often reveals no inner self at all: the Japanese self is like an onion, it reveals many levels but no core as we know it.

The we-self is characterized in both the Indian and the Japanese cultures by a strong identification with the family and other groups. The interest, reputation, and honor of the family and other groups occupies the center of the we-self. The ego ideal is one of reciprocity: responsibilities and obligations define the self. Indian and Japanese personas are duty-based rather than rights-based, predicated on connections between the me and the other, rather than on the independence of the individual. A rights-based view of personhood leads to individual freedom and differentiation. The we-self is a symbiotic self in which the ego ideal also centers around proper behavior (we might call it etiquette) in a diverse hierarchical organization of relationships. The individual first confronts this hierarchical organization of relationships within the family. He then confronts more diverse and complicated versions of hierarchical organization through interaction with specific groups, or institutional units. The sense of identity develops and is achieved within these structured groups and is fueled by emotional interdependence. Not only are children in a family or junior members in a group expected to show unquestioning loyalty, compliance, and dependence, but they can expect, in return, the nurturance and protection of the others.

The we-self is socialized from the beginning. Children are raised by their mothers to be extremely sensitive and concerned with others' feelings and needs. In return, their own needs are carefully monitored and satisfied by the mother. The nature of the we-self is the focus on the other, since people know and expect others to focus on them and their needs. Takeo Doi has called this mutual dependency "amae."[15] It is important to note that dependency characterizes each member. The child is dependent upon the mother to satisfy its needs; the satisfaction of the child's needs satisfies the needs of the mother. This model can be extended to the group outside the family so that one's self-esteem, sense of worth, and identity are determined by group, not individual, action(s). In Japan, for example, one's self-esteem is more involved with the particular school, college, or work group with which one is associated than with the amount of money one earns: the group, not the individual, is the measure of success.

Shame occurs around the we-self. The standards most important to the we-self are to avoid friction or hostility and to maintain harmonious relationships. These are the core self values. Japanese experience shame when there is a failure to do all this, for example, when the mother does not sense the needs of her child. This is an especially problematic example since children are taught not to think of themselves. Since they do not think of themselves, they are dependent on the sensitivity of the other. Failure of the other, therefore, is quite shameful.[16] Failure can, of course, occur vis-à-vis any hierarchically organized social structure or group. Shame is used in both India and Japan as one of the paramount means of instituting controls in childrearing. Bad behavior in children is immediately met with shaming and other forms of punishment. Good behavior is confirmed with subtle nonverbal expressions, since overt praise is to be avoided: praise is not only immodest, but it fosters a focus on the I-self.

Shaming the child tends to increase the interdependency between child and parent, since it focuses attention on the failure of the reciprocal relationship. Moreover, as we have seen, shame can promote dependency if it leads to forgiveness rather than to anger. Since within-group anger is not allowed in Japanese culture, and therefore the substitution of anger for shame rarely occurs, shame is likely to be owned, and therefore dissipated through forgiveness. Thus, in the Japanese culture, shame or failure followed by the forgiveness of the group are the essential elements of cohesiveness. This also is true in India. While failure, or what the Indians consider "sin," in the natural order is very common, Indian culture has many ritualistic means to expiate shame, including fasting, isolation, meditation, prayer, and confession.[17] As a general rule, this combination of shame and forgiveness, leading to dependency, seems to hold. Dyadic or group cohesiveness can be best maintained through shame and the repression of anger, combined with forgiveness. Because they are characterized by these patterns, both Japan and India are categorized as shame cultures.[18]

Let us return, for the moment, to the general principles underlying the production of shame. First, there must be a self, in this case defined as a we-self. Second, there must be a set of standards, rules, and goals. Both Japan and India have recognized social rules. Third, the self must break a rule. But can a we-self break a rule? Here my argument becomes more complex. First, even when there is a we-self definition of a person, that person must still have some separate identity. That is, things can happen to the I-self without happening to the others partially incorporated as the we-self. A good example of this is found in Shweder's account of menstruation rules among the Oriya Indians.[19] When the woman has her period, she becomes polluted. She cannot eat with her family or sleep in her husband's bed. She cannot be touched. When she is approached by her young child she must say "Mara heici. Chlu na! Chlu na!," "I am polluted. Don't touch me! Don't touch me!"

Lest we think only women in this Oriya culture have a unique I-self, pollution rules also indicate a culture wide concept of I-self: the father cannot be touched after washing and before worshipping the family deity, and a grandmother will not touch her grandchild until she takes off her outside clothes, since they may have come into contact with a lower caste, and therefore could be polluted. Even children have a game in which one child is considered polluted and tries to touch the other children in a kind of tag. Such rituals inform us about two aspects of the self. Although much of the self is defined by a we-self rather than an I-self, an I-self, bounded and unique, clearly exists. Obviously, it is "I" who am polluted and who can pollute you if we touch. If we do not touch, then I, not we, am polluted. Thus, although a we-self dominates, the I-self exists at some level, can fail, and thus can be shamed.

The next feature needed for shame is self blame. Again, how can a we-self have blame? A we-self cannot conceptualize individual blame, so again I need to argue that an I-self can coexist with a we-self. Again, the Indians show that self blame is possible within a we-self system.[20] For Hindus, the karma or the natural order can be disturbed. The disturbance of the natural order is explained by sin. The sin can be caused by an individual, the I-self. There are many personal sins, including being reborn, or being born a woman, or even having a lingering death.

The Japanese are critical of the child when she violates a we-self rule. The most important standards are the standards of the group; violation of group, rather than individual, standards is most likely to produce a shame feeling. When the standard is not the group's, violation is less likely to be shameful. Thus, behavior that might be shameful in the context of the group can take place and not be shameful when it does not take place in relation to the group. Consider aggression and rage. Because these are not tolerated within the group, their expression in the group is shameful. However, their expression outside of the group can occur and then is not considered wrong. This inner and outer group differentiation is confusing for Westerners since our sense of what is incorrect behavior, in theory, does not depend on in- or out-of-group considerations. It also seems to explain the rage commonly associated with the Japanese culture, a culture which appears to be highly ritualized and polite.[21] Roland suggests that Japanese culture reveals a strong dissociation of anger feelings caused by failure of we-self or "amae" rules: "Their dependency and narcissistic needs are so interspersed, considerable anger [for us shame-anger] is generated by disappointed expectations, slights and lack of reciprocity."[22] In Japanese culture, these feelings of anger may manifest themselves as aggressive out-group behavior (their warlike history) or in economic competition and hard work (contemporary history). For the Indians, Roland suggests that the repressed shame and anger leads to hysterical, obsessive, and compulsive symptoms. In fact, outbursts of rage are rare, but when they occur they can give rise to amnesia.

The Japanese, of course, differ from the Indians in many ways. One of the most relevant differences for this discussion of shame has to do with achievement. Most Japanese are more achievement-oriented than most Indians. Their drive for achievement is fueled by shame. While mothers in both cultures establish a strong symbiotic emotional relationship with their children, in Japan, mothers insist on achievement and accomplishment as a sign of love and respect. Thus, to fail places children in a highly shamed situation since they fail in the we-self relationship.

———— • ————

The self system I examined in earlier chapters was the system most familiar to us, a single self independent of other selves. Is the process of shame production, as I have outlined it, dependent on belief in this Western concept of self? I think not. I believe that the available data support the view that this process has strong universal features.

Shame obviously appears in cultures that have different concepts of what the self is. But shame appears when the self, however defined, violates core standards and accepts blame for its failure, blame focused on the self rather than the action of the self. Shame can be discerned in the nature of the actions following fault, related to the self rather than to reparation. The self seeks forgiveness from its shame. Shame can also be seen in the traces it leaves; rage over failure, for example, is a sure sign of the presence of unacknowledged shame. The self that fails in a we-self culture has more to do with group than with individual standards. Failures of I-self have to do with personal failures (vis-à-vis standards) that may or may not involve others. Failures of the we-self have to do with self in group or familial failures (vis-à-vis standards) that always involve others. Internal or self blame attributions apparently can be made in either an I-self or a we-self culture, whether the self is a single self or a multiple self. Although here we have less information, it does appear that the self of the moment can accept blame for the failure of the for-the-moment standard and can make attributions involving the present self rather than the present action. There is some question as to what the present self does when shamed. Certainly, it is possible that the at-the-moment shamed self can move away from the shame by deploying another self, especially if an alternative self appropriate for the situation is available. This certainly is a problem that needs further investigation; it can be explored, at least in our culture, in multiple personality disorders.

Cultural Differences in Shame

Cultures differ in the nature of their emotional lives. Some, like the Japanese, have been characterized as shame cultures. Such a characterization may be appropriate, given the role of shaming in Japanese childrearing. Any culture that uses shaming and humiliation in childrearing is likely to register high in shame. The Japanese may experience more shame, too, because their standards involve others as well as themselves, a feature of we-self cultures.

> *Imagine that you do not study for a test and consequently receive a poor grade. You feel badly about this failure, but you know you are a good student. You determine to study harder in the future. I would say that, from your viewpoint, you feel guilty over your failure. Next, however, imagine you must tell your mother about your poor test results. She feels she has failed as a parent because you did so poorly. From her viewpoint, your failure induces shame in her. You, of course, are aware of her shame and of your involvement in it. Now you, too, feel shame. The interdependency of selves, the we-self, is likely to promote shame. However, since your shame cannot be expressed as anger, you must either become depressed or ask for forgiveness. Either outcome is likely to bind the individuals more tightly and, therefore, promote more shame which can be forgiven.*

This analysis allows us to explore cultural differences in shame. Even in the West, the degree to which groups or families are interdependent is the degree to which they are likely to experience shame, though other factors, of course, play a role. The extent to which shaming and humiliating techniques are employed in personal relations, especially the socialization of children, and the extent to which group cohesiveness is maintained through mutual respect and a tolerance for anger and differences are examples of other factors. Subcultural differences in the elicitation of and response to shame do exist. Earlier, we saw how poverty, class, and race subject people to shame and humiliation, and how increased rage, expressed toward the self by suicide and toward others by murder, characterizes these subgroups.

Religious Differences in Shame

Religious differences regarding shame are likely to exist. While it is possible to make claims in either direction, my own belief is that Judaism and mainstream Protestantism are more guilt-oriented, while Catholicism and fundamentalist Christian religions are more shame-oriented. I base this distinction on several factors including the role of forgiveness, belief in heaven (and hell), and the nature of action in this world.

The Judaic belief in God does not relieve the people from God's wrath if they fail to abide by his commandments. To lead a good life is to perform the actions prescribed by him. The Old Testament is full of prescriptions. Many sections of the first five books of the Old Testament describe what the chosen people should or should not do. The combined list is enormous and detailed. Thus, the standards, rules and goals for Jews are clear. Self blame is recognized and repentance has less to do with God's forgiveness than with the commitment to good deeds. It appears, therefore, that failure can be undone by reparation, and reparation is associated with action. As the rabbis of the Roman period would say, "We have been taught that deeds make atonement for a man, and that repentance and good deeds are the shield against punishment."[23] Notice that deeds are the key to failure in adhering to standards. To combat failure, a focus on action in the world rather than prayer for forgiveness underlies the Judaic code. For example, in Jonah we hear that after sinning "the people of Nineveh believed God and proclaimed a fast, and put on sackcloth, from the greatest of them even to the least of them . . . and God saw their *works,* that they moved from their evil ways; and God repented of the evil that He had said He would do unto them and He did it not" (3:5, 10).

Reparation as a resolution of the problem of failure, as we have seen, is a sign of guilt, not of shame. Judaism has no concept of a hereafter, a heaven or a hell where the good are rewarded and the evil are damned for eternity, according to what good or bad they did while alive. Jewish reward or punishment takes place in this world.[24]

Catholicism is predicated on an entirely different premise. To begin with, the sin of Adam and Eve has not been forgiven; its burden is borne by all the people, who are born in sin. Sin must be forgiven. Jesus takes upon himself the primordial sin and, through his suffering, redeems humanity. Note here several significant features. The major theme of Catholicism is global attribution of sin, without reference to any specific action. Again, as we have seen, global attribution without reference to specific behavior is a hallmark of shame. Forgiveness is, of course, also part of the Catholic tradition. Jesus, on the cross, forgives the people; through his priests, continuing forgiveness is always possible. Confession and absolution, no matter what the sin, will ensure God's forgiveness. Certainly, specific actions, such as avoidance of sin and prayer, are important, but the major focus is global forgiveness.

The role of heaven (and hell) and the hereafter is another indication of Catholicism's global orientation. A moral life is rewarded in heaven, not on earth. Indeed, the moral person may have a terrible earthly life, but judged after death, she will sit at the right hand of God and enjoy eternal happiness.

Protestantism, like Judaism, is associated with action in this world. Action is to be rewarded; in fact, action informs at least some of the people about their predetermined status. Forgiveness is downplayed and confession is eliminated. The people seek to expiate their guilt through good works. Even heaven and hell are downplayed. Fundamentalist Protestants, in contrast, are more like Catholics in their shame orientation. Forgiveness follows belief, not action: born-again Christians hold that salvation is made possible by the belief that Jesus Christ is God and that he died for us.

Selves Over Time

We have seen that beliefs about the nature of the self vary as a function of culture. The modern Western view that the self is a single unit, and that this unit is separate from other selves so constructed, is not universal. Even today, other culture groups differ in their conceptions of self.

Indeed, what we think of as "the Western view" itself evolved over time in response to social changes.[25] Julian Jaynes offers the controversial hypothesis that the Western notion of self underwent a radical change in pre-Hellenic times.[26] He believes the *Iliad*, written before the *Odyssey*, reflects a period before human beings had self concepts similar to our own. They lacked objective self-awareness because they could not "think" as we do today. Thinking entails integrating information from the right hemisphere with information from the left; the pre-Hellenic peoples could not do this and interpreted information from the right hemisphere as the voices of gods who advised them at times of uncertainty. Jaynes sees a change in consciousness reflected in the content of the earlier *Iliad* versus the later *Odyssey:* "The contrast with the *Iliad* is astonishing. Both in word and deed and character, the *Odyssey* describes a new and different world inhabited by new and different beings. These beings are not gods directing human action, but in fact humans acting as if they had consciousness of their action."[27] Jaynes's postulated development of consciousness through the breakdown of the bicameral mind was caused by a variety of changes, most of them cultural, for example, the weakening of the auditory mode of thinking with the advent of writing, the ineffectuality of gods in the time of historical upheavals, and the inherent fragility of hallucinatory control, among others. His book is nothing less than an attempt to explain, from a historical point of view, the development of our human objective self-awareness.

The development of consciousness, which Jaynes places somewhere around 2000 B.C., gave the self a sense of unity; the fragmentation of the bicameral mind gave way to the unity of objective self-awareness. At the same time another integrative effort began: the development of the concept of monotheism. The polytheistic world was characterized by gods for each action and even for different emotions: Eros for love, the Furies for retributive justice, Athena for wisdom, etc. These separate gods for different contexts, functions, and emotions may have corresponded to the different selves. I think it is reasonable to assume that, as the Western concept of self moved toward the idea of unity, the concept of God moved in a similar fashion. The special Judaic influence on monotheism should be noted. The Ten Commandments of God, given to the Jewish people, serve as the basis for the Western Judeo-Christian belief about the moral actions of the people. Three of the Ten Commandments concern the "one" God. A broad historical perspective indicates that the concept of self and the development of consciousness have undergone change even in our own culture.

More immediate changes in the Western idea of self and the relationship of self to others can also be seen. These changes reflect the two sets of cultural differences I have already discussed, those having to do with multiple selves, and those having to do with the I-self versus the we-self. These two sets of differences are orthogonal. It is possible to imagine an I-self which, although not defined by its relationship to others, nevertheless changes depending on action or function, if not in normal circumstances, certainly in the case of multiple personality disorder. A we-self that changes depending on the situation is also possible to imagine. Consider the Japanese, whose behavior toward familiar people is quite different from their behavior toward unfamiliar people. With each person, the we-self interacts differently. To understand these alternatives, we need to consider the development of self based on social connectedness or individuality as a different process from the interaction of formed selves in different contexts.

Let us examine some changes in the Western idea of self. In what follows I have drawn heavily on Roy F. Baumeister's "How the Self Became a Problem: A Psychological Review of Historical Research."[28] In all historical analysis, there is no ultimate criterion of correctness, so it is possible that others might disagree with these conclusions.

During the medieval period, people existed as part of society. People were assigned their places by God; fulfillment consisted of knowledge of that place and the stability of this knowledge.[29] The person's selfhood was equated with social roles, including the roles related to family, group, and God. Since one's selfhood was defined by place and context, exile was the equivalent of death. Only in the literature of the 11th and 12th centuries can we discover individuals who have a unique perspective not necessarily shared by others.[30] At about the same time, as Philippe Aries notes, the judgment of individual souls in Christianity appeared; this theological change also marks the idea of an individual.[31] However, as Baumeister observes, it is not until we reach the 16th century that the self stops being equated to its action in contexts.[32]

By the 16th century the fixed hierarchy of the Middle Ages had begun to collapse. The middle class had begun to assert itself, and social roles became unstable. At this point the I-self began to emerge, since an unstable context cannot serve as the defining feature of self.

Associated with the rise of the I-self as opposed to the we-self is the development and use of notions of privacy. There were changes both in personal habits and in physical structures to mark the separation of the self from others.[33] We see this developmentally in children of the 20th century. Although we adults insist on privacy—our infants have their own rooms, and bathroom doors usually are closed—children only begin to show their own desire for privacy at around two years of age. This desire I view as one of the measures of the emergence of selfhood. Deception and pretense also allow us to examine selves independent of their actions. The rise in the interest of theater in England and France at this time may also reflect the development of the I-self.

By the end of the 18th and beginning of the 19th centuries, personality, as a concept independent of social rank or roles, became an important self-definer. Personality refers to both an inner and an outer self. During this time, the extent of the inner self expanded. The end of the 18th century marked the change from duty-based to rights-based obligations. Individuals' roles *vis-à-vis* others, and their definition of self through them, increasingly moved them toward the assertion of individual rights and negotiation of those rights against the rights of others. Selves became defined more by their differences than by their similarities. Equality became a paramount virtue, and the belief that all people are equal made reference to rights, not characteristics. The rise of the belief that the individual had rights that transcended the social good pitted the individual *against* society, indeed, it raised the individual *above* society. People were beginning to define themselves by their separateness from the group.

The collapse of the fixed order was accompanied by a change in religious beliefs. Fulfillment had been defined for hundreds of years by the Christian idea of salvation and heavenly reward, but by the 18th century, and probably before, given the problems raised by the Reformation and ensuing conflicts, this definition became inadequate. Loss of belief in salvation turned the individual to seek fulfillment through actions of the self *for* the self, through romantic love or work, for example, two of the emerging forms of self-fulfillment.

By the 19th century, the idea of selfhood as defined by individual action was widespread, not only in political and philosophical writings, but in imaginative literature as it flowered during the Romantic movement. This movement promoted the idea that the fulfillment of the individual was achieved best by separating people from society. The belief in an innocent "natural man" who was contaminated by society was perhaps most forcefully expressed by Thoreau, who took himself out of society to live alone in the woods. Thus, the individual alone and unencumbered by others became the ideal self, the self most complete and fulfilled.

Moreover, industrialization was separating the family and driving men to work outside the home. The division of labor by sex was one obvious consequence. This change in the individual's relationship to labor served not only to alter family patterns of work but caused a redistribution of the population from the land into cities, which served to further disrupt individuals' identifications with specific places and specific others.

Theories about the nature of the individual proliferated in the emerging fields of medicine and psychiatry. Darwin's theory of evolution was popularly seen as the survival of the fittest, with individuals pitted against one another. The explorations of Charcot, Janet, and Freud into the psyche further exalted the individual. In fact, when Freud abandoned his seduction theory and introduced in its place the Oedipus complex model, he shifted psychoanalysis away from the interpersonal as an explanation of the self toward the intrapsychic.

During the first half of the 20th century, the West witnessed catastrophic wars and the collapse of the social order. The kings of Europe, and the aristocracy with them, finally disappeared. Religion continued to decline, and the secular sciences enjoyed a spectacular rise. Scientific discoveries, in almost every field, attenuated beliefs in the possibility of a permanent social order. The rise of relativism in physics at the turn of the 20th century exemplifies the fleetingness of observable order and truth. Nothing is as it appears. In such times, definitions of self move in the direction of the I-self.

Moreover, and perhaps most important, romantic love and work become the anchors of self-definition, with love defining the emotional self and work the competent self. But these, too, proved elusive. The Industrial Revolution and factory production often robbed workers of their identity. It was impossible to derive much satisfaction from a job that required the worker to assemble a single part on a conveyor belt. By its nature, romantic love is not permanent, and is all the less permanent if based primarily on sexual passion. Unfortunately, its own instability is not apparent.

Thus, in the last half of the 20th century, the quest for pleasure at one level, for simple feeling at a more basic level, determines how people choose to define and fulfill themselves. Without context—place or other—the maintenance of identity becomes the focus of activity. When asked "Who are you?," in the past we could answer, "A farmer, a son, a member of a religious group." Now, answering this question is more difficult. Earlier labels no longer define the real us. The reality of ourselves now turns on itself for definition. Feelings and thoughts become the focus of self. "If I can feel, then I exist" has replaced Descartes's famous axiom. The last phase of individuation, the separating from other selves and the process of self-defining, requires consciousness of feelings. The job of feeling now replaces the job of performing in specific roles and situations.

The job of feeling requires constant stimulation and variety. Being bored is equated with not existing. Metaphorically, people need to pinch themselves to make sure they are alive. Consumption for its own sake, for the feeling, not the need, has become the cultural norm. By purchasing and possessing things, we confirm our existence in the absence of any other way to confirm it. Individualization, by definition, must turn the self toward itself.

We focus not only on our feelings, but upon the whole of ourselves, thus fusing subject and object. The tasks that define us diminish as we take on the task of creating ourselves. The age of self also is the age of self-actualization. The theoretical base of Rogers and Maslow produces the idea of an "actualizing tendency" present in all human beings.[34] We are supposed to have a righting principle that moves us to realize our full potential. While there are social conditions that facilitate this realization—unconditional positive regard and empathy, for example—the locus of control is in the person. It is there, in the person, rather than in the relationship to others, that actualization takes place, when organismic experience, what I have called subjective self-awareness and others have called the unconscious (the inner), and objective self-awareness, or consciousness (the outer), are made congruent.[35] Of perhaps even more importance is the idea of complete empathy, unconditional love, love "because you are you." This kind of love emphasizes the global self rather than specific actions. The belief not only in the possibility of unconditional love, but in its usefulness in self-actualization, points again to the connections among individuation, self-actualization, and shame.

The psychology of self-actualization nicely illustrates the historical trend toward the I-self expressed in individuation and alienation. Not only was it a part of an emerging psychology of the self, but, perhaps more crucially, it caught the imagination of the public. Maslow's therapeutic approach fostered the view that the task of the self was to better the self. This could be accomplished in many ways. The proliferation of self-help books bears witness to the power of the notion of self-betterment. Almost all bookstores include a section devoted to these books, each directing us to still another way to become a better person, through diet, or exercise, or meditation, or the power of positive thinking. We are urged to pay attention to ourselves and to become the better person that we could be. These books, at times, do address our relationship to others, but the central concern in this age of individuation is always ourselves.[36] We can learn how to please a man or woman, fall in or out of love, or make friends. To do so, we need to effect changes in ourselves—the point of all these exertions is to make ourselves happier.

Changes in Parental Practices

Cultural values are transmitted through childrearing practices. As we explored how these practices induce shame, I noted that some were more effective in that regard than others. Parental behavior differs from subculture to subculture; thus, to suggest a particular change as characteristic of the whole culture may be to overstate. But some data do seem to suggest that the practices of working-class parents follow those of middle-class parents with a time lag of perhaps up to 30 years. This lag may be true also of regional or ethnic differences. From the 1940s to the 1960s, for example, middle-class mothers did not nurse their children. By the 1980s, most middle-class mothers did nurse their babies. Poorer mothers continued to nurse their babies after middle-class and upper-class women had stopped nursing, and switched to bottles and formula just as the middle classes were changing back to breastfeeding. Obviously, the cultural value of breastfeeding has flip-flopped twice in the last 50 years, with middle-class mothers leading a movement away from breastfeeding that lower-class mothers were slow to follow, and then leading a similar movement back.

Our information about socialization techniques in this century is limited, although we do have some data from the 1930s to the present. Parental practices should follow the general societal trends I have sketched, and therefore should reveal the transition from a we-self to an I-self that increasingly emphasizes individuation. Obvious markers include the removal of the infant from the parental bed to a separate bed, and later to its own room, and the encouragement of behaviors that not only establish individual ownership—"This is mine and this is yours"—but also support privacy. How different our cultural practices are from those of many others and how they reflect our underlying view of self can be seen by comparing them to those of a we-self culture. A Japanese couple, for example, keeps their child in the same bed with them for the first three years of life. The Conge for *infant* means "river between two banks"; the term reflects the sleeping pattern of the family. The child not only sleeps in the parents' bed, but lies between them. Most of us in the West would see this pattern as a violation of the privacy of the adults and the child alike. One of the consequences of psychoanalytic theory has been the physical separation of the child from the parents' bed on the basis of the unfounded claim that such contact is too stimulating and is likely to lead to disorder. In science, theory is likely to reflect the concurrent world view of the scientists. In this case, psychoanalytic thought supports the idea of a private and unique individual.

Social mobility is part of the problem of individuation. The breakdown of the social order promotes such mobility. No longer must the farmer's son become a farmer. That individuals no longer have a "place," that they are free to find their own paths, is an important correlate of the idea of personal freedom and liberty. The familial links which place and order maintain, dissolve. Our children no longer are bound to us because they must live on the family farm. The expectation that children will "follow in our footsteps" disappears as duty and obligation, along with order, cease to be defining. Physically, our children have the freedom to move away from us; psychologically, they have the freedom to become themselves, not replicas of us. Indeed, we wish them to be different. Children who stay at home and work are viewed with suspicion since too-close contact with parents is now viewed as pathological. Recently, a friend reported that he

was worried about Stan, the son of our mutual friend, who had graduated
from a good university, has a fine job and a girlfriend, but wants to live
close to his family and often eats dinner with them. "Why does Stan spend
so much time at home?" In another time and place, Stan's behavior would
not be suspect.

Our relationship with our children has changed in profound ways over
the last 100 years. As we have seen, the consequence of individuation is the
separation of selves. One way to combat the pressure for separation is
romantic love. Just as romantic love now looms larger in our psychic lives,
so does the love of parents for children. Duties and obligations give way to
individual rights that can be negotiated, in part, through love relationships. This shift affects parents' socialization practices.

Historically, parents' socialization practices were designed to produce a
conspecific, someone like the parent, having the same values, living in the
same social nexus, and working at the same kind of job. They centered on
specific actions, behaviors, and goals, which could be articulated because
they were known. As the child gains independence from the parent, the
parent's specific standards, rules, and goals become less important. If I am
a farmer and I expect my son to be a farmer, then I need to teach him how
to farm. Farming involves certain information, skills, rules, and standards.
Failures to remember the information, acquire the skills, follow the rules,
and meet the standards are specific. Guilt, rather than shame, is the
emotion most produced.

How different the process becomes when what is to be taught ceases to
be specific, or even to be known, since the child's future is unclear. We have
changed our approach to parenting. Now, our object of concern is the
characteristics of individuals. The standards now are related to *being* rather
than to *doing*. The focus changes from specific to global, from action to
person. This change in focus is associated with an increase in shame.

The isolation of adults as a consequence of individuation continues even
now to lead them into the same bind with their children that they
experience with other adults, to whom they are connected by love and
friendship, not by more enduring ties like kinship or shared work
obligations. Recently, I asked 10 older couples, all between ages 65 and 70,
whom they socialized with on weekends. They reported that they saw
family at least half the time. When I asked my friends in their 50s the same
question, I found that family socializing constituted less than 10 percent of
their social life.

The child used to be viewed as property, something valuable that
needed care and attention, even love. Parental behavior was duty- and

obligation-based. Now the child is viewed as friend rather than property. The relationship between friends differs from the relationships between owner and property or between adult and child. The focus shifts from "What is best for my child?" to "What will my child think of me if I do this?" Moreover, the child as friend is capable of affecting the parents' own self attributions in a way not seen before. Recall the example of the parent's upset over the child's upset about having to obey. Parents have no logical reason to assume that children should be happy complying with a rule they do not like; their upset stems from the nature of this new relationship. The upset of the child has become the upset of the "friend." The "friend's" upset reflects on the character of the parent. Thus, parents are more readily shamed by their children when friendship, rather than the old order of property, duty, and responsibility, underlies the relationship.

As personal freedom gained acceptance as the underlying value for selves, the use of particular types of socialization practices became less appropriate. For example, swaddling of babies was discontinued in the West since personal freedom included the notion of physical mobility. Swaddling disappeared first from those Western countries where the ideal of individual freedom was the strongest and took longer to disappear in those countries not so committed to the value of freedom. Similarly, the use of physical punishment declined as the rights of the child—*independent of the parent*—increased. We all recognize that physical abuse is destructive and dangerous to the child, but no evidence indicates that physical punishment, delivered appropriately, is harmful. Our distaste for this form of socialization is predicated more on aesthetic than scientific study. Given the decline in this form of punishment, other forms must be used more often. Certainly, the use of reasoning or inductive techniques has increased. Even here, however, we have seen that these techniques are often accompanied by facial expressions of shame, disgust, contempt, and humiliation. Moreover, the use of love withdrawal has increased as physical punishment has decreased.

Parental practices concerning the use of praise have also been affected. Praise is used to highlight success since it is believed that its use is beneficial. A child's bowel movement is greeted with "What a good girl!" and a preschooler who holds back his tears after scraping his knee is told "Such a big boy!" We think of praise as a positive reward. But praise may be problematic since it is a global attribution that focuses the child on itself. Recall that the Japanese parent avoids praise. Praise techniques, while successful, are likely to lead to and promote feelings of individuality and therefore shame.

As I have tried to show, changes in parental behavior toward children and their transgressions reflect changes in the Western view of the nature of persons. Western society has put an ever-accelerating emphasis on the person as an individual, defined as an I-self. Socialization techniques enhance the movement toward individuation. Our experience as children growing up with our parents is the cauldron for self-conscious emotions, the source of our growing feelings of alienation and shame.

The number of problems associated with shame is increasing. The rise in narcissistic disorders, rage against others (expressed as child abuse, for example, and as random societal aggression), and multiple personality disorders all suggest problems associated with shame. Across cultures people differ in the amount and nature of their shame experience. No cultures or people, now or in the past, escape the shame experience. Cultures and individuals may differ in the amount of shame they experience; they surely differ in what causes shame and how they respond to it, but all know shame. The absence of shame is pathological. It makes little sense to say that a particular culture does not (did not) have anger, or fear, or, for that matter, shame. While Culture X may not have the words for these emotions, the people of Culture X do feel them. An excess of shame is also pathological. We might expect some cultures with an excess to have particular problems. Certainly, some societies appear to be overly aggressive, and it may well be that their aggression is shame-driven. Hitler fueled his rise to power 60 years ago by turning Germany's national sense of shame to his advantage: he blamed Germany's loss of World War I and postwar economic collapse on traitors, Communists, and Jews, and promised to end Germany's shame. He transformed his nation's shame into aggression, and caused World War II. The United States now continually goes to war: with the Germans and Japanese, Koreans, Vietnamese, Russians, Iranians, and Iraqis. Desert Storm, the 1991 war in the Iraqi desert, was believed by some to undo the shame of our loss in Vietnam. We also war among ourselves, as evidenced by our high murder and suicide rates, our random violence and child abuse. Even when we want to solve a problem, we use war as our model: for instance, the war on poverty. It could be that our high degree of individuation produces a high degree of shame, which is then transformed into aggression.

Cultures change over time. Our culture has become more shame-driven as we have turned toward personal freedom, and beyond it to narcissism. The self, now the object and the subject, is more likely to experience shame. And we have simultaneously rid ourselves of the religious institutions that are capable of absorbing shame, so many of us lack mechanisms for securing forgiveness.

We stand today more alone and more focused on ourselves than we have ever been. We sense in this condition a powerful freedom to be what we want, yet, at the same time, we are unhappy. Freedom to succeed is also freedom to fail. The self must often bear the blame for such failure. Shame, then, as a close shadow, haunts us, and we fear it.

Epilogue

If I am not for myself, who will be for me? If I am for myself only, what am I? If not now—when?

—Talmudic saying

Cultures differ; times change. The modern Western drive toward individuation has left us trapped by a mirror. By eliminating context and other people as the explanation for who we are once we become, we are left with nothing to see but ourselves. The rise of narcissism and related disorders is no accident. Narcissus himself, caught by his own reflection in a pool, is an appropriate icon for our age.

Our philosophies look into the mirror and attempt to define the image and give it meaning. Perhaps nowhere is there a clearer statement of the drama of the mirror than in the philosophy of existentialism, which frames the individual as a unique and separate unity, existing alone even against other such unities and the contexts that give rise to its unity. The existential individual is by his nature unbounded, unencumbered, and undefined. Such a self must exist with shame.

Jean-Paul Sartre, the most articulate spokesman of modern existentialism, declared: "Existence precedes essence." Existentialism is both an *expression* and an *end product* of individuation, as well as a *justification* for it. In *Being and Nothingness,* Sartre tries to analyze the nature of our identity and the feelings it produces. He points to consciousness as the defining principle. Human beings are marked by their consciousness; consciousness is a mode of being that exists *for* itself (what he calls "being-for-itself"). Objects—that is, not people—exist only *in* themselves ("being-in-itself"). "Consciousness is a being, the nature of which is to be conscious of the nothingness of its being."[37]

The understanding gained through consciousness, in Sartre's view, is the understanding that our nature does not dispose us toward anything. A chair has being-in-itself: its essence is chairness, and it cannot change itself into something else. A person is a being-for-itself, which is "what it is not and not what it is." We have no essence. For Sartre, this consciousness of self is what frees us. We are not bounded by an essence but free to be whatever we wish to be. Sartre's human being is the quintessential I-self, unbounded and undefined.

In my view, objective self-awareness, itself a process, not a structure, has no content. Other types of knowledge have structure, since they grow out of our specific adaptive needs.

What a perfect metaphor for people without context! Existentialism is the rationalization of individuation. I describe Sartre's views not to challenge them, but rather to show how they stand as the justification of what we have become.

But even Sartre recognizes the anguish that must arise from his definition of being. Yes, consciousness may lead to freedom, the freedom to become what you want to be, but this freedom has its price: anxiety and shame. Acceptance of true freedom is not easy. Sartre's philosophical contribution is not only to describe what we have become, but to rejoice in it. Surviving the anguish of individuation is the highest achievement of humanity. What, then, of other people?

Our relationship to others provides no solution. Sartre is very adamant about this point. Anxiety over being and nothingness cannot be resolved by the we-self. Sartre sees relationships as bondage since we are no more than objects to other selves and, as objects (self-in-itself), we lose the self for itself, which is what marks us as unique: "I am incapable of apprehending for myself the self which I am for the other, just as I am incapable of apprehending on the basis of the other-as-object which appears to me, what the other is for himself."[38]

There is no way out of this bind. The self, as Sartre sees it, is caught between the states of freedom with anxiety or bondage with no anxiety. For individuals, the noblest moments occur when they stand exposed and alone, the determinants of their own essence. Their anguish is the price they must pay for this freedom.

Erich Fromm, writing at about the same time as Sartre, confronts the dilemma of the modern self in a somewhat different way. In *Escape from Freedom*, he also sees our movement toward individuation and increased individual rights as leading to freedom, defined by him politically as the end of the authority of the medieval church and state. The consequence of freedom for him, as for Sartre, is isolation from others. Lack of freedom has a plus side, belongingness, while freedom has a negative side, insecurity. The challenge for humans that Fromm envisions is coping with the anxiety associated with freedom. Burdened by anxiety, humans seek to escape their freedom; this escape often leads to blind devotion to a cause, a leader, or a state. With vivid clarity Fromm outlines the ways in which people, overwhelmed by their isolation and anxiety, seek to surrender their freedom to avoid anxiety.

> Freedom, though it has brought him independence and rationality, has made him isolated and, thereby, anxious and powerless. This isolation is unbearable and the alternatives he is confronted with are either to escape from the burden of this freedom into new dependency and submission, or to advance to the full realization of positive freedom which is based upon the uniqueness and individuality of man.[39]

What is Fromm's solution? It is to seek self-actualization, a solution also suggested by Carl Rogers. Here his analysis, like that of all who seek complete freedom (the I-self), seems to fail. According to Fromm, self-actualization "is accomplished not only by an act of thinking but also by the realization of man's total personality, by the active expression of his emotional and intellectual potentialities."[40] These potentialities are present in all of us. The path to freedom "consists in the spontaneous activity of the total integrated personality."[41] However true this might be, it is of little prescriptive help. Fromm leads us closer to a definition when he suggests that spontaneity is the springboard to an integrated personality and that love is the foremost component of spontaneity. It is unclear how he arrives at this idea, but he does. However, his love is not love "as the dissolution of the self in another person, not love as the possession of another person, but love as spontaneous affirmation of others, as the union of the individual with others on the basis of the preservation of the individual self."[42]

This love is complex since it is derived from the anxiety of freedom and separateness, but "leads to oneness—and yet that individuality is not eliminated."[43] His suggestion, then, is a we-self bonding in order to maintain the I-self, a solution fraught with considerable difficulty. We must remember that for Fromm the idea of personal liberty is of such value that its surrender in any form is viewed with apprehension. Even so, he understands that a we-self is needed to overcome the anxiety of individuality.

Besides love, he suggests still another way, that of commitment to work. By work, he means meaningful, creative activity. But, as we already have seen, love and work may be illusory and impermanent.

It is impossible to understand human nature without accepting the fact that a person is easiest to define within a context or a group of contexts. The only aspect of personhood independent of context is our biological rumbles, the noise of our bodies going about their functions of self-regulation and adaptation. There is little meaning to be found there.

Humankind is social and our definitions reside in a social nexus. Alone we have nothing to understand nor any way to do so.

Interestingly, Søren Kierkegaard, considered by many to be the earliest existential philosopher, saw a solution to this problem.[44] That I turn now to Kierkegaard is both strange and appropriate. It is strange because he lived a solitary life with no friends or companions. He was misshapen, and ashamed. He wrote under a variety of pseudonyms. In a way, he surrounded himself with the imaginary people of his pseudonyms, split-off parts of his self. Although he wrote about 150 years ago, his description of isolation prefigures our current plight. He claimed that the movement away from roles and context leads to alienation and individuation.

Kierkegaard argued that loss of identity comes about through the loss of commitment. Roles, and therefore relationships, can be maintained only through commitment. Lack of commitment is the cause of the identity problem: "a world-defining commitment not only makes a difference to me; it also tells me what difference everything else in my life makes to me."[45] It is commitment, therefore, that defines us, and by committing ourselves to what we are now, our past becomes meaningful.

Kierkegaard offers both a prescription and a paradox. We usually believe that the meaningful past creates meaning for the future. What we are like now can be traced to what we were like in the past. To make commitments in the present, we must know of our past commitments. Kierkegaard turns this common belief on its head. It is not the past that gives meaning to the present or future, but the present that gives meaning to the past: "Events in the past do not determine the commitment I have, rather the commitment I have gives me an interpretation of the events of my past. At the same time, my commitment has to make sense of the events in my past, not someone else's. It seems clear that not every object of commitment has this ability."[46]

Kierkegaard calls this process "essential contingency" and claims that it reflects a person who has a self. For Kierkegaard, the result of failure to make a commitment is emptiness. Nevertheless, we fear making a commitment since we cannot, *a priori*, know whether it is the correct one, that is, the one that will lead to the essential contingency. The existential dilemma is choosing between emptiness and anxiety. When we declare a choice, we begin to be something. When we declare a choice, we are able to stand both in opposition and in agreement.

What does the analysis of Sartre's, Fromm's, and Kierkegaard's view of the self tell us about shame? First, individuation and personal freedom have a cost. While the old order connects us and restricts our actions, it also defines us. Without these definitions, we are set free, but adrift, the paradox of existential being. Second, freedom makes self-consciousness the defining characteristic of the self: "I am I" replaces all other statements of selfhood. Third, self-consciousness increases the likelihood of shame and all its concomitant ills, and, because of our lack of bonds, we have no way to seek forgiveness. The shame is beyond endurance, and we are likely to flee either to a new order or to pleasure and self-involvement. In the former case, we give up our freedom. In the latter case, we only perpetuate what we already are. Is there no way out of this paradox, the dialectic between freedom and imprisonment?

The way out is commitment. We can never be sure that any commitment is correct, but that lack of security does not matter. Commitment, by its nature, frees us from ourselves and, while it stands us in opposition to some, it joins us with others similarly committed. Commitment moves us from the mirror trap of the self absorbed with the self to the freedom of a community of shared values.

Notes

CHAPTER 1. Shame in Everyday Life

1. See, for example, Lewis, H. B., 1971; Morrison, A. P., 1989; Nathanson, D. L., 1987a, b, c; Tomkins, S. S., 1963.
2. *New York Times*, 1/29/89.
3. Fromm, E., 1941, p. 107.

CHAPTER 2. Our Emotional Lives

1. James, W., 1890.
2. Bard, P. A., 1928; Cannon, W. B., 1929.
3. Some have located this state in the soma (for example, James, W., 1890), in the autonomic nervous system (Wenger, M. A., Jones, F. N., & Jones, M. H., 1956), in the central nervous system (Cannon, W. B., 1929; Olds, M. E., & Forbes, J. L., 1981), in the endocrine hormonal system, and in all three (Izard, C. E., 1972). Following Darwin (1872/1969), who observed external manifestations of these presumed internal emotional states in the facial, vocal, and postural behavior of men and beasts, people more recently have looked at facial expressions as a direct measure of these states (see Tomkins, S. S., 1962, 1963; Izard, C. E., 1977; Ekman, P., Friesen, W., & Ellsworth, P., 1972).
4. R. Zajonc (1980) has most clearly articulated the idea that emotional states need not require cognition.
5. Freud, S., 1915/1959.
6. See Lewis, M., & Michalson, L., 1983.
7. See Plutchik, R., 1962, pp. 41–42.
8. Izard, C. E., 1977; Tomkins, S. S., 1963.
9. Moreover, and perhaps even worse, we have little empirical research to inform us about the relationship between them. The relationship between these forms

of expression may be important. It may be the case that inhibition of one expressive system leads to the accentuation of a second. For example, if children who have stranger anxiety are forced to sit in a chair and watch the approach of a stranger without being able to move away, they are more likely to show more intense and prolonged facial expression than if they are not placed in a physical restraining situation and the same condition occurs. This should not be surprising. If one of the features of emotional expression is its communicative value, then the inhibiting of some feature of that communicative message—in this case, running away—should result in the accenting of other features.

As we will see, the occurrence of language, which is a feature of emotional expression unique to humans, may serve in and of itself to dampen the expressive behavior found in the face. Thus, one interaction between expression systems may be a reciprocal one, such that suppression of one leads to the accenting of others. Alternatively, expression in one modality may enhance expression in another. One can think of the training of soldiers in this regard. To enhance physical violence or bodily expression of anger, soldiers are taught to use vocal behavior, that is, to scream and yell obscenities at the "dummy" enemy. It is assumed that the yelling enhances the motor expression of aggression and anger.

10. The exact number and type is open to considerable discussion. The reader is referred to other sources for more elaborate discussions concerning children's and adults' ability to produce faces and to understand and discriminate the meaning of faces (Lewis, M., & Michalson, L., 1983).

11. Consider the following observations.

Benjamin is a 1-year-old child who has been left alone in his room. His mother closes the door and walks out. Unbeknownst to him, we are photographing his behavior and we notice the following behavior. Benjamin cries. A simple, short whinelike sound. He stops and pauses and looks to see whether the cry brings his mother to the room. Hearing no sounds of approach, he cries again.

Contrast this behavior with that of another child, who, when left alone, starts to cry and does not pause to listen to the effect of her cry. We would argue that these two children are using vocal expression for different purposes. For Benjamin, the cry represents an instrumental response designed to get his mother to return to the room. It may or may not index his internal state. The cry of the second child, however, is a measure of the child's internal distress since the child does not appear interested in the effect of her cry. The second example occurs in a somewhat older child.

Felicia is 20 months old and she is playing in the yard by herself while her mother watches her from her study window where she is preparing her teaching lesson. During the course of play, Felicia stumbles and bangs her knee. She starts to cry but, looking around and seeing no one there, stops crying and resumes her play. She continues to play happily for the next 10 minutes. She then stops her play and, skipping and running, moves toward the entrance to the house. She enters the house through the back door and walks to her mother's study where, upon opening the door, Felicia starts to cry.

Here again, facial and vocal expression appear to represent the child's instrumental action rather than reflecting her internal state. From her mother's viewpoint, her internal state for the past 10 minutes appears to be that of a happy and playful child. That the child cries upon seeing the mother cannot represent the child's emotional state at that moment. At best, it represents a communication about some event in the past. These, and many more examples, can be presented to show that expression does not bear a one-to-one correspondence to our internal emotional states, even in early life.

12. Lewis, M., Stanger, C., & Sullivan, M. W., 1989.
13. Ekman, P., & Friesen, W. V., 1975; Saarni, C., 1979.
14. Davidson, R. J., & Fox, N. A., 1982.
15. Recently, P. Ekman (1984) tried to find a relationship between the autonomic nervous system responses of heart rate and skin temperature and particular emotions. He reports rather exciting findings that show, for example, that high skin temperature accompanied by high heart rate is associated with anger, whereas low skin temperature with high heart rate is associated with fear and sadness. These findings suggest that, in the future, we may be able to map specific emotions, such as shame, with specific physiological responses. However, at the moment, this is not the case.
16. Scherer, K. R., 1979, 1981.
17. Lewis, H. B., 1987; Tomkins, S. S., 1963.
18. McDougall, W., 1923.
19. Tomkins, S. S., 1962, p. 23.
20. Nathanson, D. L., 1987a, b, c.
21. Geppert, U., 1986.
22. Izard, C. E., 1971, 1977, 1979; Rutter, M., Izard, C. E., & Read, P., 1986.
23. Geppert, U., 1986; Heckhausen, H., 1984; Schneider, K., Hanne, K., & Lehmann, B., 1989.
24. Barrett, K. C., & Zahn-Waxler, C., 1987.
25. Lewis, M., Sullivan, M. W., Stanger, C., & Weiss, M., 1989.
26. Buss, A., 1980; Geppert, U., 1986.
27. Lazarus, R. W., 1982.
28. Darwin, C., 1872/1969, p. 325.
29. Darwin, C., 1872/1969, p. 327.

30. Darwin, C., 1872/1969, p. 345.

31. Tomkins, S. S., 1963.

32. Tomkins, S. S., 1963, p. 123.

33. Tomkins, S. S., 1963, p. 194.

34. It is hard to know the direction of the causal chain between interrupt and shame, because careful sequential analysis of facial patterns prior to or during shame has not been seriously undertaken. It seems reasonable to think of shame as causing an interrupt of excitement and enjoyment and being caused by the interrupt of excitement and enjoyment. I suspect the former causal chain is closer to the truth, especially given the results of our studies on the interrupt of learning and the resultant emotions of anger and sadness (see Alessandri, S., Sullivan, M. W., & Lewis, M., 1990; Lewis, M., Alessandri, S., & Sullivan, M. W., 1990).

35. Lewis, H. B., 1971.

36. Izard, C. E., 1977, p. 389, italics added.

37. Erikson, E. H., 1950; Klein, M., 1975.

38. The exception may be the drive reduction theorists, most represented by classical psychoanalysis. Because their theory centers around repression of unacceptable thoughts and impulses, the phenomenology associated with violations of one's own standards and values is anxiety rather than shame. Given the nature of repression and the unavailability to conscious reflection of certain feelings, states, and representations, even the phenomenology of shame is suspect. There is some truth to be found in this caution.

39. Janis, I. L., 1965.

CHAPTER 3. The Self and Its Development

1. There is some evidence that the chimpanzees, great apes, and even dolphins, among all other nonhumans, may be capable of self reflection.

2. Freud, S., 1933/1961.

3. Discussion of cultural and historical differences in self will have to wait until chapter 11.

4. Lewis, M., & Brooks-Gunn, J., 1979.

5. Freud's tripartite division of id, ego, and superego is too well known to be detailed here. What is important, however, is that Freud showed us that particular actions are features of ourselves. We credit Freud with our understanding that there were aspects of the self of which we have no awareness. While the notion of instincts or drives was considered as aspects of ourselves long before his formulation, it was Freud's extension of the self's actions which stands as one of his most significant contributions. Slips of the tongue, dreams, and accidents all were shown to be related to aspects of the self. Until the turn of this century we did not consider these things to be

features of the self. It is quite remarkable to think that there was a time, not too long ago, when such behaviors were not considered to represent aspects of the self. Dreams were explained by reference to concepts as diverse as the food we ate before sleep or the voices of spirits guiding us (Jaynes, J., 1976).

6. It would take me too far away from my goal to pursue these problems. As I proceed with my analysis of the self, I will suggest that there are functions of the self, situational as well as ontogenetically, that are available to our selves, and there are functions of the self that are not available. These functions have goals and a variety of means to these goals, some of them learned and some of them not learned. They are goal-directed, and therefore intentional. They often compete with one another, but, because they are different aspects of the self and have different functions, they are apt to have different goals.

    This makes sense to me. For example, consider the case where a student wishes to pass an exam and get a good grade. Here, clearly, is an objective goal. What is not objective, however, is her past experience of failure. Because of past experiences, she developed another ideal that she is likely to fail under situations marked by competition. When she objectively formulates her goal to get a good grade, she has not thought of the other aspect of her behavior, namely, her fear of competition. Therefore, one set of goals competes with another learned set of behaviors. This conflict between various goals and subroutines leads her to perform behaviors that are likely to be in conflict with the goal of passing the exam. B. Weiner (1986), in his book on self attribution, makes clear that some of these competing goals are apt to cause some of the conflicts that we tend to see in human behavior.

7. This topic will be taken up in chapter 11, when I discuss cultural and historical differences in the idea of self. See also Geertz, C., 1984; Ornstein, R. E., 1973; and Ross, C. A., 1989.

8. Pribram, K. H., 1984, p. 25.

9. LeDoux, J., 1989, p. 265.

10. Weiskrantz, L., 1986.

11. LeDoux, J., 1989, p. 265.

12. Lewis, M., 1990.

13. Duval, S., & Wicklund, R. A., 1972.

14. Given these definitions of objective and subjective self-awareness, we are confronted with the following question: Is all information that is subjectively known capable of being objectively known? From an epistemological point of view, the general issue of knowledge takes a similar turn. Benjamin Lewis pointed this out to me. For example, when I say "I know X," is it the case that I know that I know X? Is it the case that when I know X, I *must* know that I know X? Or is it the case that when I know X, I *can* know that I know X? If it is the case that when I know X, I *can* know that I know X, when is it the case that I *do* know that I know X? These kinds of epistemological questions

require different ways of knowing. Such questions are difficult to answer, and we do not have enough information to do a satisfactory job. It seems that there are many bodily functions of which there may be subjective awareness that we cannot make objective. Certain biochemical functions that take place in our body and that alter states, moods, and the like may not ever be objectively known. This conclusion may need to be modified, given research in behavioral medicine. If we could be taught or could train ourselves to focus on certain sensations and processes, there might be no limit to our ability to convey them from subjective to objective awareness. In a more remote fashion, it seems reasonable to assume that unique training, such as in Yoga or in other Eastern arts, allows people to come to control autonomic functioning, including temperature regulation, oxygen intake, and the like, through the objectification of subjective knowledge (Nowles, D. P., & Kamiya, J., 1970).

15. James, W., 1890, p. 176.
16. Wittgenstein, L., 1953/1963.
17. Baldwin, J. M., 1899/1903.
18. Piaget, 1926/1955, p. 197.
19. Wallon, H., 1949; Merleau-Ponty, M., 1964.
20. Cooley, C. H., 1909/1962.
21. Mead, G. H., 1934/1972, p. 173.
22. Eagle, M. N., 1989.
23. Detrick, D. W., & Detrick, S. P., 1989.
24. Erikson, E. H., 1950; Mahler, M. S., Pine, F., & Bergman, A., 1975.
25. Stern, D. N., 1985.
26. I have recently questioned the developmental framework of Stern's idea (Lewis, M., 1990). The problem has to do with the description of the nature of the self at each level of development. In particular, the description of the self is more than one of simple reflexes. Even at this age, there is no sense of self/other undifferentiation as in Mahler's theory. In fact, Stern stands in major opposition to her view. He states that "there is no confusion between self and other in the beginning or at any point during infancy" (p. 10). Not only is this self at the beginning not tied in any symbiotic way to another, this self is a highly organized and capable creature. Because of the capacities of perception and learning, the infant is capable of experiencing itself. "I am suggesting that the infant can experience the process of emerging organization, as well as the result, and it is this experience of emerging organization that I call the *emergent sense of self*. It is the experience of a process as well as a product" (p. 45). For Stern, the self, even from the beginning, has extraordinary capacities.

I think there are some difficulties with such a view of self development. First, it must rest on the belief that infants are highly capable of actions including perception, thought, and learning. While the infant has been shown to be highly capable in terms of some early capacities, these appear to be more reflexive in nature than cognitively based. The extreme dependency of the child on its caregiver speaks to the evolutionarily tied connectiveness between infant and adult. Such selected interdependency is difficult to reconcile with the cognitive capacities necessary to experience one's own emergent self.

The view of the self Stern presents does not allow for much self development. If by birth, the child is capable of experiencing the self, then this self is a self capable of objective self-awareness. The use of such a concept gives rise to problems. Although Stern uses the concept of levels, he imparts higher level activity to lower level forms. This difficulty, especially as it relates to self, has historically appeared before.

Because of this lack of objective awareness, it is difficult to see how we can ascribe to the infant states dependent on self-awareness. Stern explicitly sees the infant capable of experiencing its own emergent properties. This problem has been viewed by others (Kernberg, O. F., 1976, 1980; Lacan, J., 1968). They all claimed that the young infant is capable of experiencing its emergent self, and therefore of experiencing anxiety over its nonexistence. This is quite similar to Otto Rank's notion of birth anxiety (1929/1952). Freud, in his critique of this view, rightly points out that anxiety is a signal and, as such, has to be experienced. Only the ego can experience it: "The id cannot be afraid, as the ego can; it is not an organization, and cannot estimate situations of danger" (1936/1963, p. 80). Since the ego emerges only slowly, certainly not at birth, there can be no objective experience. The problem resides in the fact that any anxiety over nonexistence, or experiencing the emergent self as an adult might experience it, cannot occur to an organism who has no objective self-awareness. It is not possible for an organism to experience itself or to be anxious about its existence prior to the capacity to think about itself as existing, that is, prior to being able to experience itself and prior to its being able to imagine its nonexistence.

The core self and the issue of intersubjectivity as discussed presents us with the same type of problem we saw for the first period. Intersubjectivity, as Stern has defined it, is related to objective self-awareness. It might be possible to have intersubjectivity without objective awareness. We can think of intersubjectivity as simply a statement of knowledge, or even reflexive, for example, smiling when another smile appears. Under such a definition, intersubjectivity becomes simply a set of complex behavior patterns that are triggered by other behaviors. Intersubjectivity is less controlled by complex cognitions and more by simple rules, such as circular reactions. It is not based on intentions in terms of complex means-ends representation, but is more like automatic social responses. Intersubjectivity between a mother and her 8 month old can take place as a function of a complex pattern system, one that may be present in any species. However, intersubjectivity that involves human objective awareness should not be possible at this age. This conclusion, of course, depends on how intersubjectivity is defined. If the ability of the child to share experiences, to match, align, or attune its behavior, is based on its knowledge of itself and the other's self then intersubjectivity, at this age, is not possible without objective self-awareness.

It may well be that not only do we need to consider the various levels of self development, but various levels of intersubjectivity. If this is the case, then we can define low levels of intersubjectivity as automatic-like patterns of social responsivity. It is only at latter levels that intersubjectivity of the kind we usually refer to when we talk about empathic behavior, that is, putting the self in the place of the other, occurs. Intersubjectivity, like imitation or any other processes such as deception and knowledge, has a developmental sequence related to self development.

The verbal self is when the child acquires the personal pronouns and, where, through the use of language, the child is able to gain objective awareness. As I do, Stern marks this period in the second half of the second year of life, a date consistent with almost all theoretical descriptions of the emergence of objective awareness.

27. In *Social Cognition and the Acquisition of Self* (1979), we undertook a series of studies in which we observed children's self-recognition as an attempt to study self development. In *Children's Emotions and Moods* (1983), we focused upon emotional development and the role of self in its development. From the series of studies and work we have done in this area, I have articulated a theory of self development.

28. Gallup, G. G., Jr., 1973, 1977.

29. Tolman, C. W., 1965.

30. Zazzo, R., 1948.

31. Gesell, A., 1928.

32. Fraiberg, S., & Adelson, E., 1976.

33. Fischer, K., 1980.

34. The reflexive nature of this knowledge is apparent when we perform a simple experiment. We allow the child to reach for an object. At about 5 months the child can do so successfully. However, the second time the child reaches toward the object we cover either the object or the child's hand. The movement toward the object immediately comes to a halt. It seems that the child's ability to reach for the object is related to an eye-hand connection that when severed terminates the behavior. This reflex arc between hand and eye seems to be in the service of getting things into the child's mouth, perhaps reflecting some adaptive significance. What is important to note here is that this knowledge of objects in space is determined solely by a sensorimotor mode of knowing.

35. It has been pointed out that the ability to remember objects allows the child to make comparisons (Schaeffer, H. R., 1966; Duval, S., & Wicklund, R. A., 1972). Without memory the child cannot make a comparison of *A* and *B* when

they are separated in space/time. If a child looks at object *A* and then turns to object *B,* the representation of *A* allows the child knowledge of *A* as it is observing *B.* This ability of comparison must underlie the child's capacity to form primitive categories and should support the child's knowledge about its various actions and people. Consider actions first. The child is able to remember, and therefore to represent that a particular movement obtained a certain object. When, in subsequent trials, the movement that the child is performing does not result in obtaining the object, the memory of another movement may enable the child to obtain the object. In some sense, then, comparison based upon memory allows for more sophisticated development.

36. Kernberg, O. F., 1976.
37. Lewis, M., 1990.
38. Ross, C. A., 1989.
39. Kaye, K., 1982.
40. Kohut, H., 1971; Fairbairn, W. R. D., 1952.
41. Cornielson, F. S., & Arsenian, I., 1960.
42. Duval, S., & Wicklund, R. A., 1972, p. 44.
43. Such findings suggest, as has G. Mandler (1975), that objective self-awareness comes about in situations that are conflictual. By "conflictual," I mean situations in which a plan is completed and a new one is needed, or a plan is interrupted and needs attention.

CHAPTER 4. Self Thoughts and Shame

1. Nathanson, D. L., 1987a, b, c.
2. Fenichel, O., 1945.
3. Freud, S., 1923/1959.
4. Freud, S., 1930/1960, p. 126.
5. Freud, S., 1923/1959, p. 56.
6. Freud, S., 1905/1953, p. 178.
7. See Sullivan, H. S., 1953; Rank, O., 1945/1972; Horney, K., 1939; Klein, M., 1948/1975.
8. Erikson, E. H., 1950, pp. 223–224.
9. Erikson, E. H., 1950, p. 224.
10. Lewis, H. B., 1971, 1987; Piers, G., & Singer, M. B., 1953; Wurmser, L., 1981; Broucek, F., 1982; Nathanson, D. L., 1987a; Morrison, A. P., 1986a, b, 1989.
11. J. P. Tangney's (1989a) recent work on situations likely to elicit shame and guilt supports this view. It is not in situations themselves, where for the most part we can find evidence for specific elicitors.
12. See Schacter, S., and Singer, J. E., 1962, for the argument concerning

emotions as epiphenomenological, and P. Zajonc (1980, 1984) for an argument concerning the primacy of emotions.

13. For a similar view, see Weiner, B., 1986.

14. The knowledge can be acquired through a passive or an active process. In the passive view, we are acted upon by cultural forces; in the active view, humans act upon these forces (Overton, W., 1984). In the passive view, the causes of behavior, action, or thought are forces that act on the organism, causing it to acquire information. These may be internal biological features of our species or the external social control of conspecifics, determined by the shaping effect of the differential rewards. In contrast to this passive view is the constructionist paradigm, based upon the world view that the organism acts on its environment and participates in it (see Lewis, M., 1979, 1990). The organism has desires and plans. These desires and goals are constructed, as are most of the actions that enable the organism to behave adaptively within its culture.

One particular aspect of the active process is the child's observation of how people behave toward one another. One of the most curious facts about the study of this problem has been what I have called the error of the didactic method. The didactic method leads us to conclude that children or adults learn through direct interaction between the "teacher," the person extending the information, and the "learner," the person receiving the information. Most of our learning does not come about through this didactic method, but through other less direct methods.

For example, consider the case of the 5-year-old girl who has a 2-year-old sibling. The 5 year old receives some crayons as a present and takes those crayons and colors on the walls of their house. The 2 year old watches as her older sister does this. Mother appears and starts to yell at the 5 year old, exclaiming, "Don't you know you are not supposed to write on the walls? For this I'm going to punish you; give me your crayons and go to your room," at which point the 5 year old is reduced to tears.

In fact, she may not have known the rule, and the violation of it comes as a surprise. She now has learned the rule and, under most circumstances, is unlikely to color on the walls again. But what about the 2 year old? Here we see something quite different. The 2 year old has not crayoned on the wall, nor has she been yelled at, yet I think it is safe to say that this child will not crayon on the walls since she has learned indirectly about a standard.

Lest we think that such indirect learning is somehow restricted to the very young, consider this example.

Recently I attended a formal dinner party held in honor of a visiting dignitary. The dinner table was magnificently set, with at least five forks and as many spoons. A multiple course dinner was being served, and it was clear that the different silverware was meant to be used with different courses. It was unclear, however, to several people at the dinner party, which fork should be used for the first course. They learned the rule by watching others and imitating them. They learned, indirectly, through the behaviors of others.

15. See the research work of Harris, P., & Lipian, M. S., 1989, and Lewis, M., 1989b, for studies on emotional scripts.

16. In exploring this problem we observed large numbers of mothers and children from 3 to 24 months of age. We went into their homes and we observed what mothers did when children cried. What we found reflects the imposition of standards, rules, and goals. Our observation of the mothers and children indicated that mothers were highly likely to go to their children when they cried. There was little difference between their behavior to their boy or girl children. Over the first two years of life, mothers went to their children less frequently when their children signaled distress through crying, that is, mothers' frequency of comforting during stress decreased as their children grew older. Not only did mothers decrease the frequency of comforting as a function of amount of distress the child displayed, but they also increased the latency, the time before they acted, by attending to their children once they started to cry. In other words as children got older, mothers not only comforted them less frequently, but took longer to start comforting behavior. Clearly, mothers were teaching children an important standard, namely, do not cry to signal distress. With the advent of language, mothers were encouraging their children to use language rather than crying to signal distress. Although this age function held for both males and females, mothers were significantly less likely to go to their boy children when they were distressed, and when they went they had longer latencies (Lewis, M., & Michalson, L., 1983). Very early in the socialization process, children are being socialized around standards, rules, and goals, and these standards vary as a function of sex.

17. Pervin, L. A., 1989.

18. Skinner, B. F., 1938.

19. I once observed a 2-year-old girl riding a train on the way to the circus in New York City.

The train ride was about an hour long, and I watched the little girl as she jumped up and down in her seat and marked the dirty train window with her finger. During the course of the child's actions, the mother repeatedly *rewarded* and *punished* her behavior. In one instance, when the child's dress was raised by her movement, the mother scolded her and said, "Little girls don't let their panties show." On another occasion, when the child was moving her fingers around the window and dirtying herself with the grime on them, the mother said, "Little girls don't get dirty."

This example is meant to demonstrate how children's behavior can be shaped by the rewards and punishments of their parents, even at extremely early ages. While such effects do occur, it is more likely that one of the primary tasks and functions of humans is the learning and adopting of standards in an active fashion.

20. Heckhausen, H., 1984; Stipek, D. J., 1983.

21. Lewis, M., Sullivan, M. W., Stanger, C., & Weiss, M., 1989.

22. Weiner, B., 1986.

23. Seligman, M. E. P., 1975; Seligman, M. E. P., Peterson, C., Kraslow, N., Tanenbaum, R., Alloy, L., & Abramson, L., 1984.

24. Dweck, C. S., & Leggett, E. L., 1988.

25. Seligman, M. E. P., 1975; Beck, A. T., 1967, 1979.

26. Janoff-Bulman, R., 1979.

27. Global attributions for negative events are generally uncorrelated with global attributions for positive events. It is only when positive or negative events are taken into account that relatively stable and consistent attributional patterns are observed.

28. This point is well made by H. B. Lewis, especially in her volume *Psychic War in Men and Women* (1976). I will return to this topic in considerable detail in later chapters.

29. I use here the Greek term *hubris* to differentiate this emotion from pride, with which it is too often confused. As I have warned before, word usage issues associated with these emotions render careful analysis most difficult. Not only do we have the problems of differentiating shame from guilt, embarrassment, and shyness, but we also have the difficulty of distinguishing between different kinds of pride. One can think of pride in terms of its use in two ways. On the one hand, I think of pride in terms of achievement, the feeling one has when being successful in fulfilling a particular goal and activity. In my discussion of achievement motivation, I noted how children learn to feel proud about their achievements in terms of a particular standard, rule, or goal. On the other hand, I also use the term pride to indicate a negative emotional state. I speak of the proud man or the proud woman with some disdain. The Bible speaks of pride coming before the fall; throughout the Old and New Testaments, we find examples of false pride and how this pride brings down the man. It is clear that the term pride carries a surplus of meaning; if we are to understand the term at all, we need to distinguish between specific pride and global pride. I have done so by using the term "hubris" to represent global pride and "pride" to represent specific achievement.

30. Morrison, A. P., 1986a, 1989.

31. The same type of distinction has been drawn by others, including Lindsey-Harty, J., 1984, and Tangney, J. P., 1989a.

32. Heckhausen, H., 1984, for example.

33. Dweck, C. S., & Leggett, E. L., 1988.

34. Izard, C. E., & Tyson, M. C., 1986.
35. Buss, A., 1980.
36. Eysenck, H. J., 1954; Kagan, J., 1981; Reznick, J. S., & Snedman, N., 1988.
37. Lewis, M., & Feiring, C., 1989.
38. Izard, C. E., 1979; Tomkins, S. S., 1963.
39. See Edelman, R. J., 1987; Geppert, U., 1986; Lewis, M. Stanger, C., Sullivan, M. W., 1989.
40. If this analysis is correct, then it is possible that each of the four self-conscious emotions has a less intense form. This requires further consideration.

CHAPTER 5. The Origins of Shame

1. Elaine Pagels, in *Adam, Eve, and the Serpent* (1988), points out that this violation is as central to Christianity as it is to Judaism.
2. There can be no denying that, in the Old Testament, the notion of adhering to the rules of God, the Commandments, is of primary importance. The violation of God's rules disturbs the relationship between humans and God. Repeatedly, the Jewish scriptures focus on the special relationship of the chosen people to God. Throughout the history of the Jews, violation of this unique relation with God and God's law inevitably leads to serious problems for the Jewish people (see Paul Johnson's *The History of the Jew* [1987]. The violation of God's word in the Judaic tradition is complex because Jewish theology did not include the notion of heaven or hell. When the Old Testament Jews fail to fulfill their obligations to God, he turns his back on their worldly suffering. Only later, under the influence of Christianity, does the notion of suffering on earth become joined to the idea of eternal suffering in an afterlife. The difference in the consequences of sin for the two religions may highlight the differences I have already discussed between shame and guilt. Sin in Judaism has no specific punishment but does have a specific reparation, while Christianity (certainly Catholicism) developed the idea of forgiveness and eternal punishment. Thus, we might argue that Judaism focuses on guilt, whereas Christianity focuses on shame.
3. Maccoby, E. J., & Jacklin, C. N., 1974.
4. Freud, S., 1925/1959.
5. Kohlberg, L., 1976.
6. Gilligan, C., 1982.
7. As I already mentioned in chapter 2, there is some disagreement as to what are the primary emotions. This is an important consideration: if shame and guilt are primary emotions, then they exist from the start, and a developmental model is moot. While I do not hold to this view, some theorists suggest that shame and guilt can be seen in the earliest months of life. S. S. Tomkins (1963) believes that infants who turn away their heads during certain interactions

with their mothers index a shame response. I see no reason to call such responses shame. The faces of the infants show none of the behaviors we consider to index shame. Moreover, I prefer R. Plutchik's definition (1962) of primary and secondary emotions: the primary emotions *do not* involve the self, while the secondary emotions do involve the self. So, for my purposes, I do not see the primary emotions as including shame or guilt or, for that matter, pride. In the early months of life, the primary emotions—including joy, fear, anger, sadness, disgust, and surprise—emerge.

8. Bridges, K. M. B., 1932.

9. These examples point to the fact that, although objective self-awareness is a part of adult human capacity, it is not always the case that objectification is desirable. It may be quite harmful because it can interfere with on-going behavior. It is important, therefore, to have a mechanism that makes objective self-awareness aversive. Obviously, it cannot be too aversive since it is a necessary and important capacity. The solution, then, is for objectification to result in a slightly negative but intense reaction. This is a compromise between using the capacity when needed and not using it at all times.

It is interesting to note that in all religions that value meditation, the function of meditation is to remove objective self-awareness. Only through the removal of this capacity can the individual return to a oneness with the world. Here, then, is another attempt to reduce the presence of the self for the self. That such a state is viewed as ideal speaks to the belief that objectification separates the self from others and that true peace can be found only in its reunification (see R. E. Ornstein, ed., *The Nature of Human Consciousness* [1973]).

10. Lewis, M., Sullivan, M. W., Stanger, C., & Weiss, M., 1989.

11. See also Amsterdam, L., 1972; Lewis, M., & Brooks-Gunn, J., 1979.

12. See also Hoffman, M. L., 1988.

13. Hoffman, M. L., 1977; Sagi, A., & Hoffman, M. L., 1976; Zahn-Waxler, C., & Radke-Yarrow, M., 1982.

14. Borke, H., 1973.

15. Halperin, M., 1989.

16. See also Hoffman, M. L., 1982.

17. Heckhausen, H., 1984; Kagan, J., 1981.

18. Bretherton, I., 1987.

19. See H. Heckhausen's 1984 review.

20. Geppert, U., & Kuster, U., 1983. One interesting finding was that, although children as young as 30 months showed expressions of pride when they achieved a goal, expressions of shame or guilt were not observed until some months later. It was suggested that there may be some asymmetry in the evaluations of success versus failure, with a developmental sequence taking

place earlier for success. However, the work of Zahn-Waxler and Radke-Yarrow indicates the emergence of guilt and shame at about 30 months, so there is no reason to assume an asymmetry in their emergence.

21. See Tomkins, S. S., 1963; Lewis, H. B., 1987; Nathanson, D. L., 1987.

22. Emde, R. N., 1980.

23. Alessandri, S., Sullivan, M. W., & Lewis, M., 1990; Lewis, M., Alessandri, S., & Sullivan, M. W., 1990; White, R. W., 1959.

24. For a few subjects, pride and shame were shown on easy and difficult tasks, respectively. This should not surprise us since evaluation, regardless of our standards, is always included in the process of goal setting.

25. Stipek, D. J., Recchia, S., & McClinton, S., 1990, p. 2.

26. See also J. Kagan's 1981 data on this same process.

27. Piaget, J., 1932/1965.

28. See Rehm, L. P., & Carter, A. S., 1990.

29. See Freud, S., 1925/1959; Hoffman, M. L., 1977; Zahn-Waxler, C., & Kochanska, G., 1990.

30. See Barrett, K. C., & Zahn-Waxler, C., 1987.

31. Tangney, J. P., 1989b.

CHAPTER 6. The Socialization of Shame

1. Zahn-Waxler, C., & Kochanska, G., 1990.

2. Hoffman, M. L., 1970.

3. Harter, S., 1989.

4. See Zahn-Waxler's work with children of depressed mothers, Zahn-Waxler, C., Radke-Yarrow, M., & King, R. A., 1979.

5. This applies to all self-conscious emotions. If we do not blame or praise ourselves, no self-conscious evaluative emotion occurs. Shame, guilt, hubris, and pride all require our internalized blame or success.

6. Morrison, A. P., 1986a, b, 1989.

7. Seligman, M. E. P., Peterson, C., Kraslow, N., Tanenbaum, R., Alloy, L., & Abramson, L., 1984.

8. C. Dweck and E. Leggett (1988) provide a useful discussion in this regard. Their analysis allows for the consideration of all these different terms.

9. Witkin, H., 1965; Witkin, H., Dyk, R., Goodenough, D., Faterson, H., & Karp. S., 1962.

10. Lewis, H. B., 1976.

11. Given that attribution style differs for negative versus positive events, it is not easy to reconcile how field dependence could be related to a style. It might be the case that it is related to attribution for negative events. However, the

sample H. B. Lewis observed was small and the study not well reported. Tangney (personal communication) was unable to replicate the findings.

12. DiBiase, R., & Lewis, M., 1989.
13. Zahn-Waxler, C., & Kochanska, G., 1990.
14. Deaux, K., 1976; Dweck, C. S., & Leggett, E. L., 1988; Nicholls, J. G., 1984.
15. Minuchen, P. P., & Shapiro, E. K., 1983.
16. Kohut, H., 1972.
17. Morrison, A. P., 1986a, p. 360.
18. Miller, A., 1979/1981.
19. Hesse, H., 1920/1970.
20. Interestingly, some individuals appear more shamed by such action than others. So, for example, men and boys often are described as "ranking" on each other. This means they are engaged in what often is termed as playful, teasing, or aggressive behavior. Interviews with young men who engage in such ranking reveal that they do not always feel humiliated or shamed when this occurs. In fact, for some, it appears to be a positive activity, one eagerly engaged in by others and accompanied by positive smiling and interactive behavior. For some, it is a far cry from shaming situations where one would expect a lack of smiling, avoidance behavior, and a desire not to continue such games.
21. While I will not be able to go into detail, let me briefly define these terms. *Reasoning* is the parental technique by which parents explain the causes for errors and the ways to rectify them. *Power assertion* utilizes such statements as "You will do it because I tell you to." Little or no reasoning takes place here. The other techniques are self-evident and will be discussed in more detail.
22. Hoffman, M. L., 1970; Zahn-Waxler, C., & Kochanska, S., 1990.
23. Love withdrawal is likely to lead to shame not only with children but also with adults. My observations of couples in interaction reveal that one source of shame for men and women is the love withdrawal of the partner. One couple, in particular, exhibited an extreme version of this pattern.

During an argument the wife would withdraw from her husband. As a consequence of the fight, she would stop talking and go to her room, severing all contact. This response tended to enrage her husband. They came to see me because of his rage behavior. The wife complained that he could not make up after a fight and stayed very angry for a very long time. The husband confirmed his wife's report, stating that after a fight he felt very angry, "In spite of myself." It became clear that her withdrawal, as a consequence of the fight, made him feel shamed, and that he was experiencing bypassed shame in the form of rage. We discussed how, following a fight, it was necessary for both of them to reconfirm their love and care for each other, and for the wife, in particular, to let her husband know that, although she was angry at him for some specific action, she was not *generally* angry at him. This seemed to work, at least in reducing his rage outbursts and increasing his ability to make up faster.

24. Bowlby, J., 1969.
25. Bowlby, J., 1973, p. 204.
26. I differ from most of the object relations theorists since I am of the opinion that the impact of the parent-child relationship cannot make itself felt until the child is capable of representing both itself and the significant other. This is not likely to be the case until the middle of the second year of life. The similarity of my view with object relations theory lies in the fact that we both see the withdrawal of love by the significant other (whether we are children or adults) as having a profound effect on our sense of ourselves, in particular, our feelings of shame.
27. Buss, A. H., 1980; Modigliani, A., 1968.
28. Tangney, J. P., 1989b.
29. There were few situations that elicited just shame. This is consistent with my view that it is not so much what happened as how the event is construed by the person. The shame versus guilt differences in the Tangney (1989a) study were in the form and focus (global vs. specific) of the situational descriptions, not the situations themselves.
30. Pervin, L. A., 1968.

CHAPTER 7. Reacting to Our Feelings

1. Nathanson, D. L., 1987a, b, c.
2. Lewis, H. B., 1987.
3. Lewis, H. B., 1971.
4. Lewis, H. B., 1971, p. 173.
5. Ross, C. A., 1989.
6. Lewis, H. B., 1971, p. 243.
7. Lewis, H. B., 1971, p. 233.
8. M. N. Eagle (1989), in a critique of psychoanalysis, has recently written, "I do not know of a single experimental study that has succeeded in demonstrating convincingly the reality of the central psychoanalytic process of repression, let alone its role as a critical pathogen in the etiology of neurosis" (p. 392). Here he refers to Erwin's (1984) review on the topic, as well as to Grunbaum's (1984) epistemological critique.
9. Scheff, T. J., 1987.
10. Scheff, T. J., 1987, p. 110
11. Ross, C. A., 1989.

12. Morrison, A. P., 1989b.

13. See Izard, C. E., Hembree, E. A., & Huebner, R. R., 1987, for studies of inoculation.

14. The avoidance of comfort by men often has this quality, although the more common explanation has to do with feeling—or its lack—in males. As I now understand this phenomenon, men avoid comfort because they are actively trying to cope with unacknowledged emotion. Since comfort often centers around problems, the emotions avoided are generally negative, including shame.

15. Consistent with the notion of denial or externalization of blame, Tangney (personal communication, 1990) has found that shame is positively correlated with externalization of blame.

16. Chapman, D. J., 1976.

17. Retzinger, S. R., 1987.

18. Freud, S., 1916/1938.

19. Greig, J. Y. T., 1969.

20. It should be noted that others have suggested that guilt, not shame, is associated with a desire to confess. I suspect this is because confession is viewed as an act of reparation and as such speaks to specific action rather than global self. Indeed, both views may be correct if we assume one way to rid oneself of shame is through feeling guilty instead. Thus, confession may be one way of transferring shame into guilt, thus releasing the shame.

CHAPTER 8. Prolonged Reactions to Shame: Humiliation, Depression, and Rage

1. Levi-Strauss, C., 1958/1963.

2. Cooley, C. H., 1912; Duval, S., & Wicklund, R. A., 1972; Mead, G. H., 1934/1972.

3. Campos, J., Campos, R., & Barnett, K., 1989.

4. Of course, it can be pathological if our attributions are pathological, for example, if we have too high a standard, rule, or goal. The point I wish to make, however, is that some attributions are justified (shared by others), and that the shame we therefore feel is normal.

5. Lansky, M. R., 1987; Lewis, H. B., 1987; Morrison, A. P., 1986b; Nathanson, D. L., 1987c; Scheff, T. J., 1987.

6. Miller, A., 1981; Nathanson, D. L., 1987a, b, c.

7. Morrison, A. P., 1989, p. 119.

8. See M. N. Eagle, 1989, for example.

9. Freud, S., 1917/1957.

10. See Alloy, L. B., 1988, and Cicchetti, D., & Schneider-Rosen, K., 1984, for reviews.

11. Freud, S., 1917/1957.

12. Bibring, E., 1953; Bowlby, J., 1969; see also H. Kohut's view, 1977.

13. Kernberg, O. F., 1976, 1980.

14. As I have tried to point out, one way of dealing with an experience of shame is to disassociate the self from the self being shamed, that is, to become an onlooker to the shamed self. This disassociation, or this engagement of the self from the point of view of the individual, in a particular experience can be quite successful. However, under prolonged and continual shaming of the self, the use of such techniques may lead to disengagement through disassociation of the various parts of the self. Recently, C. A. Ross (1989) reported on his work with multiple personality disorder patients. His work indicates that, under intense and prolonged shame, individuals are likely to adopt an ideation such as the following: "That is not me who is being shamed; it is someone else." In other words, the disassociation of the self from the shamed self in its extreme form leads to the breakdown of the integrated self system.

15. See W. Hobilitzelle, 1987, and N. K. Morrison, 1987, for a similar discussion.

16. See H. B. Lewis, 1987, for a more complete review.

17. Brown, G., Harris, T., & Bifulco, A., 1986.

18. Bowlby, J., 1973.

19. Temper tantrums are not rage responses but the breakdown of angry behavioral patterns under the pressure of frustration or goal blockage. The tantrums do look like rage. Parents, not discriminating between the two different states, respond as if temper tantrums are rage, not frustration. Shame and rage require an objective self system. Anger does not, and its early display may be related to frustration.

20. Scheff, T. J., 1987.

21. Nietzsche, F., 1909/1966.

22. Kohut, H., 1977.

23. See M. Lewis, 1990, for a fuller discussion of the difference between anger and rage.

24. Retzinger, S. R., 1987; see also S. Miller's book, *The Shame Experience*, 1985.

25. Reid, J. B., 1986.

26. According to a *New York Times* (5 February 1990, p. B9), article, between 1976 and 1985 13 percent of all killings in the United States involved spouses, former spouses, or lovers, 34 percent involved acquaintances, 8 percent other family members, and 16 percent strangers; 29 percent were undetermined.

27. Katz, J., 1988.

28. Lansky, M. R., 1987.

29. A variety of studies indicate that psychological attacks on the self—insult,

humiliation, or threats—make aggressive reactions probable. Threats to the self-concept lead to aggression (Averill, J. R., 1982; Barron, R. A., 1977).

30. Dodge, K. A., 1986; Slaby, R. G., & Guerra, N. G., 1988.

31. Chandler, M. J., 1973; Bandura, A., 1973; Blaska, D. M., Bordwin, C. M., Henggeler, S. W., & Mann, B. J., 1989.

32. Stattin, H., & Klachenberg-Larsson, I., 1989.

33. Slaby, R. G., & Guerra, N. G., 1988.

34. Toch, H., 1969, p. 148.

35. Feshbach, N. D., 1982.

36. Rank, O., 1945/1972.

37. Lansky, M. R., 1988, p. 29.

38. Lansky, M. R., 1988, p. 6.

CHAPTER 9. Pathologies of Self: Narcissism and Multiple Personalities

1. Much has been written on narcissism. The reader is referred, for a historical review and the arguments pertaining to its meaning, measurement, and clinical signs, to A. Morrison, ed., *Essential Papers on Narcissism* (1986a), and his recent book, *Shame: The Underside of Narcissism* (1989).

2. Freud, S., 1914/1957.

3. Kohut, H., 1972.

4. Nietzsche, F., 1904/1964; Rank, O., 1945/1972; White, R. W., 1959; Lewis, M., 1990.

5. *Diagnostic and Statistical Manual of Mental Disorders*, 1987.

6. While finishing this book, I came across Morrison's 1989 book. I was familiar with some of his ideas as expressed in the earlier edited volume, and I was glad, therefore, to see our agreement on the relation between shame and narcissism.

7. Roland, A., 1988.

8. Kernberg, O. F., 1975.

9. This situation has changed with a succession of new books (Bliss, E. L., 1986; Hawthorne, T., 1983; Hilgard, E. R., 1977; Kluft, R. P., 1983; Putnam, F. W., 1989; Ross, C. A., 1989).

10. See Newell, A., 1982, for an example.

11. Lewis, M., 1990.

12. See also Rorty, A. O., 1989.

13. Ross, C. A., 1989.

14. LeDoux, J., 1989.

15. Weiskrantz, L., 1986.

16. Ross, C. A., 1989.

17. Oesterreich, T. K., 1974.

18. Prince, M., 1978.

19. Hilgard, E. R., 1977.

20. Browne, K., Davies, C., & Stratton, P., 1988.

21. Jones, E. M., 1953, p. 246, italics added.

22. Breuer, J., & Freud, S., 1895/1986, p. 76.

23. Ross, C. A., 1989, p. 180.

24. Ross, C. A., 1989, p. 217.

25. Ross, C. A., 1989, p. 218.

CHAPTER 10. Individual Differences and Shame Fights Between Couples

1. As I just have pointed out, multiple personality disorder should be considered as the diagnosis for many disorders, including borderline personalities, hysteria, and other disassociative illnesses. Since MPD is caused almost in all cases by sexual abuse, and by the shame accompanying this abuse, it could be argued that many more disorders are shame-caused than we might imagine.

2. The same can be said for some men, although the difficulties and shame over body image may take other forms, for example, body building and the taking of steroids.

3. Lewis, M., Stanger, C., & Sullivan, M. W., 1989.

4. Barrett, K. C., & Zahn-Waxler, C., 1987.

5. Masson, J. M., 1984.

6. Freud, S., 1896/1962.

7. Freud, S., 1933/1961, p. 132.

8. Lewis, H. B., 1987, p. 31.

9. Lewis, H. B., 1987, p. 13.

10. Gilligan, C., 1982.

11. Also see Harter, S., 1989.

12. See Lerner, R. M., & Brackney, B. E., 1978.

13. Chodorow, N., 1978.

14. Zahn-Waxler, C., & Kochanska, G., 1990.

15. Hoffman, M. L., 1975.

16. See, for example, N. D. Feshbach's (1982) and N. Eisenberg and R. Lemon's (1983) reviews of sex differences in empathic behavior.

17. Dweck, C. S., & Leggett, E. L., 1988.

18. Retzinger, S. R., 1989, p. 5.

19. Chodorow, N., 1978.

20. See Lamb, M., 1981; Lewis, M., 1987; Mackey, W. C., 1985.

21. Bernstein, D., 1983.

CHAPTER 11. Stigma

1. Goffman, E., 1963.

2. Lerner, R. M., & Brackney, B. E., 1978; Lerner, R. M., & Jovanovic, J., 1990; Lerner, R. M., Karabenick, S. A., & Stuart, J. L., 1973; Lerner, R. M., Lerner, J. V., Hess, L. E., Schwab, J., Jovanovic, J., Talwar, R., & Kucher, J. S., 1991; Markus, H., Jamill, R., & Sentis, K. P., 1987; Mathes, E. W., & Kahn, A., 1975; Rosenblum, G. A., 1995.

3. Working with young infants, Langlois has been able to demonstrate that fineness of facial features and symmetrical proportions are universally considered, even by young infants, to be attractive and that they are more attention-holding than cross-featured and asymmetrical faces. (Langlois, J. H., Roggman, L. A., Casey, R. J., Ritter, J. M., Rieser-Danner, L. A., & Jenkis, V. Y., 1987).

4. In general, the corrective surgery has been found to be less effective than one might hope, in part because stigmas are not only associated with physical appearance, but also with how people act. Thus, although one might be able to correct some physical stigma, if there are underlying conditions such as mental retardation, then, in fact, all of the stigmas may not disappear with cosmetic surgery.

5. Jones, E. E., Farina, A., Hastorf, A. H., Markus, H., Miller, D. T., & Scott, R. A., 1984.

6. Jones et al., 1984, pp. 1–4.

7. Reiss, S., & Benson, B. A., 1984.

8. Levinson, R. M., & Starling, D. M., 1981; Siperstein, G. N., & Gottlieb, J., 1977.

9. Because the literature on mental retardation is so extensive on this subject, it is here that we turn our attention.

10. Childs, R. E., 1981; David, A. C., & Donovan, E. H., 1975; Hurley, A. D., & Hurley, F. J., 1987; Margalit, M., & Miron, M., 1983; Peat, M., 1991; Rimmerman, A., & Portowicz, D. J., 1987.

11. Frey, K. S., Greenberg, M. T., & Fewell, R. R., 1989.

12. Frey et al., 1989.

13. Nixon, C. D., & Singer, G.H.S., 1993, p. 670.

14. Marvin, R., & Pianta, R., 1994.

15. Foley, G. M., 1986.

16. Gath, A., 1992; see also Shulman, S., 1988.

17. Jones et al., 1984.

18. If the presence among normals markedly exposes the stigmatized person with invasion of privacy, this has important implications for any programs

of mainstreaming. In mainstreaming, one tries to destigmatize by exposing the person to the public good. By exposing children, for example, to the normal, we may be doing them harm. Goffman (1963, p. 11) states: "Within such capsula congenitally stigmatized child can be carefully sustained by means of information control. Self-belittling definitions are prevented from entering the charmed circle . . . leaving the encapsed child as a fully qualified ordinary human being." Thus, there is reason to believe that mainstreaming may not, in fact, protect the person from the effects of being stigmatized. Several studies looking at the change in children with retardation feelings of self have indicated that mainstreaming does very little good for them in terms of feeling stigmatized by their dysfunction.

19. Borkowski, J. G., Weyhing, R. S., & Turner, L. A., 1986; Cook, R. E., 1983; Gibbons, F. X., 1985; Turner, L. A., 1994; Turner, L. A., Dofny, E. M., & Dutka, S., 1994; Wehmeyer, M. L., 1994.

20. Weiner, B., 1993.

21. Responsibility can change as a function of new knowledge and information or of a change in social values. When illness was regarded as a form of punishment imposed for wrongdoing, then illness could be thought of as something to be blamed on the person with the illness. However, when the idea of disease caused by a germ was introduced, the germs originated outside of the individuals and thus were not their responsibility. A changing technology impacts on beliefs about responsibility. The idea of controlability therefore must play a very important part in our attribution theories. Weiner's attempt to focus our attention on responsibility is an important addition to our understanding in this regard.

22. In this regard, the attempt to alter the perception of others by altering their language, for example, by talking about a person who has disability, rather than a disabled person, is an attempt to remove the stigma as the defining element of the person and thus to remove the power of the stigma to reflect upon the total self.

23. Angrosino, M. V., 1992; Gibbons, F. X., 1985; Reiss, S., & Benson, B. A., 1984; Rogers, S. J., 1991; Szivos-Bach, S. E., 1993; Taylor, A. R., Asher, S. R., & Williams, G. A., 1987; Varni, J. W., Setoguchi, Y., Rappaport, L. R., & Talbot, D., 1992.

CHAPTER 12. Shame Across Time and Place

1. Hallowell, A. I., 1955.
2. Geertz, C., 1984, p. 126.
3. Geertz, C., 1984, p. 126.
4. Geertz, C., 1984, p. 128.
5. Geertz, C., 1984, p. 133.

6. Geertz, C., 1984, p. 130.

7. Rosaldo, M. Z., 1984; Read, K. E., 1955.

8. Rosaldo, M. Z., 1984, p. 148.

9. Rosaldo, M. Z., 1984, p. 149.

10. Shweder, R. A., & Bourne, E. J., 1984.

11. Luria, A., 1976.

12. The question arises as to whether these cultural differences in the nature of the self give rise to different phenomenological experiences of shame? While such a question is central to the understanding of the role of self consciousness in shame, we have little data to answer the question. Our choices are either to assume that the particular self-at-the-moment experiences shame as we do or that different selves have different experiences of shame. This question remains open. See also Ross, C. A., 1989, for a discussion of multiple selves and MPD.

13. See R. Emde's (1983) analysis of this as well.

14. Roland, A., 1988; Shweder, R. A., 1985; Benedict, R., 1946.

15. Doi, T., 1973.

16. I am reminded of this failure to take care of the other as it applies to eating together. In Japan, one does not pour a drink for oneself but for another. If the other does not remember to pour your drink, you may go thirsty. When I was first taught this practice, I failed to watch my dinner partner's glass, and several times I caught him looking at me politely, but impatiently, waiting for me to take care of his glass.

17. Shweder, R. A., & Miller, J. G., 1985.

18. See Benedict, R., 1946.

19. Shweder, R. A., 1985.

20. Shweder, R. A., & Miller, J. G., 1985.

21. Benedict, R., 1946.

22. Roland, A., 1988, p. 256.

23. Eban, A. 1968, p. 14.

24. See also Johnson, P., 1987.

25. Because of the problems with historical records and analysis, much of what we say about ancient history or even more modern history is open to a variety of interpretations. For almost every statement, we are likely to find a historian who differs.

26. Jaynes, J., 1976.

27. Jaynes, J., 1976, p. 273.

28. Baumeister, R. F., 1987.

29. Nisbet, R., 1973.

30. Hanning, R. W., 1977.

31. Aries, P., 1977/1981.

32. Baumeister, R. F., 1987.

33. Aries, P., 1960/1962.

34. Rogers, C. R., 1959; Maslow, A. H., 1943.

35. While it takes place in the individual, it does have an impact on, and is impacted on, other people. Nevertheless, the change is seen in the individual and the measures of change are measures of the individual.

36. Self psychology and even object relations theory do focus upon the origins of the self in its relationship to the social nexus, but the outcome of the relationship is a whole and integrated self, an I-self. Failures in this developmental process can be addressed through the therapeutic relationship of patient and analyst.

37. Sartre, J ., 1943/1966, p . 86.

38. Sartre, J. 1943/1966, p. 327.

39. Fromm, E., 1941, p. viii.

40. Fromm, E., 1941, p. 261.

41. Fromm, E., 1941, p. 258.

42. Fromm, E., 1941, p. 261.

43. Fromm, E., 1941, p. 261.

44. Kierkegaard, S., 1846/1962.

45. Rubin, J., 1989, p. 135.

46. Rubin, J., 1989, p. 145.

References

Note: The English-language editions of translated works are referenced first in this listing.

Abelson, R. (1976). Script processing in attitude formation and decision making. In J. S. Carroll & J. Payne (Eds.), *Cognition and social behavior.* Hillsdale, NJ: Erlbaum.

Acquarone, S. (1992). What shall I do to stop him crying? Crying infants and their mothers/parents. *Journal of Child Psychotherapy, 18*(1), 33–56.

Alessandri, S., Sullivan, M. W., & Lewis, M. (1990). Violation of expectancy and frustration in early infancy. *Developmental Psychology, 26,* 738–744.

Alloy, L. B. (Ed.). (1988). *Cognitive processes in depression.* New York: Guilford Press.

Amsterdam, L. (1972). Mirror self-image reactions before age two. *Developmental Psychology, 5,* 297–305.

Angrosino, M. V. (1992). Metaphors of stigma: How deinstitutionalized mentally retarded adults see themselves. *Journal of Contemporary Ethnography, 21*(2), 171–199.

Aries, P. (1962). *Centuries of childhood: A social history of family life.* New York: Random House. (Original work published 1960)

Aries, P. (1981). *The hour of our death.* New York: Knopf. (Original work published 1977)

Asch, S. (1956). Studies of independence and conformity: 1. A minority of one against a unanimous majority. *Psychological Monographs, 70,* 1–70.

Averill, J. R. (1982). *Anger and aggression: An essay on emotion.* New York: Springer-Verlag.

Baldwin, J. M. (1903). *Mental development in the child and the race.* 2d ed. New York: Macmillan. (Original work published 1899)

Bandura, A. (1973). *Aggression: A social learning analysis.* Englewood Cliffs, NJ: Prentice-Hall.

Bard, P. A. (1928). A diencephalic mechanism for the expression of rage with special reference to the sympathetic nervous system. *American Journal of Physiology, 84,* 490–515.

Barrett, K. C., & Zahn-Waxler, C. (1987, April). Do toddlers express guilt? Poster presented at the meetings of the Society for Research in Child Development, Toronto.

Barron, R. A. (1977). *Human aggression.* New York: Plenum.

Baumeister, R. F. (1987). How the self became a problem: A psychological review of historical research. *Journal of Personality and Social Psychology, 52,* 163–176.

Baxter, C. (1989). Investigating stigma as stress in social interactions of parents. *Journal of Mental Deficiency Research, 33,* 455–466.

Beck, A. T. (1967). *Depression: Clinical, experimental, and theoretical aspects.* New York: Harper & Row.

Beck, A. T. (1979). *Cognitive therapy and the emotional disorders.* New York: Times Mirror.

Bender, J. (1970). The relative proneness to shame and guilt as a dimension of character style. *Dissertation Abstracts International, 32,* 1833B. (University Microfilms No. 71–23697).

Benedict, R. (1946). *The chrysanthemum and the sword.* Boston: Houghton Mifflin.

Bernstein, D. (1983). The female superego: A different perspective. *International Journal of Psycho-Analysis, 64,* 187–202.

Bibring, E. (1953). The mechanism of depression. In P. Greenaire (Ed.), *Affective disorders* (pp. 13–48). New York: International Universities Press.

Birenbaum, A. (1988). Courtesy stigma revisited. *Mental Retardation, 30*(5), 265–268.

Blaska, D. M., Bordwin, C. M., Henggeler, S. W., & Mann, B. J. (1989). Individual, family, and peer characteristics of adolescent sex offenders and assaultive offenders. *Developmental Psychology, 25,* 846–855.

Bliss, E. L. (1986). *Multiple personality, allied disorders, and hypnosis.* New York: Oxford University Press.

Bogie, C. E., & Buckhalt, J. A. (1987). Reactions to failure and success among gifted, average, and EMR students. *Gifted Child Quarterly, 31*(2), 70–74.

Borke, H. (1973). The development of empathy in Chinese and American children between 3 and 6 years of age: A cross-cultural study. *Developmental Psychology, 9,* 102–108.

Borkowski, J. G., Weyhing, R. S., & Turner, L. A. (1986). Attributional retraining and the teaching of strategies. *Exceptional Children, 53*(2), 130–137.

Bower, T. R. (1974). *Development in infancy.* San Francisco, CA: Freeman.

Bowlby, J. (1969). *Attachment and loss: Vol. 1. Attachment.* New York: Basic Books.

Bowlby, J. (1973). *Attachment and loss: Vol. 2. Separation.* New York: Basic Books.

Bracegirdle, H. (1990). The acquisition of social skills by children with special needs. *British Journal of Occupational Therapy, 53*(3), 107–108.

Bretherton, I. (1987). New perspectives on attachment relations: Security, communication, and internal working models. In J. D. Osofsky (Ed.), *Handbook of infant development,* (2nd ed., pp. 1061–1100). New York: Wiley.

Bretherton, I., Fritz, J., Zahn-Waxler, C., & Ridgeway, D. (1986). Learning to talk about a functionalist perspective. *Child Development, 57,* 530–548.

Bretherton, I., McNew, S., & Beeghly-Smith, M. (1981). Early person knowledge as expressed in gestural and verbal communication: When do infants acquire a "theory of mind"? In M. E. Lamb & L. R. Sherrod (Eds.), *Infant social cognition* (pp. 333–373). Hillsdale, NJ: Erlbaum.

Breuer, J., & Freud, S. (1986). Studies on hysteria. In J. Strachey (Ed and Trans.), *The standard edition of the complete psychological works of Sigmund Freud* (*Vol. 2,*) London: Hogarth Press. (Original work published 1895)

Bridges, K. M. B. (1932). Emotional development in early infancy. *Child Development, 3,* 324–334.

Brooks-Gunn, J., & Lewis, M. (1982). Affective exchanges between normal and handicapped infants and their mothers. In T. Field & A. Fogel (Eds.), *Emotion and early interaction* (pp. 161–188). Hillsdale, NJ: Erlbaum.

Broucek, F. (1982). Shame and its relationship to early narcissistic developments. *International Journal of Psycho-Anaysis, 65,* 369–378.

Brown, G., Harris, T., & Bifulco, A. (1986). Long-term effects of early loss of parent. In M. Rutter, C. Izard, & P. Read (Eds.), *Depression in young people* (pp. 251–296). New York: Guilford Press.

Browne, K., Davies, C., & Stratton, P. (Eds.) (1988). Introduction. *Early prediction and prevention of child abuse.* (pp. 3–12). Sussex, England: Wiley.

Buber, M. (1958). *I and Thou* (2d ed.). New York: Scribner's.

Buss, A. H. (1980). *Self-consciousness and social anxiety.* San Francisco, CA: W. H. Freeman.

Campos, J., Campos, R., & Barnett, K. (1989). Emergent themes in the study of emotional development and emotion regulation. *Developmental Psychology, 25,* 394–402.

Cannon, W. B. (1929). *Bodily changes in pain, hunger, fear, and rage.* New York: Appleton.

Capute, A. J. (1984). Primitive reflex profile: A quantitation of primitive reflexes in infancy. *Developmental Medicine and Child Neurology, 26,* 375–383.

DiBiase, R., & Lewis, M. (1989). Temperament and emotional expression in infancy: A short-term longitudinal study. Unpublished doctoral dissertation, Temple University, Philadelphia.

Dodge, K. A. (1986). Social information-processing variables in the development of aggression and altruism in children. In C. Zahn-Waxler, E. M. Cummings, & R. Iannotti (Eds.), *Altruism and aggression* (pp. 280–302). Cambridge: Cambridge University Press.

Doi, T. (1973). *The anatomy of dependence.* Tajoko, Japan: Kodansha International.

Duval, S., & Wicklund, R. A. (1972). *A theory of objective self-awareness.* New York: Academic Press.

Dweck, C. S., & Leggett, E. L. (1988). A social-cognitive approach to motivation and personality. *Psychological Review, 95,* 256–273.

Eagle, M. N . (1989). *The epistemological status of psychoanalysis.* Social Research, 56, 383–419.

Eban, A. (1968). *Civilization and the Jews.* New York: Heritage Press.

Edelman, R. J. (1987). *The psychology of embarrassment.* Chichester, England: Wiley.

Eisenberg, N., & Lemon, R. (1983). Sex differences in empathy and related capacities. *Psychological Bulletin, 94,* 100–131.

Ekman, P. (1984). Expression and the nature of emotion. In K. R. Scherer & P. Ekman (Eds.), *Approaches to emotion* (pp. 319–344). Hillsdale, NJ: Erlbaum.

Ekman, P., & Friesen, W. V. (1975). *Unmasking the face.* Englewood Cliffs, NJ: Prentice-Hall .

Ekman, P., Friesen, W. V., & Ellsworth, P. (1972). *Emotion in the human face: Guidelines for research and an integration of findings.* New York: Pergamon.

Emde, R. N. (1980). Levels of meaning for infant emotions: A biosocial view. In K. R. Scherer & P. Ekman (Eds.), *Approaches to emotion* (pp.77–107). Hillsdale, NJ: Erlbaum.

Emde, R. N. (1983). The prerepresentational self and its affective core. *Psychoanalytic Study of the Child, 38,* 165–192.

Emde, R. N. (1988). Development terminable and interminable: 2. Recent psychoanalytic theory and therapeutic considerations. *International Journal of Psycho-Anaysis, 69,* 283–296.

Erikson, E. H. (1950). *Childhood and society.* New York: Norton.

Erwin, E. (1984). The standing of psychoanalysis. *British Journal of Philosophy of Science, 35,* 115–128.

Eysenck, H. J. (1954). *The psychology of politics.* London: Routledge & Kegan Paul.

Fairbairn, W. R. D. (Ed.). (1949). *Steps in the development of an object-relations theory of the personality.* New York: Basic Books.

Chandler, M. J. (1973). Egocentrism and antisocial behavior: The assessment and training of social perspective-taking skills. *Developmental Psychology, 9,* 326–337.

Chapman, D. J. (Ed.). (1976). *Humor and laughter: Theory, research, and applications.* London: Wiley.

Childs, R. E. (1981). Maternal psychological conflicts associated with the birth of a retarded child. *Maternal-Child Nursing Journal, 21,* 175–182.

Chodorow, N. (1978). *The reproduction of mothering.* Berkeley and Los Angeles: University of California Press.

Cicchetti, D., & Schneider-Rosen, K. (1984). Toward a transactional model of childhood depression. *New Directions for Child Development, 26,* 5–27.

Coates, S. (1978). Sex differences in field dependence among preschool children. In R. Friedman, R. Reichart, & R. Vande Weile (Eds.), *Sex differences in behavior.* (pp. 259–277). New York: Wiley.

Cook, R. E. (1983). Why Jimmy doesn't try. *Academic Therapy, 19*(2), 155–162.

Cooley, C. H. (1912). *Human nature and the social order.* New York: Scribner's.

Cooley, C. H. (1962). *Social organization: A study of the larger mind.* New York: Schocken. (Original work published 1909)

Cornielson, F. S., & Arsenian, I. (1960). A study of the responses of psychotic patients to photographic self-image experience. *Psychiatric Quarterly, 34,* 1–8.

Csikszentmihalyi, M. (1975). *Beyond boredom and anxiety: The experience of play in work and games.* San Francisco, CA: Jossey-Bass.

Darwin, C. (1969). *The expression of the emotions in man and animals.* Chicago: University of Illinois Press. (Original work published 1872)

Davidson, R. J. & Fox, N. A. (1982). Asymmetrical brain activity discriminates between positive versus negative affective stimuli in human infants. *Science, 218,* 1235–1237.

Deaux, K. (1976). Sex: A perspective on the attribution process. In J. Harvey, W. Iches, & R. Kidd (Eds.), *New directions in attributional research* (Vol. 1). Hillsdale, NJ: Erlbaum.

Deaux, K., & Emswiller, T. (1974). Explanations of successful performance on sex-linked tasks. What is skill for male is luck for the female. *Journal of Personality and Social Psychology, 29,* 80–85.

Detrick, D. W., & Detrick, S. P. (1989). *Self-psychology: Comparisons and contrasts.* Hillsdale, NJ: Analytic Press.

Dewey, J. (1922). *Human nature and conduct.* New York: Henry Holt.

American Psychiatric Association. (1987). *Diagnostic and statistical manual of mental disorders* (3rd ed., rev.). Washington, DC.

David, A. C., & Donovan, E. H. (1975). Initiating group process with parents of multihandicapped children. *Social Work in Health Care, 1*(2), 177–183.

Fairbairn, W. R. D. (1952). *Object-relations theory of the personality.* New York: Basic Books.

Fenichel, O. (1945). *The psychoanalytic theory of neuroses.* New York: Norton.

Feshbach, N. D. (1982). Sex differences in empathy and social behavior in children. In N. Eisenberg (Ed.), *The development of prosocial behavior* (pp. 315–338). New York: Academic Press.

Fischer, K. (1980). A theory of cognitive development: The control and construction of hierarchies of skills. *Psychological Review, 87,* 477–531.

Foley, G. M. (1986). Emotional development of children with handicaps. *Research in Affective Development, 18,* 57–73.

Fraiberg, S., & Adelson, E. (1976). Self-representation in young blind children. In Z. Jastrzembska (Ed.), *The effects of blindness and other impairments on early development* (pp. 48–96). New York: American Foundation for the Blind.

Freud, S. (1938). *Wit and its relation to the unconscious: The basic writings of Sigmund Freud.* (A. A. Brill, Trans.) London: Kegan Paul, Trench, & Trubner. (Original work published 1916)

Freud, S. (1953). Three essays on the theory of sexuality. In J. Strachey (Ed. and Trans.), *The standard edition of the complete psychological works of Sigmund Freud* (Vol. 7, pp. 153–243). London: Hogarth Press. (Original work published 1905)

Freud, S. (1957). *On narcissism: An introduction. (Vol.* 14, pp. 67–102). London: Hogarth Press (Original work published 1914)

Freud, S. (1957). Mourning and melancholia. In J. Strachey (Ed. and Trans.), *The standard edition of the complete psychological works of Sigmund Freud* (Vol. 14, pp. 243–258). London: Hogarth Press. (Original work published 1917)

Freud, S. (1959). Repression. In E. Jones (Ed.) and J. Riviere (Trans.), *Collected papers* (Vol. 4, pp. 84–97). London: Hogarth. (Original work published 1915)

Freud, S. (1959). The ego and the id. In J. Strachey (Ed. and Trans.), *The complete psychological works of Sigmund Freud* (Vol. 19, pp. 3–66). London: Hogarth Press. (Original work published 1923)

Freud, S. (1959). Some psychical consequences of the anatomical distinction between the sexes. In J. Strachey (Ed. and Trans.), *The standard edition of the complete psychological works of Sigmund Freud* (Vol. 19, pp. 241–258). London: Hogarth Press. (Original work published 1925)

Freud, S. (1960). Civilization and its discontents. In J. Strachey (Ed. and Trans.), *The standard edition of the complete psychological works of Sigmund Freud* (Vol. 21, pp. 51–145). New York: Cape & Smith. (Original work published 1930)

Freud, S. (1961). New introductory lectures on psychoanalysis. In J. Strachey (Ed. and Trans.), *The standard edition of the complete psychological works of Sigmund Freud* (Vol. 22, pp. 5–182). New York: Norton. (Original work published 1933)

Freud, S. (1962). *The etiology of hysteria.* In J. Strachey (Ed. and Trans.), *The standard edition of the complete psychological works of Sigmund Freud* (Vol. 3, pp. 187–221). London: Hogarth Press. (Original work published 1896)

Freud, S. (1963). *The problem of anxiety.* (H. A. Bunker, Trans.) New York: Norton. (Original work published 1936)

Frey, K. S., Greenberg, M. T., & Fewell, R. R. (1989). Stress and coping among children: A multidimensional approach. *American Journal on Mental Retardation, 94*(3), 240–249.

Fromm, E. (1941). *Escape from freedom.* New York: Rinehart and Co.

Gallup, G. G., Jr. (1973). *Towards an operational definition of self-awareness.* Paper presented at the 9th International Congress of Anthropological and Ethological Sciences, Chicago.

Gallup, G. G., Jr. (1977). Self-recognition in primates: A comparative approach to the bidirectional properties of consciousness. *American Psychologist, 32,* 329–338.

Gath, A. (1992). The brothers and sisters of mentally retarded children. In F. Boer & J. Dunn (Eds.), *Children's sibling relationships: Developmental and clinical issues* (pp. 101–108). Hillsdale, NJ: Erlbaum.

Geertz, C. (1984). On the nature of anthropological understanding. In R. A. Shweder & R. A. Levine (Eds.), *Cultural theory: Essays on mind, self, and emotion.* Cambridge: Cambridge University Press.

Geppert, U. (1986). *A coding-system for analyzing behavioral expressions of self-evaluative emotions.* (Technical Manual.) Munich: Max-Planck Institute for Psychological Research.

Geppert, U., & Kuster, U. (1983). The emergence of "wanting to do it oneself": A precursor of achievement motivation. *International Journal of Behavioral Development, 6,* 355–370.

Gesell, A. (1928). *Infancy and human growth.* New York: Macmillan.

Gibbons, F. X. (1985). Stigma perception: Social comparison among mentally retarded persons. *American Journal of Mental Deficiency, 90*(1), 98–106.

Gilligan, C. (1982). *In a different voice.* Cambridge: Harvard University Press.

Gleick, J. (1987). *Chaos: Making a new science.* New York: Viking.

Gleser, G., Gottschalk, L., & Springer, K. (1961). An anxiety scale applicable to verbal samples. *Archives of General Psychiatry, 5,* 593–605.

Goffman, E. (1963). *Stigma.* Englewood Cliffs, NJ: Prentice-Hall.

Greenberg, J. R., & Mitchell, S. A. (1983). *Object relations in psychoanalytic theory.* Cambridge: Harvard University Press.

Greig, J. Y. T. (1969). *The psychology of laughter and comedy.* New York: Cooper Square.

Grunbaum, A. (1984). *The foundations of psychoanalysis: A philosophical critique.* Berkeley and Los Angeles: University of California Press.

Hallowell, A. I. (1955). The self and its behavioral environment. In A. I. Hallowell (Ed.), *Culture and experience* (pp. 75–110). Philadelphia: University of Pennsylvania Press.

Halperin, M. (1989, April). *Empathy and self-awareness.* Paper presented at the Society for Research in Child Development meeting, Kansas City.

Hanning, R. W. (1977). *The individual in twelfth-century romance.* New Haven, CT: Yale University Press.

Harris, P., & Lipian, M. S. (1989). Understanding emotion and experiencing emotion. In C. Saarni & P. Harris (Eds.), *Children's understanding of emotion* (pp. 241–258). Cambridge: Cambridge University Press.

Harter, S. (1989). *Adolescent self and identity development.* Unpublished manuscript.

Hartmann, H. (1964). Comments on the psychoanalytic theory of the ego. In *Essays on ego psychology.* New York: International Universities Press.

Hawthorne, T. (1983). *Multiple personality and the disintegration of literary character.* New York: St. Martin's Press.

Heckhausen, H. (1984). Emergent achievement behavior: Some early developments. In J. Nicholls (Ed.), *The development of achievement motivation* (pp. 1–32). Greenwich, CT: JAI Press.

Hesse, H. (1970). A child's heart. In *Klingsor's last summer* (pp.1–42). (R. Winston & C. Winston, Trans.) New York: Harper & Row. (Original work published 1920)

Hilgard, E. R. (1977). *Divided consciousness: Multiple controls in human thought and action.* New York: Wiley.

Hinde, R. A. (1979). *Towards understanding relationships.* London: Academic Press.

Hobilitzelle, W. (1987). Differentiating and measuring shame and guilt: The relation between shame and depression. In H. B. Lewis (Ed.), *The role of shame in emotion formation* (pp. 207–236). Hillsdale, NJ: Erlbaum.

Hoffman, M. L. (1970). Moral development. In P. H. Mussen (Ed.), *Handbook of child psychology* (3rd ed., Vol. 2, pp. 261–359). New York: Wiley.

Hoffman, M. L. (1975). Sex differences in moral internalization and values. *Journal of Personality and Social Psychology, 32,* 720–729.

Hoffman, M. L. (1977). Empathy, its development, and prosocial implications. In H. E. Howe, Jr., *Nebraska symposium on motivation* (pp. 169–218). Lincoln: University of Nebraska Press.

Hoffman, M. L. (1982). Development of prosocial motivation: Sympathy and guilt. In N. Eisenberg (Ed.), *The development of prosocial behavior* (pp. 281–313). New York: Academic Press.

Hoffman, M. L. (1988). Moral development. In M. Lamb & M. Bornstein (Eds.), *Developmental psychology: An advanced textbook* (2nd ed., pp. 497–548). Hillsdale, NJ: Erlbaum.

Horney, K. (1939). *New ways in psychoanalysis.* New York: Norton.

Hubel, D. H., & Weisel, T. N. (1962). Receptive fields, binocular interaction, and functional architecture in the cat's visual cortex. *Journal of Physiology, 160*, 106–154.

Hurley, A. D., & Hurley, F. J. (1987). Working with the parents of handicapped children. *Psychiatric Aspects of Mental Retardation Reviews, 6*(11), 53–57.

Izard, C. E. (1971). *The face of emotion.* New York: Appleton-Century-Crofts.

Izard, C. E. (1972). *Patterns of emotion: A new analysis of anxiety and depression.* New York: Academic Press.

Izard, C. E. (1977). *Human emotions.* New York: Plenum Press.

Izard, C. E. (1979). The Maximally Discriminative Facial Movement Coding System (MAX). Newark, DE: Instructional Resources Center, University of Delaware.

Izard, C. E., Hembree, E. A., & Huebner, R. R. (1987). Infants' emotion expressions to acute pain: Developmental change and stability of individual differences. *Developmental Psychology, 23*, 105-113.

Izard, C. E., & Tyson, M. C. (1986). Shyness as a discrete emotion. In W. H. Jones, J. M. Cheek, & S. R. Briggs (Eds.), *Shyness: Perspectives on research and treatment* (pp. 147–160). New York: Plenum Press.

Jacobson, E. (1964). *The self and the object world.* New York: International Universities Press.

James, W. (1890). *The principles of psychology.* New York: Holt.

Janis, I. L. (1965). Psychodynamic aspects of stress tolerance. In S. Z. Klausner (Ed.), *The quest for self control* (pp. 215–246). New York: Free Press.

Janoff-Bulman, R. (1979). Characterological versus behavioral self-blame: Inquiries into depression and rape. *Journal of Personality and Social Psychology, 37*, 1798–1809.

Jaynes, J. (1976). *The origins of consciousness in the breakdown of the bicameral mind.* Boston: Houghton Mifflin.

Johnson, P. (1987). *The history of the Jews.* New York: Harper & Row.

Jones, E. E., Farina, A., Hastorf, A. H., Markus, H., Miller, D. T. & Scott, R. A. (1984). *Social stigma: The psychology of marked relationships.* New York: W. H. Freeman

Jones, E. M. (1953). *Sigmund Freud: Life and work* (Vol. 1). London: Hogarth Press.

Kagan, J. (1981). *The second year.* Cambridge: Harvard University Press.

Katz, J. (1988). *Seductions to crime.* New York: Basic Books.

Kaye, K. (1982). *The mental and social life of babies.* Chicago: University of Chicago Press.

Kernberg, O. F. (1975). *Borderline conditions and pathological narcissism.* New York: Aronson.

Kernberg, O. F. (1976). *Object relations theory and clinical psychoanalysis.* New York: Aronson.

Kernberg, O. F. (1980). *Internal world and external reality: Object relations theory applied.* New York: Aronson.

Kierkegaard, S. (1962). *The present age* (A. Duc, Trans.). New York: Harper & Row. (Original work published 1846)

King, S. M., Rosenbaum, P., Armstrong, R. W., & Milner, R. (1989). An epidemiological study of children's attitudes toward disability. *Developmental Medicine and Child Neurology, 31*(2), 237–245.

Klein, M. (1975). *"Envy and gratitude" and other works, 1946–1963: On the theory of anxiety and guilt.* New York: Delacorte Press. (Original work published 1948)

Kluft, R. P. (Ed.). (1983). *Childhood antecedents of multiple personality disorders.* Washington, DC: American Psychiatric Press.

Kohlberg, L. (1976). Moral stages and moralization: The cognitive-developmental approach. In T. Lickona (Ed.), *Moral development and behavior: Theory, research, and social issues* (pp. 31–53). New York: Holt, Rinehart & Winston.

Kohut, H. (1971). *The analysis of the self.* New York: International Universities Press.

Kohut, H. (1972). Thoughts on narcissism and narcissistic rage. *Psychoanalytic Study of the Child, 28,* 360–399.

Kohut, H. (1977). *The restoration of the self.* New York: International Universities Press.

Lacan, J. (1968). *Language of the self.* Baltimore, MD: Johns Hopkins University Press.

Lamb, M. (Ed.) (1981). *The role of the father in child development* (2d ed.). New York: Wiley.

Langlois, J. H., Roggman, L. A., Casey, R. J., Ritter, J. M., Rieser-Danner, L. A., & Jenkis, V. Y. (1987). Infant preferences for attractive faces: Rudiments of a stereotype? *Developmental Psychology, 23,* 363–369.

Lansky, M. R. (1987). Shame and domestic violence. In D. L. Nathanson (Ed.), *The many faces of shame* (pp. 335–362). New York: Guilford Press.

Lansky, M. R. (1988, November 5). Shame and the problem of suicide: A family system's perspective. Paper presented at the symposium "Suicide and the Family." Sponsored by Los Angeles Suicide Prevention/Family Service for Los Angeles.

Lazarus, R. W. (1982). Thoughts on the relations between emotion and cognition. *American Psychologist, 37,* 1019–1024.

LeDoux, J. (1989). Cognitive and emotional interactions in the brain. *Cognition and Emotion, 3,* 265–289.

Lerner, R. M., & Brackney, B. E. (1978) The importance of inner and outer body parts: Attitudes in the self-concept of late adolescent. *Sex Roles, 4,* 225–238.

Lerner, R. M., & Jovanovic, J. (1990). The role of body-image in psychosocial development across the lifespan: A developmental perspective. In T. T. Cash & T. Pruzinsky (Eds.), *Body-images: Development, deviance and change* (pp. 110–127). New York: Guilford Press.

Lerner, R. M., Karabenick, S. A., & Stuart, J. L. (1973). Relations among physical attractiveness, body attitudes, and self-concept in male and female college students. *Journal of Psychology, 85,* 119–129.

Lerner, R. M., Lerner, J. V., Hess, L. E., Schwab, J., Jovanovic, J., Talwar, R., & Kucher, J. S. (1991). Physical attractiveness and psychosocial functioning among early adolescents. *Journal of Early Adolescence, 11,* 300–320.

Levinson, R. M., & Starling, D. M., (1981). Retardation and the burden of stigma. *Deviant Behavior: An Interdisciplinary Journal, 2,* 371–390.

Levi-Strauss, C. (1963). *Structural anthropology.* (C. Jacobson & B. Grunefest Schoepf, Trans.). New York: Basic Books (Original work published 1958)

Lewis, H. B. (1971). *Shame and guilt in neurosis.* New York: International Universities Press.

Lewis, H. B. (1976). *Psychic war in men and women.* New York: New York University Press.

Lewis, H. B. (1987). Shame: The "sleeper" in psychopathology. In H. B. Lewis (Ed.), *The role of shame in symptom formation* (pp. 1–28). Hillsdale, NJ: Erlbaum.

Lewis, M. (1979). The self as a developmental concept. *Human Development, 22,* 416–419.

Lewis, M. (1987). Social development in infancy and early childhood. In J. Osofsky (Ed.), *Handbook of infancy* (2nd ed., pp. 419–493). New York: Wiley.

Lewis, M. (1989a). Chaos: Making a new science. [Review of J. Gleick, *Chaos, making a new science*]. *Human Development, 32,* 241–244.

Lewis, M. (1989b). Cultural differences in children's knowledge of emotional scripts. In P. Harris & C. Saarni (Eds.), *Children's understanding of emotion* (pp. 350–373). New York: Cambridge University Press.

Lewis, M. (1989c, June 20–24). Why women cry and men do not: The origins of emotional differences. [Speech.] International Academy of Sex Research, Princeton , NJ.

Lewis, M. (1990). The development of intentionality and the role of consciousness. *Psychological Inquiry, 1,* 231–248.

Lewis, M. (in press). The development of anger and rage. In S. P. Roose & R. Glick (Eds.), *Rage, power and aggression: Their relationship to motivation and aggression.* New Haven, CT: Yale University Press.

Lewis, M., Alessandri, S., & Sullivan, M. W. (1990). Expectancy, loss of control, and anger in young infants. *Developmental Psychology, 26,* 745–751.

Lewis, M., & Brooks-Gunn, J. (1979). *Social cognition and the acquisition of self.* New York: Plenum Press.

Lewis, M., & Feiring, C. (1989). Infant, mother, and mother-infant interaction behavior and subsequent attachment. *Child Development, 60,* 146–156.

Lewis, M., & Michalson, L. (1983). *Children's emotions and moods.* New York: Plenum Press.

Lewis, M., Stanger, C., & Sullivan, M. W. (1989). Deception in three-year-olds. *Developmental Psychology, 25,* 439–443.

Lewis, M., Sullivan, M. W., Stanger, C., & Weiss, M. (1989). Self-development and self-conscious emotions. *Child Development, 60,* 146–156.

Lewis, M., Sullivan, M. W., & Vasen, A. (1987). Making faces: Age and emotion differences in the posing of emotional expressions. *Developmental Psychology, 23,* 690–697.

Lewis, M., & Weinraub, M. (1979). Origins of early sex-role development. *Sex Roles, 5,* 135–153.

Lindsey-Harty, J. (1984). Contrasting experience of shame and guilt. *American Behavioral Scientist, 27,* 689–704.

Luria, A. R. (1976). *Cognitive development: Its cultural and social foundations.* Cambridge: Harvard University Press.

Maccoby, E. J., & Jacklin, C. N. (1974). *The psychology of sex differences.* Stanford, CA: Stanford University Press.

Mackey, W. C. (1985). *Fathering behaviors: The dynamics of the man-child bond.* New York: Plenum Press.

Mahler, M. S. (1968). *On human symbiosis and the vicissitudes of individuation: Vol. 1. Infantile psychosis.* New York: International Universities Press.

Mahler, M. S., Pine, F., & Bergman, A. (1975). *The psychological birth of the infant.* New York: Basic Books.

Main, M., Kaplan, K., & Cassidy, J. (1985). Security in infancy, childhood, and adulthood. A move to the level of representation. In I. Bretherton & E. Waters (Eds.), *Crowing points of attachment theory and research. Monographs of the Society for Research in Child Development, 50* (1–2, Serial No. 209), 66–104.

Makas, E. (1988). Positive attitudes toward disabled people: Disabled and non-disabled persons' perspectives. *Journal of Social Science Issues, 44*(1), 49–61.

Mandler, G. (1975). *Mind and emotion.* New York: Wiley.

Margalit, M., & Miron, M. (1983). The attitudes of Israeli adolescents toward handicapped people. *Exceptional Child, 30*(3), 195–200.

Markus, H., Jamill, R., & Sentis, K. P. (1987). Thinking fat: Self schemas for body weight and the processing of weight-relevant information. *Journal of Applied Social Psychology, 17,* 50–71.

Marvin, R. & Pianta, R. C. (1994, May 5–7). Attachment in locomotor and non-locomotor preschool children: The regulation of emotion and motor behavior. Paper presented at the 4th Annual Conference of the Center for Human Development and Developmental Disabilities, "Emotional Development in Atypical Children," New Brunswick NJ.

Maslow, A. H. (1943). A theory of human motivation. *Psychological Review, 50,* 370–396.

Masson, J. M. (1984). *The assault on the truth: Freud's suppression of the seduction theory.* New York: Farrar, Strauss, and Giroux.

Mathes, E. W., & Kahn, A. (1975). Physical attractiveness, happiness, neuroticism and self-esteem. *Journal of Psychology, 90,* 267–275.

McDougall, W. (1923). *An introduction to social psychology.* London: Methuen. (Original work published 1908)

Mead, G. H. (1972). *Mind, self, and society.* Chicago: University of Chicago Press. (Original work published 1934)

Meltzoff, A. N., & Moore, M. K. (1977). Imitation of facial and manual gestures by human neonates. *Science, 198,* 75–78.

Merleau-Ponty, M. (1964). In J. Eddie (Ed.), *Primary of perception.* Evanston, IL: Northwestern University Press.

Miller, A. (1981). *The drama of the gifted child.* New York: Basic Books. (Original work published 1979)

Miller, A. (1986). Depression and grandiosity as related forms of narcissistic disturbances. In A. P. Morrison (Ed.), *Essential papers on narcissism* (pp. 323–347). New York: New York University Press.

Miller, C. T., Clarke, R. T., Malcarne, V. L., Lobato, D., Fitzgerald, M. D., & Brand, P. A. (1991). Expectations and social interactions of children with and without mental retardation. *Journal of Special Education, 24*(4), 454–472.

Miller, S. (1985). *The shame experience.* Hillsdale, NJ: Erlbaum.

Minuchen, P. P., & Shapiro, E. K. (1983). The school as a context for social development. In P. Mussen & E. M. Hetherington (Eds.), *Handbook of child psychology,* (4th ed., Vol. 4, pp. 197–274). New York: Wiley.

Modigliani, A. (1968). Embarrassment and embarrassability. *Sociometry, 31,* 313–326.

Morrison, A. P. (Ed.). (1986a). *Essential papers on narcissism.* New York: New York University Press.

Morrison, A. P. (1986b). The eye turned inward: Shame and the self. In D. L. Nathanson (Ed.), *The many faces of shame* (pp. 271–291). New York: Guilford Press.

Morrison, A. P. (1989). *Shame: The underside of narcissism.* Hillsdale, NJ: Analytic Press.

Morrison, N. K. (1987). The role of shame in schizophrenia. In H. B. Lewis (Ed.), *The role of shame in emotion formation* (pp. 207–236). Hillsdale, NJ: Erlbaum.

Morrow, R. D. (1987). Cultural differences—be aware! *Academic Therapy, 23*(2), 143–149.

Mounoud, P. (1976). Les revolutions psychologiques de l'enfant. *Archives de Psychologie, 44,* 103- 114.

Nathanson, D. L. (Ed.). (1987a). *The many faces of shame.* New York: Guilford Press.

Nathanson, D. L. (1987b). The shame/pride axis. In H. B. Lewis (Ed.), *The role of shame in symptom formation* (pp. 183–206). Hillsdale, NJ: Erlbaum.

Nathanson, D. L. (1987c). A time table for shame. In D. L. Nathanson (Ed.), *The many faces of shame* (pp. 1–63). New York: Guilford Press.

Newell, A. (1982). The knowledge level. *Artificial Intelligence, 18,* 81–132.

Nicholls, J. G. (1984). Achievement motivation: Conception of ability, subjective experience, task choice, and performance. *Psychological Review, 91,* 328–348.

Nietzsche, F. (1964). *Will to power.* New York: Russell & Russell (Original work published 1904)

Nietzsche, F. (1966). *Beyond good and evil.* (W. Kaufman, Trans.). New York: Random House. (Original work published 1909)

Nisbet, R. (1973). *The social philosophers: Community and conflict in Western thought.* New York: Crowell.

Nixon, C. D., & Singer, G.H.S. (1993). Group cognitive-behavioral treatment for excessive parental self-blame and guilt. *American Journal on Mental Retardation, 97*(6), 665–672.

Nowles, D. P., & Kamiya, J. (1970). The control of electroencephalographic alpha rhythms through auditory feedback and the associated mental activity. *Psychophysiology, 6,* 476–484.

Oesterreich, T. K. (1974). *Possession, demoniacal and other.* Secaucus, NJ: Citadel Press. (Original work published 1905)

Olds, M. E., & Forbes, J. L. (1981). The central basis of motivation: Intracranial self-stimulation studies. *Annual Review of Psychology, 32,* 523–576.

Ornstein, R. E. (Ed.). (1973). *The nature of human consciousness.* San Francisco, CA: Freeman.

Overton, W. (1984). World views and their influence on psychological theory and research: Kuhn-Lakatos-Lauden. In H. W. Reese (Ed.), *Advances in child development and behavior.* (Vol. 18, pp. 191–226). New York: Academic Press.

Peat, M. (1991). Community based rehabilitation-development and structure: Part 2. *Community Rehabilitation, 5,* 231–239.

Pegals, E. (1988). *Adam, Eve, and the serpent.* New York: Random House.

Pervin, L. A. (1968). Ideographic and nomothetic aspects of affect. In L. Van Langenhove, J. M. De Waele, & R. Harre (Eds.), *Individual persons and their actions.* Brussels: Free University of Brussels.

Pervin, L. A. (Ed.). (1989). *Goals and concepts in personality and social psychology.* Hillsdale, NJ: Erlbaum.

Piaget, J. (1952). *The origins of intelligence in children* (M. Cook, Trans.) New York: International Universities Press. (Original work published 1936)

Piaget, J. (1954). *The construction of reality in the child* (M. Cook, Trans.) New York: Basic Books. (Original work published 1937)

Piaget, J. (1955). *Language and thought of the child* (M. Gabain, Trans.) New York: Harcourt Brace. (Original work published 1926)

Piaget, J. (1965). *The moral judgment of the child* (M. Gabain, Trans.) New York: Free Press. (Original work published 1932)

Piers, G., & Singer, M. B. (1953). *Shame and guilt.* New York: Norton.

Plutchik, R. (1962). *The emotions: Facts, theories, and a new model.* New York: Random House.

Plutchik, R. (1980). A general psychoevolutionary theory of emotion. In R. Plutchik & H. Kellerman (Eds.), *Emotion: Theory, research, and experience* (Vol. 1, pp. 3–33). New York: Academic Press.

Pribram, K. H. (1984). Emotion: A neurobehavioral analysis. In K. R. Scherer & P. Ekman (Eds.), *Approaches to emotion* (pp. 13–38). Hillsdale, NJ: Erlbaum.

Prince, M. (1978). *The disassociation of a personality.* New York: Oxford University Press. (Original work published 1905)

Putnam, F. W. (1989). *Diagnosis and treatment of multiple personality disorders.* New York: Guilford Press.

Quine, L. (1986). Behaviour problems in severely mentally handicapped children. *Psychology Medicine, 16,* 895–907.

Rank, O. (1952). *The trauma of birth.* London: Kegan, Paul/Trench & Trubner. (Original work published 1929)

Rank, O. (1972). *Will therapy and truth and reality.* New York: Knopf. (Original work published 1945)

Read, K. E. (1955). Morality and the concept of the person among the Gahuku-Gama. *Oceania, 25,* 253–282.

Rehm, L. P., & Carter, A. S. (1990). Cognitive components of depression. In M. Lewis & S. M. Miller (Eds.), *Handbook of developmental psychopathology* (pp. 341–351). New York: Plenum Press.

Reid, J. B. (1986). Sexual-interaction patterns in families of abused and nonabused children. In C. Zahn-Waxler, E. M. Cummings, & R. Iannotti (Eds.), *Altruism and aggression* (pp. 238–255). Cambridge: Cambridge University Press.

Reiss, S., & Benson, B. A. (1984). Awareness of negative social conditions among mentally retarded, emotionally disturbed outpatients. *American Journal of Psychiatry, 141*(1), 88–90.

Retzinger, S. R. (1987). Resentment of laughter: Video studies of the shame-rage spiral. In H. B. Lewis (Ed.), *The role of shame in symptom formation* (pp. 151–181). Hillsdale, NJ: Erlbaum.

Retzinger, S. R. (1989). *Marital conflict: The role of emotion.* Unpublished paper.

Reznick, J. S., & Snedman, N. (1988). Biological bases of childhood shyness. *Science, 240,* 167–171.

Richardson, S. A., Hastorf, A. H., & Dornbusch, S. M. (1964). Effects of physical disability on a child's description of himself. *Child Development, 35,* 893–907.

Riggen, K., & Ulrich, D. (1993). The effects of sport participation on individuals with mental retardation. *Adapted Physical Activity Quarterly, 10,* 42–51.

Rimmerman, A., & Portowicz, D. J. (1987). Analysis of resources and stress among parents of developmentally disabled children. *International Journal of Rehabilitation Research, 10*(4), 439–445.

Rogers, C . R. (1959). A theory of therapy, personality, and interpersonal relationships, as developed in the client-centered framework. In E. Koch (Ed.), *Psychology: A study of science* (Vol. 3, pp. 184–256). New York: McGraw-Hill.

Rogers, S. J. (1991). Observation of emotional functioning in young handicapped children. *Child Care Health and Development, 17,* 303–312.

Roland, A. (1988). *In search of self in India and Japan.* Princeton, NJ: Princeton University Press.

Rorty, A. O. (1989). *Mind in action.* Boston: Beacon Press.

Rosaldo, M. Z. (1984). Toward an anthropology of self and feeling. In R. A. Shweder & R. A. Levine (Eds.), *Cultural theory: Essays on mind, self, and emotion* (pp. 137–157). Cambridge: Cambridge University Press.

Rosenblum, G. A. (1995). Body image, physical attractiveness and psychopathology during adolescence. Unpublished doctoral dissertation, Rutgers University, New Brunswick, NJ.

Ross, C. A. (1989). *Multiple personality disorder.* New York: Wiley.

Rubin, J. (1989). Narcissism and nihilism: Kohut and Kierkegaard on the modern self. In D. W. Detrick & S. P. Detrick (Eds.), *Self psychology* (pp. 131–150). Hillsdale, NJ: Analytic Press.

Russell, J. A. (1980). A circumflex aspect of the human conceptual organization of emotions. *Journal of Personality and Social Psychology, 45,* 1281–1288.

Rutter, M., Izard, C. E., & Read, P. (Eds.). (1986). *Depression in young people.* New York: Guilford Press.

Saarni, C. (1979). Children's understanding of display rules for expressive behavior. *Developmental Psychology, 15,* 424–429.

Sagi, A., & Hoffman, M. L. (1976). Empathic distress in newborns. *Developmental Psychology, 12,* 175- 176.

Sartre, J. P. (1966). *Being and nothingness.* New York: Washington Square Press. (Original work published 1943)

Schacter, S., & Singer, J. E. (1962). Cognitive, social, and physiological determinants of emotional state. *Psychological Review, 69,* 379–399.

Schaeffer, H. R. (1966). The onset of fear of strangers and the incongruity hypothesis. *Journal of Child Psychology and Psychiatry, 7,* 95–106.

Scheff, T. J. (1987). The shame-rage spiral: A case study of an interminable quarrel. In H. B. Lewis (Ed.), *The role of shame in symptom formation* (pp. 109–150). Hillsdale, NJ: Erlbaum.

Scherer, K. R. (1979). Nonlinguistic vocal indicators of emotion and psychopathology. In C. E. Izard (Ed.), *Emotions in personality and psychopathology* (pp. 495–529). New York: Plenum Press.

Scherer, K. R. (1981). Speech and emotional states. In J. Darby (Ed.), *Speech evaluation in psychiatry* (pp. 189–220). New York: Grune & Stratton.

Scherer, K. R. (1986). Vocal affect expression: A review and a model for future research. *Psychological Bulletin, 99,* 143–165.

Schneider, K., Hanne, K., & Lehmann, B. (1989). The development of children's achievement-related expectancies and subjective uncertainty. *Journal of Experimental Child Psychology, 47,* 160–174.

Seligman, M. E. P. (1975). *Helplessness: On depression, development, and death.* San Francisco: Freeman.

Seligman, M. E. P., Peterson, C., Kraslow, N., Tanenbaum, R., Alloy, L., & Abramson, L. (1984). Attributional style and depressible symptoms among children. *Journal of Abnormal Psychology, 39,* 235–238.

Shulman, S. (1988). The family of the severely handicapped child: The sibling perspective. *Journal of Family Therapy, 10,* 125–134.

Shweder, R. A. (1985). Menstrual pollution, soul loss, and the comparative study of emotions. In M. A. Kleinman & B. Good (Eds.), *Culture and depression* (pp. 182–215). Berkeley and Los Angeles: University of California Press.

Shweder, R. A., & Bourne, E. J. (1984). Does the concept of the person vary cross culturally? In R. A. Shweder & R. A. Levine (Eds.), *Cultural theory: Essays on mind, self, and emotion* (pp. 158–199). Cambridge: Cambridge University Press.

Shweder, R. A., & Miller, J. G. (1985). The social construction of the person: How is it possible? In K. J. Gergen & K. E. Davis (Eds.), *The social construction of the person* (pp. 41–69). New York: Springer-Verlag.

Siminov, P. V. (1969). Studies of emotional behavior of humans and animals by Soviet psychologists. *Annals of the New York Academy of Sciences, 159,* 3.

Siminov, P. (1986). *The emotional brain.* New York: Plenum Press.

Siperstein, G. N., & Gottlieb, J. (1977). Physical stigma and academic performance as factors affecting children's first impressions of handicapped peers. *American Journal of Mental Deficiency, 81,* 455–462.

Skinner, B. F. (1938). *The behavior of organisms.* New York: Appleton-Century Crofts.

Slaby, R. G., & Guerra, N. G. (1988). Cognitive mediators of aggression in adolescent offenders: 1. Assessment. *Developmental Psychology, 24,* 580–588.

Spitz, R. (1946). The smiling response: A contribution to the ontogenesis of social relations. *Genetic Psychological Monographs, 34,* 57–125.

Stattin, H., & Klachenberg-Larsson, I. (1989). Delinquency as related to parents' preferences for their child's gender. (Rep. No. 696). Sweden: University of Stockholm, Department of Psychology.

Stern, D. N. (1985). *The interpersonal world of the infant.* New York: Basic Books.

Stipek, D. J. (1983). A developmental analysis of pride and shame. *Human Development, 26,* 42–54.

Stipek, D. J., Recchia, S., & McClinton, S. (1990). *Achievement-related self-evaluation in young children.* Unpublished manuscript.

Sullivan, H. S. (1953). *The interpersonal theory of psychiatry.* New York: Norton.

Szivos-Bach, S. E. (1993). Social comparisons, stigma and mainstreaming: The self-esteem of young adults with a mild mental handicap. *Mental Handicap Research, 6*(3), 217–236.

Tangney, J. P. (1989 a). *Situational determinants of shame and guilt in young adulthood.* Unpublished manuscript.

Tangney, J. P. (1989, August b). Shame and guilt in young adulthood: A qualitative analysis. Paper presented at American Psychological Society Meetings, New Orleans.

Taylor, A. R., Asher, S. R., & Williams, G. A. (1987). The social adaptation of mainstreamed mildly retarded children. *Child Development, 58,* 1321–1334.

Toch, H. (1969). *Violent men.* Chicago: Aldine.

Tolman, C. W. (1965). Feeding behavior of domestic chicks in the presence of their own mirror image. *Canadian Psychologist, 6,* 227. (Abstract)

Tomkins, S. S. (1962). *Affect, imagery, and consciousness: Vol. 1. The positive affects.* New York: Springer.

Tomkins, S. S. (1963). *Affect, imagery, and consciousness: Vol. 2. The negative affects.* New York: Springer.

Trevarthen, C. (1979). Communication and cooperation in early infancy: A description of primary intersubjectivity. In M. Bullowa (Ed.), *Before speech: The beginning of interpersonal communication* (pp. 321–347). London: Cambridge University Press.

Turner, L. A. (1994, May 5–7). Attributional beliefs of students with retardation. Paper presented at the 4th Annual Conference of the Center for

Human Development and Developmental Disabilities, "Emotional Development in Atypical Children," New Brunswick, NJ.

Turner, L. A., Dofny, E. M., & Dutka, S. (1994). Effect of strategy and attribution training on strategy maintenance and transfer. *American Journal on Mental Retardation, 98*(4), 445–454.

Varni, J. W., Setoguchi, Y., Rappaport, L. R., & Talbot, D. (1992). Psychological adjustment and perceived social support in children with congenital/acquired limb deficiencies. *Journal of Behavioral Medicine, 15*(1), 31–44.

Wallon, H. (1949). *Les origines du caritere chez l'enfant: Les preludes du sentiment de personality* (2d ed.). Paris: Presses Universitaires de France.

Walton, A. (1989, August 20). Willie Horton and me. *New York Times Magazine,* pp. 52–53.

Weiner, B. (1986). *An attributional theory of motivation and emotion.* New York: Springer-Verlag.

Wehmeyer, M. L. (1994). Perceptions of self-determination and psychological empowerment of adolescents with mental retardation. *Education and Training in Mental Retardation and Developmental Disabilities,* 9–21.

Weiner, B. (1993). On sin versus sickness: A theory of perceived responsibility and social motivation. *American Psychologist, 48*(9), 957–965.

Weiskrantz, L. (1986). *Blindsight: A case study and implications.* Oxford: Oxford University Press.

Wenger, M. A., Jones, F. N., & Jones, M. H. (1956). *Physiological psychology.* New York: Holt.

Werner, H. (1961). *Comparative psychology of mental development.* New York: Science Editions.

White, R. W. (1959). Motivation reconsidered: The concept of competence. *Psychological Review, 66,* 297–323.

Widom, C. (1989). Cycle of violence. *Science, 244,* 160–166.

Witkin, H. (1965). Psychological differentiation and forms of pathology. *Journal of Abnormal Psychology, 70,* 317–336.

Witkin, H., Dyk, R., Goodenough, D., Faterson, H., & Karp, S. (1962). *Psychological differentiation.* New York: Wiley.

Wittgenstein, L. (1963). *Philosophical investigations.* (G. E. M. Anscombe, Trans.) New York: Macmillan. (Original work published 1953)

Wurmser, L. (1981). *The mask of shame.* Baltimore: Johns Hopkins University Press.

Zahn-Waxler, C., Cummings, E. M., & Iannotti, R. (Eds.). *Altruism and aggression.* Cambridge: Cambridge University Press.

Zahn-Waxler, C., & Kochanska, G. (1990). The origins of guilt. In R. Thompson (Ed.), *36th Annual Nebraska Symposium on Motivation: Socioemotional Development* (pp. 183–258). Lincoln: University of Nebraska Press.

Zahn-Waxler, C., Kochanska, G., Krupnick, J., & McKnew, D. (1990). Patterns of guilt in children of depressed and well mothers. *Developmental Psychology, 26,* 51 -59.

Zahn-Waxler, C., & Radke-Yarrow, M. (1982). The development of altruism: Alternative research strategies. In N. Eisenberg-Berg (Ed.), *The development of prosocial behavior* (pp. 109–138). New York: Academic Press.

Zahn-Waxler, C., Radke-Yarrow, M., & King, R. A. (1979). Child rearing and children's prosocial imitations toward victims of distress. *Child Development, 50,* 319–330.

Zajonc, R. B. (1980). Feeling and thinking: Preferences need no inferences. *American Psychologist, 35,* 151–175.

Zajonc, R. B. (1984). On primacy of affect. In K. R. Scherer & P. Ekman (Eds.), *Approaches to emotion* (pp. 259–270). Hillsdale, NJ: Erlbaum.

Zazzo, R. (1948). Images du corp et conscience du soi. *Enfance, 1,* 29–43.

Index

Printed in the United States
36815LVS00008BA/130